SHIPMATES

SHIPMATES
Inside the Royal Navy Today

Christopher Terrill

CENTURY

Published by Century in 2005

1 3 5 7 9 10 8 6 4 2

This book is based on the television series *Shipmates*
produced for the BBC by Shine Limited in association with Uppercut Films.
Series Producer: Christopher Terrill
Executive Producer: Olivia Lichtenstein
BBC Executive Producer: Maxine Watson

Picture credits:
© Crown Copyright/MOD: pages: 2, 68, 78-9, 142-3, 191, 226, 233, 235,
249, 252 (top, larger pic), 260 (top, larger pic), 278-9, 287, 288-9, 292-3.
© Nelson's Island Excavation: pages: 224, 227.

First published in the United Kingdom in 2005 by Century
The Random House Group Limited
20 Vauxhall Bridge Road, London SW1V 2SA

Random House Australia (Pty) Limited
20 Alfred Street, Milsons Point, Sydney,
New South Wales 2061, Australia

Random House New Zealand Limited
18 Poland Road, Glenfield, Auckland 10, New Zealand

Random House (Pty) Limited
Isle of Houghton, Corner Boundary Road & Carse O'Gowrie,
Houghton, 2198, South Africa

The Random House Group Limited Reg. No. 954009
www.randomhouse.co.uk

A CIP catalogue record for this book is available from the British Library

ISBN 1 8441 3791 0

Papers used by The Random House Group Limited are natural, recyclable products
made from wood grown in sustainable forests; the manufacturing processes conform
to the environmental regulations of the country of origin

Typeset by SX Composing DTP, Rayleigh, Essex
Design & make-up by Roger Walker

Printed and bound in Germany by
Appl Druck, Wemding

To My First Shipmates
My mother and father, Joan and Clive, and my sisters,
Rosalind and Debbie

ME AND MY TEAM – ALI AND HEATHER

Acknowledgements

This book arises from the TV series of the same name made for the BBC by Shine Ltd and Uppercut Films. My initial thanks go, therefore, to Liz Murdoch, Paul Hamann, and Mike Tait for their enduring support for the project since it was but a twinkle in all of our eyes. As the project took form and substance many people at Shine contributed enormously to its development, notably the holy trinity of Joe Mclusky (Director of Production), David Surtees (Chief Financial Officer) and John Gilbert (Legal Eagle *extraordinaire*). At the front line of day-to-day organisation were Fiona MacDonald and Hannah Riesner – their eyes constantly on a speeding and often spinning ball. Latterly, Sam Anthony entered the fray as Creative Director Factual Programmes; he provided constant support and encouragement, as did Rachel House and John Villeneau.

At the BBC I would like to extend my gratitude to Richard Klein, for his wise counsel at all stages of production, as well as Maxine Walson, my Executive Producer at The BBC, for her understanding and guidance.

I would particularly like to thank Olivia Lichtenstein, my other Executive Producer and good friend, for her encouragement and advice throughout all the production stages and for sharing her own special insights into the constant mystery that is film-making.

I am eternally grateful to my long-suffering and hugely talented film editors, Joel Legate and Julie Buckland, for giving themselves so wholeheartedly to the project as well as always encouraging my work on this book. Few people, other than film editors who work in the hothouse of the cutting room, understand better the pain of creative film making. Joel and Julie are two of that special breed that simply 'make it happen'.

I reserve special thanks to my researcher/assistant producer and friend Ali Beattie, who grasped the nettle of production with both hands. It was a sharp learning curve for her but she rose to the challenge magnificently and we would never have achieved what we did without her supreme organisational abilities as well as her very special 'people' skills. When she announced halfway through the production period that she had become engaged to her long-term boyfriend Joe, I became aware of a deep sense of disappointment throughout the male ranks of the Royal Navy and the Royal Marines!

My heartfelt thanks go also to everybody at Uppercut Films and Oasis Television for their extraordinary support throughout the long and very demanding post-production period.

At Random House I received wonderful encouragement from Oliver Johnson, who first encouraged me to write a book to go with the series. Thereafter, I benefited from the constant and unstinting advice of Tim Andrews, who kept a watchful eye on the developing manuscript. He was always there to provide wise editorial suggestions that greatly benefited the final drafts of the book.

Kate Watkins as well provided magnificent support and lent her keen and imaginative eye to the books layout and design.

Thanks also to the talented designer, Roger Walker.

I am indebted to Rick Jolly, the author of *Jackspeak* the definitive guide to Royal Navy language – which I have drawn upon throughout the book.

The films and the book would never have seen the light of day if it had not been for the extraordinary support and good faith of the Royal Navy. I would particularly like to thank Captain Brian Warren of the Directorate of Defence Publicity (Royal Navy) for his amazing ability to see with two sets of eyes – the eyes of the military as well as the eyes of the creative media – and to combine both into a workable and productive whole. Similarly, I am forever grateful to Lieutenant Commander Jon Green who helped the whole project off the ground in the first place. Lieutenant Commander Adrian Mundin and Commander Russ Tuppen deserve a special word of thanks for their eagle-eyed proofreading of the book and their invaluable advice over technical details. A word of gratitude must go also to Micky Goble, my very good friend who I first met on HMS *Brilliant* over ten years ago, who was always on the end of the line to answer another question about shipboard life and mess-deck culture.

I must thank also my friend Anna Shelmerdine, not only for her proofreading of the initial chapters but also her constant and unstinting encouragement. By the same token I am eternally grateful to Glen and all the guys at the Fitzroy Lodge Amateur Boxing Club for their interest in this project, their support and for beating me up every Saturday without fail!

I would like to thank everyone at the Devonport Naval Base Media Liaison Office for their support and advice throughout the period of production – especially Lorraine Coulton, Guy Boswell and Nicki Dunwell.

Enormous gratitude goes to Lieutenant Heather Tuppen, the Project Officer allocated to the production of *Shipmates*. Heather has had to deal with the professional demands of her own Service as well as those I threw at her on a daily basis over an entire year. Hers has not always been an easy task as she has had to reconcile her own interests of positive publicity for the Navy with my overriding concern for honest reporting and 'telling it like it is'. Sometimes it seemed like we were on opposite sides but Heather's sparkling and ever smiling personality never let pragmatics get in the way of friendship. Thanks, Heather, for keeping the faith!

Above all others, however, I must extend an enormous vote of thanks to the men and women of the Royal Navy who welcomed me into their world. Specifically I would like to thank the ships' companies of HMS *Chatham*, HMS *Bulwark* and HMS *Ocean* as well as their Commanding Officers: Captain Steve Chick, Captain Jerry Stanford and Captain Tony Johnstone-Burt. They were always very proud of their ships and everyone who served on them and, as I was to find out, with great good reason. I would like to thank Commodore James Fanshawe for his constant support and belief in the project from the beginning as well as his excellent company on many occasions. Also, I would like to thank Commodore David Pond for the privileged access he allowed me to HMS *Raleigh*, the famous RN training establishment in Plymouth that trains young sailors and readies them for service in the fleet.

I leave the Royal Navy after a year spent within its ranks. It has been a pleasure, an honour and an inspiration, as well as a series of unforgettable adventures. It has resulted in a major TV series as well as this book, but for me, most importantly, it has given me a host of new naval friends – all of whom I am proud to call 'shipmates'.

Christopher Terrill, London.

Author's Note

This book is a record of events in Her Majesty's Naval Base Devonport, as well as several of the ships that are based there, over the course of a year. In the case of HMS *Chatham* this meant extended times at sea in the Middle East as well as the Indian Ocean. Much of what is reported in this book is based on my own, personal diaries. Sometimes I have resorted to long-term memory as well as transcripts of tapes recorded at the time. Occasionally, I have introduced a measure of creative licence by making a few educated guesses about people's inner reactions to events, but this is only ever done to complement an otherwise closely observed reality. Any error of fact or misinterpretation is entirely my own and should not be attributed to individuals concerned. On a few occasions I have changed people's names to save them undue embarrassment but none of them was a major player in the stories I have related in the pages that follow.

Contents

Life in a Blue Suit

The Royal Navy is not only the Senior Service but also the Silent Service – hidden, secret, seaborne and mysterious. To the uninitiated landlubber the world of the British sailor can seem a strange, bizarre, even surreal world in which people live in floating grey prisons called warships (or submerged ones called submarines) for months on end; sleep in coffin-sized bunks surrounded by snoring shipmates; constantly pit their wits against the hostility of the sea, the weather or the threat of an enemy; 'run ashore' periodically for legendary beer-binges that come with the territory, and use a strange language in which 'getting a car-smash down your grid for scran' simply means having tomatoes on toast for tea!

The Royal Navy has a long and proud tradition, is fundamental to the British way of life and central to our social, economic and political history, but is none the less pitilessly parodied and caricatured by those who would make fun of what they do not understand or are quite possibly a little afraid of. Whether it is music hall, slapstick, sitcom, pantomime or high camp revue, the British sailor has always been fair game for the comics, mimics and satirists who instinctively associate shipboard life with all that is outrageous, extreme and shocking. Maybe it is the idea of so many men living together in such close quarters that has generated so much droll comment, tongue in cheek witticism, and just plain seaside postcard bawdiness. The apparently innocuous greeting 'Hello sailor!' is as pink in its innuendo as The Village People were in their rendition of 'In the Navy', and it is no coincidence that *Little Britain*'s 'Only Gay in the Village' is invariably dressed in a PVC sailor suit. On the other side of this particular coin, of course, is the counter view, just as stereotypical, that the average sailor is a serial womaniser who operates on a global scale. Again, this undoubtedly arises from the conjecture that weeks and months at sea pump up the sex drive to an exaggerated degree – hence the evergreen assumption that a sailor has 'a girl in every port', and of course the more romantic or possibly ironic postulation that 'every nice girl loves a sailor!'* Add to that the old favourite 'Worse things happen at sea' and we have a neat set of notions that have coloured our attitudes to 'life on the ocean wave'.

My theory is that we make fun of our sailors precisely because we find them so mystifying as people, and their lifestyles so perplexing and counter to our own. We do not react to soldiers or airmen in the same way – just sailors. On one level, as an island race and a seagoing people, I think we naturally identify with seafarers – we admire them. It's just that we find it difficult to understand what makes them tick. So, from Gilbert and Sullivan's *HMS Pinafore* to the lowbrow stage farce *Sailor Beware* and from Alec Guinness's perpetually seasick captain in the film *All At Sea* to the 1950s sitcom *The Navy Lark* and even from Captain Pugwash to Captain Birdseye, the Navy has long been the butt of a nation's sometimes mischievous but mostly affectionate humour.

In stark contrast to the inherent humour of 'things naval', we are informed by a literature rich in seafaring tales such as Nicholas Monsarrat's *The Cruel Sea*, C.S. Forester's adventures of Horatio Hornblower and Patrick O'Brian's classic novels like *Master and Commander*. For all their rousing derring-do, however, all these fictions find more than their measure in historical fact, for it is on the Navy that the destiny of this island nation has so often depended. And here all the joking stops, because when it comes down to war the Royal Navy is, and always has been, deadly serious. Consider the amazing capture of the entire French fleet at the Battle of Sluys in 1340; the extraordinary vanquishing of the Spanish Armada in 1588; the decisive battle of Quiberon Bay in 1759; the great revenge battle against the Germans in the Falklands in 1916; and then, in the Second World War, the great convoy action for the relief of Malta, the gruelling battle against U-boats and surface raiders in the Atlantic; and not least, two hundred years ago, Admiral Lord Nelson's legendary exploits at the Nile and then finally at Trafalgar.

In short, the Navy enthrals us but at the same time slightly intimidates us with its exotic customs, inward-looking culture and its own ingrained suspicion of anyone who is not 'Navy'.

* This stereotyping applies only to male sailors. Female sailors, have, of course, an entirely spotless reputation!

My aim in this book is not so much to examine the Navy's proud heritage, for that is a given, but to explore and examine the hidden culture of ships and sailors and find out a little bit more about what it is to be a sailor in the modern Royal Navy. Sailors call their time in the Navy 'life in a blue suit,'* so my intention has been to find out exactly what that means – from the inside. Ten years ago I had the great privilege of spending 10 weeks in HMS *Brilliant* – a Type 22 Frigate deployed to the Adriatic during the Yugoslavian War. That gave me a fascinating insight into the Royal Navy and I produced a BBC series of the same name which commanded massive viewing figures. That convinced me of the British public's fascination and great fondness for the Navy and Navy people.

* Resigned acceptance of the vicissitudes of life in the 'Andrew' (widespread nickname for the Royal Navy said to be named after Lieutenant Andrew Miller, a highly successful press-gang officer of the 18th Century).

I was delighted, therefore, when the Navy invited me back behind the scenes for the purpose of producing a new TV series about the Royal Navy in the 21st Century. My initial research actually focused on Portsmouth Command and the working title for the series started off as 'Sailor Town'. After a few weeks, however, I had a meeting with the Second Sea Lord, Vice Admiral Sir James Burnell-Nugent, who is responsible for recruiting, manning and most shore training, and he was firmly of the opinion that I should consider Plymouth Command instead. This was not because Portsmouth was not fascinating and would not have provided extraordinary opportunities for filming, but simply because he felt Plymouth was so often neglected by the media and yet had so much to offer. Initially I was unsure, but went to have a look around Plymouth anyway. I was immediately drawn in by Devonport dockyard and the people I met, so I happily agreed to refocus my attention on this historic West Country shore base.

I was promised unprecedented 'warts and all' access to the Royal Navy virtually in its entirety. Nothing was to be hidden from me and the only limitation on what I could reveal would be dictated by national security issues. The degree of access I enjoyed was unprecedented, and I applaud the Admiralty for granting it even though, for them, it was always going to be 'high risk'. I think they decided to take the plunge again for two reasons. Firstly, they know they are accountable to a taxpaying public, many of whom do not really understand what the modern Navy actually does any more and secondly, I reckon; they felt pretty confident that most of what I would find would enhance their reputation before it would tarnish it.

One other thing I need to mention in order to put my whole approach to this project in full context. As I have said, the series commissioned by the BBC, and green-lighted by the Navy, was one that would tell the story of a naval command – Plymouth. At first my idea was simply to tell the day-to-day story of this enormous shore base over a year. There was plenty to look at – the intense and continuous training of personnel, the preparation of warships and submarines for deployment, the vital maintenance of security by bomb-disposal squads and MoD police and then, on the other hand, the highly charged 'runs ashore' on Friday and Saturday nights – when Jack* hits the bars and pubs of Union Street – and the consequent policing of the town centre by naval regulators in roaming shore patrols. Certainly, all life was here.

Before I started filming, however, I attended a reception on, of all things, a Russian frigate on a goodwill visit to Devonport. At one point in the evening, after clinking vodka glasses with a group of very senior Royal Navy officers, I pointed to a row of British frigates and destroyers tied up opposite the Russian ship and said, 'You must be very proud when you see all your ships lined up in the dockyard like that'.

Without hesitation one of the officers, a commodore, replied, 'Absolutely not! When our ships are in port they are not where they should be – out there, over the horizon performing their duty.'

'We just wind them up here,' said another, 'and then let them go and do what they do best. We don't want them here collecting cobwebs'.

In that moment I realised what my concept for the series was still vitally missing. It had to go 'over the horizon' as well. If I was to tell the story of a command I also had to follow ships from that command on deployment, or else the story would only ever be half told.

To this end I spent an entire year shadowing everybody from raw recruits coming through the famous training establishment HMS *Raleigh* to the saltiest sailors on the high seas; I sailed on frigates on deployment like HMS *Chatham*; massive state-of-the-art amphibious assault ships like HMS *Bulwark* and HMS *Ocean*, the largest ship in the fleet; I joined battle-hardened Marines on manoeuvres as well as on active service in the Arabian Gulf; I shared the excitement and horror of the Royal Navy sailors who arrived in Sri Lanka days after the terrible tsunami had struck; I stood with a naval burial party in Egypt as they laid to rest thirty sailors killed two hundred years ago in the battle of the Nile; I accompanied a naval contingent to Turkey for the ninetieth anniversary of the battle of Gallipoli; I flew with the jet pilots of the Fleet Air Arm; 'ran ashore' with sailors hell-bent on beer and women;

* 'Jack' – Generic name for all Royal Navy sailors, derived from Jack Tar, the 18th and 19th century matelot with his glossy black hat, carefully dressed pigtail, and canvas breeches that, like the hair on his head, were impregnated with high grade tar. 'Jolly Jack Tar' – probably a sailor who got outside a tot or two of best rum!

went out on shore patrol with tough naval regulators; followed the Field Gun teams in their race for glory; and lined up with the rest of the Navy for a massive Fleet Review at Spithead in front of the Queen. The people I found – from the lowliest stokers, gunners and stewards to the most senior commanders, captains and commodores – were unfailingly larger than life, often delightfully eccentric, and all united by a particular brand of humour that is born of the sea and nurtured by ships and ship living. I soon found out that to understand naval humour is to understand the Navy and Navy people.

I was also impressed to find the huge degree of professionalism and dedication to the task in hand in one of the most difficult and frustrating periods the Navy has ever had to face. Gone are the great sea battles of the Second World War, gone are the ballistic threats of the Cold War, but here and here to stay for the foreseeable future is the 'asymmetric' threat of the terrorist dedicated to global destabilisation. This threat, often invisible, always unexpected and frequently exercised with horrific effect, demands a very different sort of Navy from any we have had in history – but one, none the less, that still recalls its proud heritage, most notably the courage and dedication of Nelson's Navy 200 years ago…

21 October 1805:
'England expects that every man will do his duty'

The twenty-first of October is the most important date in the naval calendar, because it was on this day in 1805 that Admiral Lord Horatio Nelson vanquished the French and Spanish navies and claimed glorious victory at the Battle of Trafalgar. Tragically, of course, Lord Nelson was shot by a French sniper at the height of battle and died soon after, but not before he knew he had won the day. This remarkable and utterly comprehensive victory changed the course of European history and ensured that the Royal Navy would 'rule the waves' for the next hundred years.

Custom dictates that every 21 October the men and women of the Royal Navy will remember and honour the man who, in life and in death, provided the standards against which all Royal Navy sailors have been expected to measure themselves ever since . . .

What follows is a story of our Royal Navy today. It is not meant to be the definitive story, because it is from a very personal perspective. It is really a chronicle of my own adventures with the many people I met while with the Navy. It will provide a frank, honest and, to some perhaps, a controversial insight into our Senior Service at a time when it is not only helping to stabilise a world spinning out of control but also fighting for its own survival amidst long-term recruiting problems, the constant threat of defence cuts and an urgent need for strategic and tactical reinvention.

I present this to my reader as a closely observed, living, dynamic story about an extraordinary body of men and women who are simply the naval generation of the moment and who carry Britannia's torch forward to future generations. The same torch has been passed down from many previous generations of British sailors – hundreds of thousands of men and women and even children who lived and sometimes died under the White Ensign. Most were ordinary people like my own father, a Fleet Air Arm Swordfish pilot in the Second World War, and indeed my own mother, a Leading Wren (Maintainer) during the same war. Some earned fame for their exploits and even greatness, such as Sir Francis Drake, Captain James Cook, Admiral Sir David Beatty and Admiral Jacky Fisher. Only one, of course, became a virtual God: a slight man known as Horace to his family but to the rest of us as Admiral Lord Horatio Nelson. His immortal memory is etched into the nation's psyche and his flagship HMS *Victory* has a permanent anchorage in British posterity.

'Thank God I have done my duty'

(*Admiral Lord Nelson on his death bed*)

Prologue

Location: HMS *Drake* wardroom, Devonport dockyard
Date: 21 October 2004
Time: 16.00

HMS *Drake* is the name given to the accommodation area within Devonport dockyard and tonight its wardroom is buzzing with activity. In the enormous, red-carpeted lobby are six Royal Marines from the Corps of Drums. They are pacing out their intricate drum and bugle routine, to be performed later this evening. The kitchens are frantically preparing for a five-course dinner for around 500 guests: the sirloin has to be marinated in coarse grain mustard and black pepper; the new potatoes need to be covered in tarragon and rosemary butter before roasting and the fine wines and vintage port need to be fetched from the cellars. In the main hall, the maître d' is giving his waiters and waitresses a final and thorough briefing.

'Tonight is very important to the Navy and there will be a lot of senior officers here with their guests. Serve the courses with care and attention to detail. This is not just another mess dinner; this is the most important dinner of the year. You must get it right . . .'

Up in the gallery the bandmaster is rehearsing the HMS *Drake* band for tonight's celebrations as well.

'We will be playing throughout the dinner to provide background music and then at the end of the evening we will provide accompaniment for all the assembled guests to sing sea shanties. Right, I just want to go through the opening section of "Glorious Victory" by Kendall and then we will run through Langford's "Fantasy on British Sea Songs".'

The guests are arriving at the front entrance of HMS *Drake* – an imposing granite building with a sweep of around twenty steps leading to its

TRAFALGAR NIGHT AT
HMS *DRAKE*

double front doors. All Naval Officers are resplendent in their dress uniforms – navy blue, with rich gold braid and a bow tie. There are one or two civilian guests in dinner suits and a few guests from the army and the air force in their own striking dress uniforms. A group of soldiers from the Cavalry regiment stand out from the sea of blue and gold with their bright red tunics, and for good measure they have arrived quite literally booted and spurred. It is an astonishing sight – imposing and extremely colourful. After cocktails in the main bar room the guests assemble in the lobby and take their positions for the display by the Royal Marines Corps of Drums. Some of the guests stand at the base of the magnificent staircase, some on the staircase itself and others go to the top landing in order to look down.

There is a distant roll of six marching drums – 'rat-a-tat, rat-a- tat'. The lobby falls silent and all eyes turn to the long corridor that leads to the lobby – 'rat-a-tat, rat-a-tat'. The roll of drums gets louder as the Marines get closer. Everybody cranes their necks to get the first view of the drummers – 'rat-a-tat, rat-a-tat, rat-a-rat-a-rat-a-tat'. The roll builds to a crescendo as six drummers with bugles hung at their side and in full military band uniform march majestically into the pool of golden light that illuminates the lobby floor. The Royal Marines march in perfect step to the centre of their stage and proceed with a display of precision drumming and marching that is utterly mesmerising. All eyes are on the drums and the drummers and not a step, not a strike, not a turn is out of place. Overlooking the lobby is a large portrait of Winston Churchill, who looks down approvingly at this scene of pageantry, naval tradition and national pride.

The display finishes with a rallying call of bugles and a burst of excited applause and cheering from the audience. The mess president, Commander Trevor Horne, steps forward.

'I would like to thank the Royal Marines from the Plymouth band for that remarkable display. And now, ladies and gentlemen, please take your places in the dining room.'

Five hundred guests file into the dining room with its long tables laid out with the best cutlery and crystal wine glasses. The lights are low but it is still possible to see the dozens of model wooden ships from the Battle of Trafalgar that permanently hang from the high ceiling.

The waiters and waitresses move endlessly from the kitchens carrying tonight's starter – four cheese terrine with a mixed leaf salad and granary bread. Wine waiters are pouring out a Yalumba unwooded chardonnay.

This is followed by sauté monkfish with sugar snaps.

The maître d' stands at the back of the room behind the top table and conducts the proceedings with silent hand movements directed at the waiting staff – one sign for 'serve' another for 'clear' – the precision of the serving is on a par with the standard of the drumming.

PARADING THE BEEF AT TRAFALGAR NIGHT

It is time for the main course but first another custom: 'The Parade of the Baron of Beef.' One of the Royal Marine drummers has changed into the uniform of his nineteenth-century counterpart and emerges from the kitchen beating his drum. Following him are four sailors also dressed in nineteenth-century uniform carrying a plinth on their shoulders; on it is a gigantic slab of sirloin beef. The beef is paraded around the whole room and the guests bang the tables approvingly with their hands in time to the drummers' beat.

The main course is finished and the plates have been cleared. The lights are lowered and a hush descends on the room. The kitchen doors are thrown open and a dozen waiters surge in carrying large chocolate models of nineteenth-century battle-of-the-line ships, each with ignited sparklers thrust into their sides. The waiters circle the room to huge applause, and there is stamping and more slapping of the tables. The chocolate ship tradition is highly symbolic, for it represents Nelson's fleet, breaking through the French fleet on course for annihilation and complete victory. Once the ships have been paraded round the entire dining hall they are set on the tables and consumed. They are followed by chocolate-and-rum-truffle mousse.

Decanters of Graham's vintage port (1983) are placed on the tables. Everybody pours themselves a glass and tradition dictates that they should then pass the decanter to the left – never to the right. Another tradition, still observed by some, is to pour the port to the very top of the glass – just to the very point of spillage but not past it. The port has to tremble at the brim, held back only by surface tension – referred to in the Navy as the 'Midshipman's Meniscus'. This is a typical example of naval bravado because to spill the port is a finable offence (with the fine invariably being another bottle of port), so officers with a particular sense of fun and mischief take their port pouring literally 'to the brink'. Should so much as a drop spill on to the table, the shout goes up 'Spillage!' followed by 'Fine!'

Once the decanters have been passed round the toasts commence. The first is to the 'Queen', the second is to 'Our Guests' and the third is to 'The Immortal Memory' of Horatio Nelson himself. The toast is made with solemnity and great gravity. Once made, however, the mood changes to one of celebration – a rousing salute to the Navy itself with the hearty rendition of sea shanties like 'What Shall We Do With the Drunken Sailor?' and stirring anthems like 'Jerusalem' and 'Heart of Oak', rounded off, inevitably, by a roof-raising, table-thumping performance of 'Rule Britannia'.

Guests retire to the bar room for more drinks and mess games – not gentle parlour games or party charades, but some of the most fiendish and violent games ever devised. The ladies and some of the older and more senior officers retreat to the sides of the room as the young blades take to the centre and brace themselves for some full-contact indoor rugby. One of the older officers, a commander, balding and somewhat short in stature, seeks extra shelter behind a large table on which have been placed dozens of ice buckets, dishes of nuts and olives, as well as multitudes of shot glasses full of vodka.

'I'm not taking any chances,' he says to a fellow officer. 'These games get emotional!'

Two teams are organised. One of them even contains some of the visiting Cavalry officers. Then, someone magically produces a rugby ball and tosses it towards the players. Simply, the idea is for each team to get the ball to one or other side of the room. Other than that, few rules seem to apply. There is great cheering as the opponents, mostly in blue and gold but some in red, hurl themselves around the room. Suddenly the ball pops out of the groaning mass of heavily breathing men and bounces over the ice-bucket table. The scrum moves ominously and unstoppably in the same direction. 'Look out!' someone cries. CRASH! There is an explosion of ice cubes, nuts, olives and vodka. 'Help!' splutters a strangled voice from somewhere beneath the mound of heaving, sweating men. People move towards the scene of destruction and gradually unpick the human knot. As the final layer of sailors and one soldier is pulled out, the supine form of the short and balding commander is revealed – flattened, soaked in vodka and blinking in astonishment.

'Buggeration!' he exclaims, peeling squashed green olives from his starched white shirt.

When people have got their breath back more games follow, including one in which the challenge is to get from one side of the room to the other without touching the floor, which involves lots of climbing over furniture. Another, 'Flight Deck Landings', involves the competitors hurling themselves headlong on to a long table-top to see how far they can slide on their stomachs.

The final guests leave HMS *Drake*. Trafalgar Night has come to an end. The one-hundred-and-ninety-ninth anniversary of the death of Nelson has been properly observed.

It has been a colourful evening of proud tradition, solemnity and celebration mixed with the rousing rumbustiousness that marks out a naval occasion like this for what it is and always should be. Trafalgar Night is not only about honouring a great sailor, it is also an expression of the intense comradeship and loyalty that must underpin any disciplined fighting force. Trafalgar Night might have its roots in the past but it is also highly relevant to the modern Navy, because tradition and heritage are the foundation blocks on which the Senior Service is built. Toasts of port to the Immortal Memory, the Midshipman's Meniscus, communal singing of sea shanties and rough-house mess games might all seem, to the outsider, like just so many outdated boarding-school rituals, but they are much more than that. They are a living expression of the Navy's heritage and proud lineage and hopefully a sign that when the chips are down on the high seas these men and women will be there for each other and their ship in the same way Nelson and his men were there for each other on this day nearly two hundred years ago.

Following this Trafalgar Night I was to meet hundreds more sailors in the year that followed and film with most of them in a wide variety of situations all over the world. It was to be an experience that more than anything else was to reveal to me a Navy in dramatic and exciting transition, a Navy reinventing itself, continually adapting to new demands, new challenges, new threats and new technologies. Nevertheless, I have always been pleased that I started with Trafalgar Night. It represented for me the Old Navy and highlighted its traditions and its customs, as I prepared to immerse myself in the modern Navy.

On the morning of 21 October 1805
The combined fleets of France and Spain were sighted sixteen miles westward of Cape Trafalgar

Nelson prayed:
'May the great God, whom I worship, grant to my Country and for the benefit of Europe in general, a great and glorious Victory: and may no misconduct, in any one, tarnish it: and may humanity after victory be the predominant feature of the British Fleet. For my self individually, I commit my life to Him who made me and may His blessing light upon my endeavours for serving my Country faithfully. To Him I resign myself and the just cause which is entrusted to me to defend.'

AMEN – AMEN – AMEN

CHAPTER ONE

Guzz

Watching Seagulls

Location: Plymouth Hoe
Date: 8 November 2004
Time: 07.30

I am watching seagulls. High over Devonport dockyard and Plymouth Sound a squadron of them are circling and screeching in ragged formation. Every now and again some break away and swoop low over the harbour waters in their constant search for food. It is what seagulls do. It is what they have always done. A hundred years ago, two hundred, five hundred, a thousand years ago, ancestors of the very birds I am watching right now would have been doing the very same thing. The birds of old, like the excited, screaming birds up there today, would have given no thought to what actually lay beneath their frenetic flight paths save for the prospect of fat fish in the sheltered waters of this natural harbour. But imagine what those ancient seagulls did look down on in times gone by. Imagine what history they witnessed, if only they realised the significance of what they were seeing from their privileged positions so far aloft.

In the thirteenth century the first ever national fleet was assembled in Plymouth by Edward I, to sortie over to south-west France for a bit of naval sabre rattling. In 1348 Edward the Black Prince sailed with a multitude of ships to Gascony 'in order to maintain my father's rights'. This led to the Battle of Poitiers and the Black Prince returning to Plymouth with the French king held captive and half of France under English control. Just fifty years later, thirty French ships from Breton attacked

DEVONPORT DOCKYARD
– A SEAGULL'S VIEW

Plymouth, setting fire to six hundred houses. In 1580 Sir Francis Drake returned to Plymouth in the *Golden Hind* after an epic global circumnavigation that established Britain as a major sea power, and just eight years after that he played his famous game of bowls before setting off to vanquish the Spanish Armada which was sailing up the channel.

And so it has continued – as long as seabirds have circled the skies above Plymouth and pillaged its waters for food, they have been unwitting observers of our seafaring history. They were there for the departure of the *Royal Sovereign*, the first one-hundred-gun ship on her way to achieve great glory as part of Nelson's fleet at the Battle of Trafalgar; for the arrival in 1815 of the captive Napoleon Bonaparte aboard *Bellerophon*, en route to exile in St Helena; for the departure of the Devonport cruisers *Cornwall* and *Caernarvon* en route to the Falklands in 1916 where, in a famous sea battle, they helped sink the mighty German flagship *Scharnhorst* and her sister ship *Gneisenau*; for the aircraft carrier *Courageous* leaving Devonport in the first weeks of the

Second World War, only to be torpedoed and sunk with the loss of 500 men; for the heroic return and tumultuous welcome of HMS *Exeter* in 1940, when she limped back to Devonport, badly damaged after playing her part in the sinking of the massive warship *Graf Spee* at the Battle of the River Plate; for the embarkation of the US Navy and American ground forces on their way to the epic invasion of Normandy on 6 June 1944; for the departure of the frigates *Ardent* and *Antelope* as part of the Falklands Taskforce in 1982 – both doomed never to return. The seabirds saw it all . . .

I am standing on the broad promenade known as the Hoe which overlooks Plymouth Sound and the massive breakwater, built in the nineteenth century by French prisoners of war, that protects it. Behind me is the statue of Sir Francis Drake looking out to sea heroically, arrogantly even, and next to him is proud Britannia, defiantly holding her shield and trident. Behind them both is the huge naval war memorial, guarded by a granite lion at each corner, and upon which is inscribed the name of every sailor killed in the two World Wars – row upon row of seemingly endless names, and of course a human story to every one if only we could know it.

Devonport today is Europe's largest naval base. Known to everybody in the Navy as Guzz,* it is an extensive, rambling array of buildings, from early Victorian to ultra modern, with dry docks, wet docks, warehouses, shipbuilding sheds, car parks, playing fields and of course warships – frigates, destroyers, amphibious assault ships, survey vessels, patrol boats and submarines. Some are tied up alongside, others are on the move – either coming into the port or heading out to sea.

Ships come and ships go – that is their nature . . .

Later today, for example, HMS *Cumberland* is due back from a seven-month deployment to the Gulf. On her return, according to tradition, she will pass the breakwater into the sheltered waters of the Sound where she will anchor for her final night at sea,† and early tomorrow

* The derivation of Guzz is a little uncertain. Some say it is an abbreviation of 'guzzle' – traditionally one of the favourite pastimes of an off-duty sailor, especially on return from a long spell at sea in the 'far flung' (anywhere abroad but especially east of Suez). Others say it derives from Plymouth's call sign during the war which some claim was Golf, Uniform, Zulu – although that is probably untrue.

† It is customary, though not compulsory, for a ship to spend her last night at sea just outside her home port. Partly this is to facilitate customs procedures, but it is also to allow the ship's company to share one final night of fun to mark the end of a long journey. Often there is a party and a ship's revue consisting of sketches and songs that sum up the deployment. Neither censorship nor restraint plays a large part in either the conception or the performance of these skits, which spare the blushes of no one from able seaman to commanding officer.

morning she will enter the harbour to tie up alongside, where waiting families will greet the ship and their loved ones on board her with the tears and cheers that have been welling in their hearts since she left over half a year ago.

Over on Frigate Alley, however, tied up at Wharf 12 is HMS *Chatham*, a Type 22 (Batch 3) Frigate, starting her final preparations for her own imminent deployment to the Gulf. In a week from now she will be sailing past the breakwater at the head of the Sound, slicing into the open seas and setting course for the Middle East and everything that great but troubled region might have to throw at her. She is of particular interest to me, because this is one of the ships I will be following over the months ahead. I will be joining her periodically on her deployment to get an idea of just what a modern Royal Navy warship actually does when she goes over the horizon. She will become a home away from home for me, just as she will to all the sailors aboard.

Half a dozen seagulls are circling the frigate's radar aerial and one by one swooping in to land on it. The perfect perch . . .

Location: HMS *Chatham*. Wharf 12, Frigate Alley
Time: 09.00

I walk up the gangway and on to the flight deck. As I look up towards the funnel, I can see the ship's personal pennant. It is a turquoise rectangle embroidered with the cartoon character Mighty Mouse and the ship's motto 'Up and At'Em'.*

I have come to visit a sailor I met recently at the Royal Navy's Novice Boxing Championships. He was a corner man for a couple of contenders from HMS *Chatham* and I got talking to him after the competition. He told me he was on the *Chatham* himself, so I arranged to come over today and say hello. He seemed friendly and it is always good to know a few people before joining a ship – especially if you are a civvy like I am. He is a 42-year-old gunner called Chris Butler but everybody knows him as Rab, after the politician R.A. Butler, who was always known as Rab, too.†

The quartermaster directs me to the helicopter hangar. 'Rab will be in there I reckon,' he says. 'Either there or racked out in his pit.'‡

I go through the doors of the hangar. The first thing I see is the grey shape of a Lynx helicopter with its rotors and tail plane neatly folded

*Shortly after the completion of HMS *Chatham* in 1989, the new ship's staff decided to look into the provision of a ship's motto. They felt the traditional Chatham Dockyard cry of 'Up and At 'Em', familiar at rugby and football pitch touchlines, was most appropriate and the Ships' Names and Badges Committee agreed. Because of this the ship has the rare honour of having an English motto – subsequently translated into the Latin *Surge et Vince* (Arise and Conquer).

† All Butlers in the Navy are known as Rab.

‡ Asleep in his bunk.

back, giving it the appearance of a giant sleeping insect. The second, just behind the Lynx, is a swinging punch bag suspended from a steel beam. The third thing I see is a big, sweaty, shaven-headed and heavily tattooed man about to unleash a big right hook.

'Hello, Rab,' I say after the shuddering punch has landed.

''Ello mate. Just 'avin' a bit of a workout. Punchin' the bag and pretending it's someone I don't like . . .' He laughs as he pulls off his gloves.

'So, this is your gym, is it?' I ask.

'Yes mate: gym, helo' house, workshop and barber's shop as well. Space is at a bit of a bleedin' premium on a frigate. Cup o'tea, mate?'

'Thanks.'

'Got a kettle here – so I guess that makes it a fuckin' tearoom as well.'

I look round the hangar. It is a strange mix of the warlike and the homely. Apart from the imposing presence of a Lynx attack helicopter there are all manner of tools, machinery, pulleys, ropes and chains. Boxes of spare parts are stacked on galleries above us and hung up on numerous racks are flying overalls, helmets and lifejackets. On the front of metal cupboard doors there are the inevitable pinups – with pride of place going to a poster-sized picture of Jordan in all her pneumatic glory. There is the kettle, now on the boil, and an array of about twenty chipped and tea-stained mugs. Next to them I notice a stack of drawers all carefully labelled. Some are marked 'Split pins', others are marked 'Bolts' and yet others 'Fuses', but then I notice one that says 'Nutty and fags – Senior Maintenance Ratings only!',* one that says 'Filth!' and one beneath that suggesting it contains 'Morale!' but with the added emphatic proviso 'Do not open!'

RAB AND HIS BELOVED PUNCH BAG

*Nutty is chocolate or sweets.

'Navy humour, mate!' says Rab with a guffaw.

'So, you're off next week then?' I say to Rab as he tosses a tea bag into a chipped mug featuring an extremely well-endowed Page Three girl.

'Yeah. Back out on the "blue and crinkly". I mean, we've still got a lot to do before we go. Got to get the weapons all sorted out in the next few days. Getting some ammo on board later today, and then tomorrow we start getting the food stores on.'

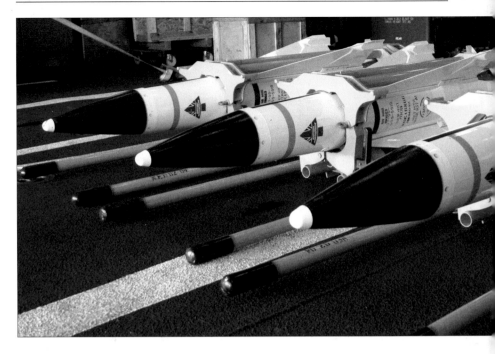

'And everybody's ready for the off?' I ask him as he pours out the boiling water.

'Yes and no really. It's strange this period leading up to deployment. You know you're leaving, but it don't seem real somehow. I mean 'ere I am in Guzz, 'avin' a cup o'tea, and next week I'll be on me way to the Gulf for six bleedin' months.'

He hands me the mug of steaming tea.

'Missing most of the football season. Be away for the Army – Navy rugby match – bugger it! I'm just pleased I'll be 'ere for the Inter Command Boxing Championships in a couple of days. I would've hated to 'ave missed that.' He jabs at the punch bag with his bare hands. 'It'll be a good crack I reckon. Always like to see the Plymouth Command beat up Portsmouth or the Marines or the Fleet Air Arm. I'm too old to box, but I help out with the coaching a bit when they let me.'

'Let you?'

'Yeah, well, I got into a bit of bovver with the gaffer down there – the lieutenant commander in charge at the Wyvern.* I got these business cards made up, see, sayin' me name, and underneaf I 'ad 'em put "Boxing Coach". Well, 'e got me in and ripped me fuckin' 'ead off didn't 'e? Said I was posing as somink I'm not and then said he didn't like my coaching style anyway. You know I'm not one of 'is PTIs, so he reckoned I was muscling in I guess.'

'Are you a coach?'

'Yeah. I do coach. I'm not officially trained exactly. I just know boxing and I know boxers.'

'Didn't you tell the gaffer that?'

'To be honest I just had to sit there and take it. It was a bit of a "one way transmission" if you know what I mean . . .'

Location: HMS *Chatham*. Ammunition Buoy, Frigate Alley
Time: 10.30

HMS *Chatham* has transferred to the ammunitioning buoy just outside Frigate Alley, and ammunition barges are coming alongside the frigate to deliver boxloads of deadly ordnance. Cranes are transferring the cargo on to the flight deck from where it is being carried to magazines around the ship. Most of the ammunition is quickly stowed, but the sensitive and powerful Sea Wolf missiles are still in their crates on the flight deck. Weapons engineering officers and weapons engineering artificers are carefully unboxing them and taking them to the dedicated missile magazine. Methodically, each British Aerospace missile, resplendent in its red and white livery, is wheeled into the hangar and slotted into a mechanical lift that will take it to its storage position. There it will stay until it is loaded into its launchers, once the ship is in theatre.

For the next six months HMS *Chatham* will be taking her place in an international taskforce of ships policing all the approaches to the Persian Gulf and Iraq. Her duty will be to monitor shipping in the area and, if necessary, stop and search individual vessels for arms, al-Qaeda suspects, drugs and illegal immigrants. The ship's company of 246 (196 men and fifty women) already know they will be on patrol over Christmas.

At the waist of the ship on the upper deck, a group of sailors watch as two tugboats, *Forceful* and *Faithful*, manoeuvre one of the massive amphibious assault ships, HMS *Bulwark*, into her space at Wharf 16. HMS *Portland* is tied up at Wharf 14 and, in between, Wharf 15 has been kept vacant – ready for the return of HMS *Cumberland* tomorrow morning. One of the watching sailors is Leading Chef Ginge Grieveson.

'Coming home is amazing – nothing like it,' he says. 'But leaving? That's bollocks if you want to know. Absolute bollocks, and it rips my heart out every time.'

He pauses as one of the tugboats delivers a long blast from her foghorn which frightens the life out of the seagulls perched on the frigate's radar. They fly off screeching their displeasure and rejoin the circling flocks above.

'I know it's what we do – being sailors,' Ginge continues, 'going to sea an' all, but it never gets any easier saying goodbye to the missus and the kids. Bleeding hate it I do. And Christmas on patrol . . . That sucks.'

I move back towards the flight deck and go into the hangar to see if Rab is still around. Sure enough he is next to his beloved punch bag where he is stacking metal boxes of shells for the new Mini Gun.

'Have you ever seen so many friggin' bullets?' he says. 'They just keep coming! This new Mini Gun is the dog's bollocks you know. Fires 3,000 rounds a minute – that's fifty rounds a second. Useful bit of kit that.'

'Nearly loaded up?' I ask.

'Yeah. The 4.5 shells for the big gun at the front are all in the magazine. Soon as the Sea Wolves are down we'll be done. Really beginning to feel like we're goin' now.'

'Ginge Grieveson doesn't seem very happy about leaving,' I say.

'Leavin'? Yeah, well, you have to deal with it the best way you can,' says Rab with a resigned smile. 'I mean, for the youngsters without ties its fuckin' great, know what I mean? They're off to foreign places – carefree, money in their pockets, with wine, women and song to look forward to. I used to be like that.'

He jabs absent-mindedly at the gently swinging punch bag.

'But now. What with being married an' all, it's a bit different – same wiv old Ginge – but I'll still 'ave a laugh. I mean, I don't know what we're going out to – you never do. The command don't tell you that much and anyway plans always change. It's a case of everythin' being a "definite maybe" in the Navy. But I reckon there will be some good runs ashore. Dubai for New Year should be a bleedin' blast.'

'Going to be a bit of a knees up is it?' I ask, already knowing the answer.

'The stuff of bleedin' legends mate. You betcha!' He grins widely before adding, 'Hope you'll be with us for that one shipmate – then we can show you some real Navy action – know what I mean?'

'Oh I expect I'll be there, Rab,' I say with a laugh. 'Put me down for half a pint of shandy.'

'Oh yeah,' he retorts. '*And* the fuckin' rest mate. You're in the Navy now!'

Matelots are by nature a friendly bunch, but I know from experience what it means to party with them and I am already bracing myself. I recall ten years ago on board HMS *Brilliant*, when we had a run ashore in Souda Bay in Crete. Some of the officers in the wardroom decided my time for initiation had come and so I was ordered to drink anything put in front of me – 'You have to down them all in one,' they insisted. 'Them's the rules!' I looked them straight in their smiling eyes and realised there was simply no retreat from the situation . . .

It started with a treble brandy, followed by another treble brandy; then came half a pint of white wine, then a double whisky; and then came . . . I really do not remember. All I can tell you is that I was found at 2.30 in the morning in the chief petty officers' mess, drinking a Campari cocktail out of my right shoe. I was carried to my bunk, strapped in on my side in case I vomited and choked, and then checked every half an hour until breakfast, when I was forced to consume a 'full English', being told it was the best possible cure for a hangover. The Navy looks after its own. I was initiated as one of 'the Mob' and my aching head throbbed with pride all day.

Now, ten years later, I have the uneasy feeling that in just a few weeks history is very likely to repeat itself in some bar full of British sailors in down-town Dubai. I ponder on the likelihood of there being an ancient Koranic law against drinking suspect concoctions out of your shoe . . .

The run ashore is part of Navy culture and is a very real part of being away for extended periods and coping with the particular stresses of life on a warship. A sailor friend of mine once pointed out to me that on a long deployment a ship might only come ashore every few weeks – whilst civilians get a Saturday night every week, sailors only get one every month or so. 'We have to make up for lost time,' he said.

Anyway, running ashore, in my view, is not so much to do with boozing but with bonding. I will never forget seeing a gigantic stoker from HMS *Brilliant* carrying one of his oppos* on his shoulders, all the way back to the ship and up the gangway after what had clearly been a terrific run ashore in Crete. The one being carried was instantly in trouble and would in due course have to pay his dues, but that was not the point. One sailor was looking after another sailor, and it was not difficult to transpose the action to another scene, for example an enemy missile attack with the same stoker carrying his badly wounded shipmate to safety.

*An 'oppo' is an especial friend or chum in a ship or unit; the term is derived from 'opposite number', the person who is on watch when you are off. The American equivalent is 'buddy'. 'Shipmate' is a more generic term that refers to anybody else on your ship, or even in the Navy as a whole.

Location: HMS *Ocean*. 2 Jetty, South Yard
Time: 11.30

Devonport dockyard is home port to three of the Navy's largest ships: HMS *Albion*, HMS *Bulwark* and HMS *Ocean*. These massive vessels, bigger than aircraft carriers, are part of the Navy's latest amphibious warfare capability. Each ship is able to insert not only heavily armed Royal Marines to an enemy beachhead via landing craft and helicopter, but also transport large numbers of tanks, lorries and other heavy equipment. HMS *Ocean*, described as an amphibious helicopter carrier, is the biggest ship in the British fleet, and I am here to see two key men in her company. One is the ship's chaplain Mike Brotherton, and the other is the ship's captain Tony Johnstone-Burt. Both these men had already persuaded me by sheer force of personality that HMS *Ocean* was a ship I simply had to get to know. As soon as I had first met Mike and Tony, on an earlier research trip, I had recognised their special qualities, not just as sailors but as men of extraordinary strength, commitment, compassion and humour, who would have shown a highly developed sense of duty in any walk of life they might have chosen. For them, however, it was the Royal Navy that gave them the best opportunity to fulfil their considerable potentials.

CAPTAIN TONY
JOHNSTONE-BURT

Tony Johnstone-Burt greets me warmly and instantly asks his steward to bring tea. I sit down in the well-appointed cabin of a man with an obvious specialisation in aviation. All over the walls are pictures of naval planes, from Second World War Swordfish to Tornadoes and Harriers, interspersed with photographs of his family – a very large family: his beautiful ex-model wife Rachel and five teenage children.

He looks at the photographs with obvious tenderness. 'We agreed that I would name the boys, so I went for English traditional: Edward, Richard and Thomas; Rachel went for Greek classical for the girls: Persephone and Antigone!'

At the other end of the cabin is a beautifully carved West African chair and other exotic memorabilia I guess he has picked up on his travels.

'I got that chair in Ghana on a visit with HMS *Montrose* – wonderful trip,' he says. 'When they heard I was a captain of a Royal Navy ship they made me an honorary paramount chief. I had to sit on that chair and get up from it three times as they chanted something extraordinary I couldn't understand. Then they told me, "You are now invulnerable." I said, "But that is fantastic. Thank you so much!" I mean, being invulnerable is terribly useful in my game – you know, high-risk war-type stuff. So far it seems to be working,' he laughs.

We get to talking about Africa, a continent I know well, and it then emerges that we have both read anthropology at Durham University.

'Goodness. What a small world. Well, as a fellow Durham man you are doubly welcome. And an anthropologist to boot. Perfect qualification for studying the Navy – we are very tribal!'

Tony Johnstone-Burt is forty-eight, but looks ten years younger. Fresh faced, ever smiling and always gracious, he is Royal Navy through and through and, not to spare his blushes, is universally respected by his seniors as well as his subordinates. I recognised this the first time I ever visited HMS *Ocean* a few weeks ago, but now I want to know exactly why this is. How does he manage to achieve this level of respect around him? How does he manage to marry firm discipline with such an obvious sense of fun and with such lightness of touch? From what I have already seen, he seems to know the first names of just about everyone on his ship as well as the details of their personal backgrounds – not because he has to but because he cares, genuinely. I am not saying this is unusual for commanding officers, but certainly, with Tony J-B as everyone knows him, he seems to take it to the next level.

The steward comes into the cabin with a silver tray on which is a teapot with two cups and saucers. I think back to my Page Three mug of tea earlier this morning with Rab Butler.

'Ships are amazing places with amazing people,' says the captain. 'It never ceases to astound me – the richness of life we have on board. Very tight communities. Highly ritualised in a way.'

'Now there's an anthropologist speaking if ever I heard one,' I quip.

'Exactly!' he laughs. 'Of course we have a command structure, but it must never be too rigid. Rank has to be respected, but that goes both ways. I would hate it if any sailor felt he could not come and talk to me, whether it is about his career or the football results.'

'But you would not want them to be too familiar.' I observe. 'You *are* the captain.'

'Well, yes. That's what I mean about respecting rank I suppose. I mean, you can't respect rank without respecting the man behind the stripes or the cap badge. Talking about "familiar" though; you'll never guess what happened today. I was coming along C deck and I saw this chap walking towards me in the most extraordinary way. He looked like a gorilla walking on hot coals.

'I said, "Whatever is wrong with you?"

'He said, "You don't want to know, sir."

'I said, "But you look like you're in agony."

' "That's 'cos I am, sir," he said with his face contorted in pain.

' "Well, for goodness sake," I said. "Why?"

' "Caught the old man in the zipper, sir."

' "What!" I said.

' "Zippered me dick, sir."

' "Good God."

' "Won't stop bleedin'."

' "Have you been to sickbay?"

' "Said they couldn't do nothin', sir. Said it would stop by itself. They just laughed, sir . . ."

' "Well, where were your boxers? Your nicks? I mean . . ."

' "I'm a marine, sir" he said haughtily, at which point he walked away like Quasimodo on a bad day.'

'So marines don't wear underwear?' I enquire.

'Considered bad form apparently,' says the captain, smiling and shaking his head. Whoever said 'worse things happen at sea' was dead on the button.

'How about *Ocean*?' I ask. 'What's the plan for her in the next few months?'

'Ah, well,' says Tony J-B, smiling widely and raising his eyebrows to the ceiling in mock frustration. 'We will have an extended period along-side, because we are being Bowmanised* at the moment and that takes time. This provides its own challenges of course because we have to keep the ship's company not only busy but happy. I reckon we would all rather be at sea like *Chatham*, but sometimes ships just have to be serviced, modernised and generally prepared for deployment.'

'So it's Plymouth for a while then for *Ocean*?'

'Well yes, but as soon as our communications are sorted out we will be working-up again – doing sea trials and then putting ourselves through BOST.† That is another huge challenge – one of the most ardu-

* Bowman is a state-of-the-art communication system, developed by the Army, which is being put into all the amphibious landing platforms like HMS *Ocean*. The conversion is very complicated and can take months to complete.

† BOST is Basic Officer Sea Training – one aspect of FOST, standing for Flag Officer Sea Training. This latter refers to the Admiral, and the generic name for his staff, responsible for devising and supervising operational sea training of RN ships, and increasingly of ships of allied navies.

ous tasks facing any ship or any sailor in the Royal Navy. We go through all manner of exercises to test us to our limits, and then every Thursday we literally go to war, just off the coast here, and it is as real as we can make it. I would love you to be with us for a Thursday War or two, because you would see a side of the Navy few ever see from the outside – they really put us through it. All of us are exposed to real tension and pressure. That's the way we get ready for deployment – stress, strain, anxiety and nerves.'

'It sounds extraordinary,' I say, 'but what happens if you fail the test?'

'Oh, we have to do it all over again till we pass,' says Tony J-B with a shrug of the shoulders. 'Failure simply is not an option because ultimately we have to go to sea and perform our duty somewhere in the world. That's the great thing about being in the Navy – you never know what you may be called upon to do, so you have to be prepared for anything.'

CAPTAIN TONY JOHNSTONE-BURT ON THE BRIDGE WING OF HMS *OCEAN*

'Well, I would love to be with you for a Thursday War. Thanks for the offer.'

'Not at all,' he replies nodding firmly, but then adding with a broad grin, 'I would also love you to come with us on a proper run ashore and see the other side of the Navy . . .'

'Really!' I say, surprised at such an unexpected offer from a senior officer. 'You mean a wobbly sailor show!'

'Exactly,' he laughs. 'I know you've seen it all on HMS *Brilliant*, but I would like you to see a proper "Rig Run". The sailors go ashore, not in their jeans and T-shirts but in naval rig. It's high risk I suppose, because they are that much more visible if anything should go wrong or if they get a bit too wobbly, but I think it's fantastic. The public seldom see sailors in uniforms these days and they love it, and the sailors love it too. It makes them quite proud I think.'

'It doesn't stop them having fun?' I enquire.

'Not at all,' Tony J-B replies. 'Uniforms are very good for trapping.* You see the best fun after midnight, in the small hours – in the clubs or the pubs or just out in the streets. There he is, Jack, hat on the back of the head, fag in the mouth, pint in the hand and a girl on either arm. Scene straight out of a black and white British war movie. Fantastic!'

* 'To trap' is to acquire a new female friend on a run ashore. In civvy speak it means to pick up.

'Well, I'll certainly be with you for that one as well,' I smile, considering the real possibility that I may have to be re-initiated on every ship I sail in, and that will not be good news – well, not for my constitution anyway. Nor my shoes come to that.

An hour later I say goodbye to Tony J-B and head down the corridor to Mike Brotherton's cabin. He is at his desk, on which he has placed a case – an ordinary-looking, medium-sized suitcase – and in his hand is a small paintbrush.

'I'm painting on the names of every ship I have ever served in,' says the ever-cheerful chaplain.

By his side are two small pots of enamel paint – one black, one gold. Carefully, he has drawn the outline of letters in black and he is now filling the letters in with gold: HMS *Ark Royal*, HMS *Boxer*, HMS *Cumberland*, HMS *Gloucester* . . . the list goes on and on.

'I carry all my robes and paraphernalia round in this,' he says. 'It was a bit plain, so I thought I would jazz it up a bit. Do you like it?'

'I do. Good way to remember all your ships.'

'Exactly,' he says filling in the d of HMS *Cumberland*. 'The straight letters are OK but the round ones are a nightmare . . . there!' He surveys his artwork with pride. 'We get very attached to our ships, us sailors.'

'I know,' I say. 'My father told me how difficult he found it, leaving a ship to join another during the Second World War. He said it was like leaving an old friend.'

'That is it precisely – and when we leave a ship we are also leaving a community, saying goodbye to good mates. You join another ship and become part of another community and so it goes on.' He pauses, looks up at me and grins hugely. 'Strange life really . . .'

'Do you have to be a bit odd to be a sailor, then, Mike?'

'Oh crikey, yes! Absolutely. What is it they say? "You don't have to be mad to work here – but it helps." That sums it up really, because I think we *are* a bit odd. Not in a bad way, because nobody has a bigger heart than a sailor, but we are definitely odd. I think that is good actually – nothing wrong with odd, a bit of healthy madness, but I think outsiders think we are from another planet.'

Mike Brotherton is legendary in the Navy. Like nearly all chaplains he is called a Bish – short for bishop* – but Mike Brotherton is known

* Bish is the most common name for a padre or chaplain in the Navy, although other variants include Devil Dodger, God Botherer, Holy Joe, Maker's Rep, Sin Bosun and Sky Pilot.

THE REVEREND MIKE BROTHERTON

to all as 'The Mad Bish'. To call him eccentric would be understating the case – like describing Mount Everest as a bit on the large side – and you only have to look around his cabin to get the idea. A large framed portrait of his all-time hero Charlie Chaplin, two stuffed monkeys, a teddy bear with flying goggles, a model of a Dalek, photographs of him on his beloved scooter and another of him in full clerical robes standing at the bow of a warship facing into the teeth of a gale with his arms splayed like Kate Winslet in *Titanic* – everywhere you look there is a visual joke, a souvenir, or a knick-knack with a story. Evidence of his vocation is there too, testaments to his calling: a pre-Raphaelite print of Christ walking on water, a Russian icon, a bible, the book of modern prayer and a car sticker saying 'Get a taste for religion – bite a cleric!'

'Glad you could pop in, Chris. Have you seen the captain?'

'Yes, just been with him,' I reply.

'Excellent. By the way, I'm doing a wedding next week if you would like to come. Proper Navy wedding at the church at HMS *Drake*. Give you a good insight into another side of our culture.'

'Great. Love to. Just so long as it doesn't clash with *Chatham* leaving because I will be going with her.'

'Oh, right. Of course. You need to do that. Off to the Gulf isn't she?'

'That's right. Away for Christmas.'

'Ah, the long goodbye. The families, the wives, the girlfriends will all be dealing with that now. Difficult time. For some, separation can be quite a strengthening thing, but for others it can be debilitating and, of course, not everyone can get through it. Coping with separation can be very difficult.'

'I know,' I say. 'I was talking to one of the cooks on *Chatham*, and he said it rips his heart out every time he goes on deployment.'

'Yes, it can hit some very hard, but, you know, that's where the community spirit kicks in on a ship. We do look after each other. Separation is hard, but it's probably usually worse for the ones left behind. Sailors soon get tucked into their own world when they go to sea. Shipmates look after each other. It's just the way it is.'

The Mad Bish looks down at his case. 'Right, still got to paint on all the shore establishments I have served in. My last one was HMS *Raleigh*. Are you covering HMS *Raleigh*, Chris? Fantastic place. I was there for two years. Loved every minute of it . . .'

Baby sailors

Location: Plymouth Railway Station
Time 11.30

I am standing next to a sign saying 'HMS *Raleigh*. Recruits report here'. It is on the main concourse of Plymouth railway station and behind it is a leading seaman holding a clipboard. He is busy ticking off the names of the latest batch of naval recruits who are starting to arrive from all over the country. Every week throughout the year the Navy takes in around sixty new recruits to its main training establishment, HMS *Raleigh* on the outskirts of Plymouth.

Right now, some as young as sixteen are stepping off Inter City trains from places like Newcastle, London, Glasgow, Liverpool and Manchester. Others have come in from Heathrow or Gatwick after long flights from their homelands – places like Fiji in the south Pacific and St Vincent in the West Indies where the Royal Navy has started a successful recruitment drive. These young men and women are about to start an intense eight-week period of Phase One training – seamanship; physical training; assault courses; teamwork; fire fighting; first aid; outward bound; swimming; sailing; kit maintenance; drill practice; and weapon handling – that will turn them from civvies off the street into 'baby' sailors.

A small girl, no more than seventeen or eighteen, with long blonde hair and big blue eyes, walks into the station from platform 3, pulling along a suitcase almost as big as she is.

'Hello,' says the leading seaman with the clipboard to the small girl. 'Name?'

'Jenny Parker,' she replies. He looks down his list and ticks her name. 'OK, just relax, but don't go far. Still waiting for a few more to arrive, and then we'll get you over to *Raleigh*.'

The small girl drags her case over to a wall and sits on it.

'How are you feeling?' I say.

'Excited! Bit nervous too. It was difficult saying goodbye at home – Mum was a bit emotional, you know. So was I!'

'Why have you chosen the Navy?' I ask.

'Oh, well, I have an uncle in the Marines, so that gave me the idea, and then I did geography for one of my A-levels and I thought I would like to become a hydrographer – you know, ocean surveys and all that. So the Navy just seemed right. Hope so!'

A male recruit wanders over with a rucksack on his back – he looks a bit older than most of the others. 'Hi, I'm Paul,' he says with a friendly grin. Jenny introduces herself and so do I. 'Pleased to meet you all,' he says with a smile.

'Forgive me for asking,' I say, 'but you're not exactly a teenager are you?'

'No spring chicken you mean,' he laughs. 'I'm thirty-two, with a couple of kids to boot.'

'So why are you joining up?'

'Well, because I want some security for my kids. Basically I want a career rather than a job, and jobs are all I've ever had. This and that, you know. Done all sorts. Time to do something that has a future.'

'And what branch do you want join after basic training?'

'Catering,' he replies immediately. 'I want to be a chef.'

'You've done cheffing before, then?'

'No, never cooked a thing in my life. Well – boiled the odd egg, but that's about it!'

A tall girl with a confident stride and determined look comes over to join us. 'What a day!' she says in a broad Scots accent. 'I've come all the way from Glasgow and had to come through London. Never been to London before – that tube system is a nightmare! Hi, my name's Sharon . . .'

All over the concourse nervous-looking young men and women are introducing themselves to each other. For many of them this is their first time away from home and they are probably still coming to terms with the farewells bid this morning to mums, dads, brothers, sisters and friends. For them it will have been the first 'goodbye' of their naval career but, as Rab Butler on HMS *Chatham* would tell them, it never gets any easier.

What strikes me most about these recruits is just how very civilian they look. I know that is hardly surprising, because that is precisely what they still are, but there is simply nothing military in their appearance or demeanour at all, nothing to suggest a naval leaning in the slightest. The boys, for instance, are generally sporting modern designer haircuts caked in gel, and the girls look just as unlikely with their make-up, fashion accessories and hair worn loose. Just how long, I think to myself, does it take to transform civilians into sailors both outwardly and inwardly?

'Hello,' says another girl approaching a small group outside the station burger bar. 'Are you all for *Raleigh*?' The group turn as one to greet the most unlikely-looking naval recruit of all of them. Bleached blonde hair halfway down her back, massive silver gypsy earrings, mini-skirt, a wrap-around, low-cut blouse and a huge bright pink suitcase. 'I'm Amy,' she says, 'from Manchester . . .' The other girls blink at her and the boys simply ogle.

By 12.30 the newly arrived recruits have been shepherded into a coach which heads for Torpoint where they experience the first sea trip of their naval careers. It is just a few minutes on a chain-driven car ferry that takes them from Plymouth to the other side of the Tamar River, where

HMS *Raleigh* is situated in rolling countryside bordering the sea. As we cross the Tamar on the lumbering boat, the recruits are pointing out to each other the array of grey warships bordering the jetties and wharfs. I look as well. There is the gigantic amphibious helicopter carrier HMS *Ocean* that I was on this morning, and her sister ship, the brand new HMS *Bulwark* recently arrived from the shipbuilders in Barrow; there is HMS *Trafalgar* the T-class hunter-killer submarine being prepared for secret missile testing in the Gulf of Mexico; there is HMS *Scott*, the survey vessel, soon to set off to South Africa and the Falklands, and over there is HMS *Chatham*, just a week away from her Gulf deployment.

Jenny, Paul, Sharon and Amy are wide-eyed as they survey the bustling scene in the famous waters of Devonport dockyard and I imagine their inner thoughts: '*We* could soon be on ships like that . . . going somewhere new . . . exciting . . . maybe even dangerous.' As I try to perceive the scene through their eyes, I recall the stories my father has told me of when he, as a young sailor of just seventeen, sailed in convoys across the North Atlantic, running the daily gauntlet of German U-boat attacks. How many young sailors, I wonder, have joined the Navy since then – that is, in the last sixty-odd years? The Navy has changed of course since my father's day, but still the world remains a dangerous and threatening place and I wonder if any of these recruits who not long ago stepped off their trains at Plymouth station are having the jitters yet or even second thoughts. That step off the train was a big one – quite literally life-changing.

We drive up to the front gate of HMS *Raleigh*. An armed Royal Marine guard stops the coach and a Ministry of Defence policeman gets on to check everyone's papers. 'Welcome to HMS *Raleigh*,' he says. 'I just need to check you are who you say you are. Your ID papers please.' The recruits dutifully pull out their IDs from a sheaf of paperwork containing the many mind-numbing forms they have been sent. Once identities are confirmed, the policeman steps off the coach, pausing only to glance back at the fresh-faced newcomers. 'Good luck you lot!' he says with a friendly smile.

We proceed, but the chatter that filled the coach up to this point has dissolved into nervous silence. The recruits peer at a bewildering array of buildings, parade-grounds and sports pitches that seem to spread for miles. At last we arrive at a modern brick-built building into which everybody is told to carry their luggage. A friendly petty officer greets the newcomers and invites them into a large classroom where there is tea and coffee available. After about ten minutes a leading hand brings in some sandwiches. ''Ere you go, shipmates,' he chirrups loudly. 'You'll get yer supper tonight, but for now a lovely choice of sarnis for you – spam and pickle or pickle and spam.'

The hungry recruits devour the sandwiches like vultures.

'They seem very nice here, don't they? Very friendly,' says Amy with the big earrings.

'They're probably just softening us up,' says a small boy with a West Country drawl and impressively sticky-out ears.

'Yes,' laughs Paul, the wannabe chef. 'Enjoy the hospitality whilst it lasts. Our days are numbered.'

'I hate spam . . .' says Jenny.

Over the next hour more recruits arrive until, eventually, fifty-two of them are congregated in the same room. It is then that a chief petty officer comes in and starts to go through a lot of routine paperwork with everyone: passport details, home addresses, ID papers and next of kin. When all this is done he calls for their attention.

'Right. Hear this!' What I have got to say is very important, so I want you to listen very, very carefully.' He pauses and looks round the room until he is sure every eye is on him. 'OK. You are about to join the Royal Navy . . . but I am telling you loud and clear I don't want you to . . .' he pauses again, '. . . no, not unless you are 100 per cent convinced you want to be here. It is a big move for each one of you, and you have to be sure it is what you want. Maybe some of you have already decided you have made a mistake, I don't know . . .'

Jenny glances at her half-eaten spam sandwich.

'. . . but if you have, don't worry. You will only have to spend the night here, and tomorrow you can be back on that train to Civvy Street and no hard feelings. If you decide to stay, your next "get out" is not for at least six weeks – we give you another chance to leave then. If you stay after that, you are in for six months with no way out. Beyond that we're talking life sentence! Well not exactly, but me – I've been in twenty-five years. That's longer than most of you have been sucking air.'

The recruits shift a little uneasily in their seats. At first I wonder why the chief seems almost to be putting them off the idea of joining the Royal Navy, but then he makes it clear.

'If you don't want to join the Navy, then don't,' he continues in a firm but sympathetic tone. 'It must be *your* decision. If you are here because your dad pushed you into it, or because someone else pressured you, then you should leave. We don't do press-gangs any more. OK? We want you if you want us – simple as that. It costs £30,000 to train each one of you over the next eight weeks, so we want to know you are a good investment.'

The chief petty officer pauses once again to look around the room, giving his message time to sink in.

'Later on today you will be invited to sign your naval contract. If you are sure, then sign it. If you want to sleep on it, do so and tackle the decision tomorrow morning. Plenty of people do that – we call them "sleepers". Any questions?'

There are no questions.

'OK, enough said. Next on the agenda does not apply to females – so ladies, stand fast! Haircuts. You men, if you have anything shorter than a buzz-cut number two you are probably OK. Otherwise you will be invited to take a haircut with us, and of course you will accept. For that privilege we will stop £4 from your first pay day.'*

We proceed to the basement where a jolly lady called Cynthia stands waiting next to a barber's chair. In her left hand she is wielding a metal comb and in her right hand an electric hair-clipper. She presses the button twice to test the motor and cuts the air with it as if she is about to fell a Giant Redwood with a chainsaw. Satisfied all is in cutting order she then invites the first of her clients to take a seat. A blond recruit with highlights slumps miserably into the chair, as if it is one of those they plug into the mains in Texan penitentiaries. Then, as the hair clipper is activated, the victim closes his eyes and waits for the inevitable. One by one the gel-reinforced designer haircuts that cost an arm and a leg on Civvy Street are levelled to just so much head bristle. Cynthia, happy in her work, remains cheerful throughout – smiling and joking, oblivious of the torment she is inflicting.†

Next, the girls and the now shaven-headed boys are able, if they want, to sign their naval contracts. They do not have to, as they have already been told, but for all the recruits there seems to be no doubt at this stage and they are eager to sign, literally, on the dotted line. There are no sleepers.

In a room immediately adjacent to Cynthia's Salon there are about a dozen naval officers and non-commissioned officers, seated at small tables with another vacant chair at each one. Recruits file in and each

*Re pay for trainees £11,774 p.a.

† The recruits can in fact regrow their hair to a reasonable length. This initial 'head-beasting' is just a symbolic exercise in discipline and conforming. There is a real sense too that all the male recruits start with a common and shared experience that in some way unites them. Female recruits do not have to have their hair cut, but neither are they allowed to wear it loose. Long hair has to be worn as a bun.

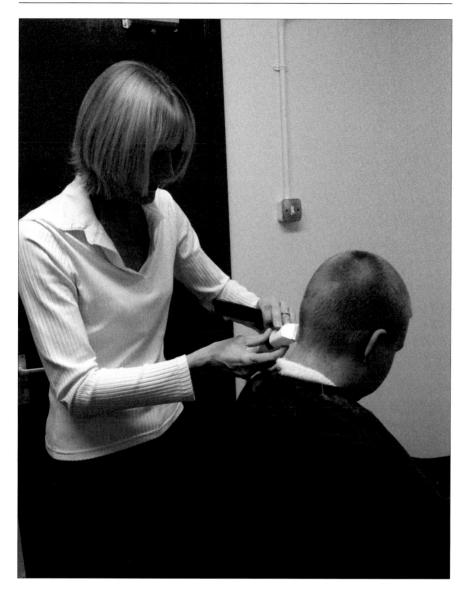

A RECRUIT IS SHORN

one sits opposite one of the officers. The rest of the recruits remain at the door and wait their turn. The officers go through yet another MoD form with each recruit in private, before asking them individually: 'Are you ready to sign yourself into the Navy?'

'Yes' come the answers, some more resolute than others, but 'yes' none the less.

The recruits, called the 'Forty-Sixers' because they have all joined up in week forty-six, are told to muster outside. It is 4 p.m. – 16.00 as they must learn to think of it – and they have to proceed to the Slops stores* to collect uniforms. It is about 200 yards away.

* Slops store or clothing store.

'OK you lot,' says a chief petty officer who wears his peaked cap low over his eyes and stands in boots as shiny as polished ebony. 'We 'ave to get ourselves from 'ere to over there. How are we goin' to do it?'

'Walk,' suggests one recruit.

'Wrong!'

'Drive,' suggests another, hopefully.

'Are you 'aving a laugh, mister?'

'March, sir,' says yet another.

'Right. As new recruits you will march everywhere. No bimbling, strolling or walking. You march everywhere. Standard pace, or double time if you are in a hurry. And you do not call me "sir", you call me "Chief". You call officers "sir". Leading seamen instructors you will call "Staff". If you are confused as to what rank we are in your first few days, just resort to "Staff" – but *always* give us a title. There you are that's your first get out of jail free card.'

The recruits try hard not to look confused.

'Right, get fell in. Two ranks. Shortest on the right, tallest on the left!'

The recruits do their best to organise themselves in some semblance of order and eventually approximate to two vaguely neat lines.

'OK, not bad, but some of you seem to have an exaggerated sense of your own heights. Oi, Lofty. How tall are you?'

'Five foot five, sir . . . Staff. I mean Chief.'

'So why are you standing between two ten-foot beanpoles? Move down the line.'

'Lofty' does as he is told.

'Listen up,' continues the chief. 'You will be receiving drill instruction as part of your training, so for now just do your best and use your common sense. Listen carefully to my orders. Ready. Right turn!'

Most people manage to turn right – but some turn left, leaving them staring into the face of a fellow recruit.

'Come on, people! You 'ad a fifty-fifty chance of getting that one right! OK, try this one. By the right, quick march!'

Chaos ensues. Some people lead with their right foot, some with their left, one person does a complete about turn and about six remain rooted to the spot.

Somehow, the Forty-Sixers make it to the Slops store. In fact, by the time they get there they are beginning to get the hang of marching – that is to say, marching in a straight line. Right or left wheels and about turns on the march are still accidents waiting to happen.

The recruits collect bags of uniform, boots and other clothing and then march with them back to their dormitories or 'mess decks' to try them all on.

In the girls' mess deck Jenny has pulled on a long-sleeved turquoise games shirt and is currently wrestling with two enormous black boots. Sharon is trying on a thick navy-blue jumper and Amy – earrings, wrap-around blouse and mini-skirt discarded – is looking down suspiciously at the fatigue trousers she has just climbed into.

'Not exactly flattering is it?' she says, looking over her shoulder at her reflection in a mirror.

'It's not meant to be high fashion, Amy,' laughs Sharon.

'I know, but I wonder when we will get the chance to wear our own clothes again, to look like girls again.'

'Don't hold your breath. We've got to dig in for eight weeks.'

Each recruit has also been given a pair of orange epaulettes – the sign of their rank, or should I say absence of rank? They will never be lower in the naval food chain than they are today and, in fact, for the whole of this week. Right now they are the latest intake into the Royal Navy, but next week there will be a new entry of recruits who will assume the lowest rung on the ladder, and today's arrivals will have gained one week's seniority – the first step on a career path geared to promotion.

'How are you doing Forty-Sixers?' says a cheery voice from the doorway. The new recruits look up to see a smiling brunette who promptly walks in.

'Hello, I'm Jane from the Forty Twos. Just came to say hi and see if you want any help.'

'Hello,' say the Forty-Sixers.

'Can you show us how we are meant to fold our clothes and stack them in the cupboards?' says Sharon. 'These instructions are doing my head in!'

'Yeah, no probs. Give us your shirt and I'll show you,' says Jane. 'You have to fold everything so it is the shape of an A4 piece of paper – no bigger. It's because you will have such small storage spaces on board ships.' She folds the shirt expertly and then measures it against an A4 piece of cardboard.

'There,' she says, 'it's easy when you know how. It's all about conformity. Military conformity. If you don't fold your clothes right and stow 'em right, they will just pull everything out of the cupboard and throw the lot all over the room. It can blow your mind if you let it, but you get used to it. Just don't let it get to your emotions.'

Clearly, conformity and discipline are essential to the sense of order demanded by shipboard living as well as to the regulation and organisation essential to sailing, maintaining and replenishing a ship, not to mention fighting a war at sea. However, sailors are not robots – far from it. In my experience sailors are often great individuals and studied non-conformists – but only outside the requirements of duty. A sailor on-duty is a very different animal to a sailor off-duty when he or she is very much his own man or woman, very much the individual. It is because of the demands of an ordered and conformist existence that Jack has to exercise his alter ego just to balance things out. Maybe, I ponder, that is why sailors have gained their reputations for exuberance and high living as well as their celebrated sense of humour and mischief.

At 17.35 the Forty-Sixers are marching again – this time it is to the dining room for their supper. With the prospect of food there is a definite spring in their step and the arms are swinging high, but then a tannoy makes an announcement.

'Two minutes to Sunset.'

The petty officer in charge of the recruits brings them to a halt and stands them at ease.

'In two minutes it will be 'Sunset Routine', he explains. 'That is to say the naval flag – the White Ensign at the front gate – will be lowered at dusk. As a sign of respect you will face in the direction of the flag and you will salute on my orders.'

The Forty-Sixers stand and wait.

In just under two minutes the tannoy announces, 'Ten seconds to Sunset.'

'Parade! Parade, attention! Parade, right turn!'

'Pipe the still,' echoes the tannoy.

'Parade will salute to the front, salute!'

A shrill note from a bosun's whistle signals 'Sunset', and the White Ensign on the main parade ground and another at the entrance of HMS *Raleigh* are slowly lowered.

The Sunset Routine is observed every day on board every ship, wherever it is in the world as long as it is alongside, and every member of the Royal Navy on the upper deck or within sight of the Ensign, normally flown at the stern of a ship, will stand to attention and salute. (The sunrise routine is called Colours, when the Ensign is raised for the day, and so the cycle continues.) It is one of those many embracing rituals that will begin to beat out a whole new rhythm in the daily life of these newcomers. At this moment they are joining with all the other sailors and officers of all ranks currently saluting the White Ensign throughout the naval base as the sun dips beneath the horizon.

Twenty seconds later the tannoy announces, 'Pipe the carry on.'

The bosun's whistle duly obliges.

Location: Plymouth Town Centre
Time: 21.00

Plymouth's Union Street is the hub of the town's nightlife and off-duty naval personnel flock to its numerous pubs and clubs on a nightly basis. Most are just after a good time, but problems can and do occur. Alcohol-fuelled revelling sometimes leads to fights – occasionally amongst servicemen, but more usually between servicemen and civilians – and so naval police or regulators, wearing stab-proof body armour and carrying batons and handcuffs, patrol the streets, ready to pounce on any troublemakers.

I have joined a team of two regulators for their night patrol in a large van marked 'Service Police', complete with blue lights and sirens. In charge is Leading Regulator Marie Maddocks from Liverpool – five foot

SCOUSE AND MARIE
ON THE BEAT

two and bubbly, but tough as nails. Her partner and tonight's driver is Leading Regulator 'Scouse' Ashton, also from Liverpool. He is tall and imposing, but sports a bright and cheery countenance – despite a telling scar across his lower lip and chin.

'Plymouth can be a very violent place sometimes,' says Scouse as he stops at a zebra crossing to let a crowd of jeering city youths over the road, 'especially down here in Union Street, and our job is first and foremost to assist libertymen ashore. We don't want to nick them if we don't have to; we want to stop them getting into trouble or getting hurt in the first place. We also help sailors get back to their ships – especially if they've had a skinful. Always best to get them back where they belong and out of harm's way.'

'But you do nick them if you have to?' I say.

'Oh yes. Then they have to face naval discipline which can be a lot more severe than what they might get in Civvy Street. That's why a lot of them would always prefer to be nicked by the civvy police rather than us.'

'It will be fairly quiet now,' adds Marie. 'They're all in the pubs and the clubs, but once they shut down that's when we can get aggro. That's when everybody spills out on to the streets, all boozed up, wired and looking for a taxi . . . or trouble. It only takes a civvy to take a pop at a sailor, or the other way round, and you've got yourself a bundle!'

'They can be as good as gold sometimes – civvies and sailors,' says Scouse. 'Usually at the end of the month when the cash is short, so there's not so much drinking done – but at other times all hell can let loose. You can never tell. But it will always be a minority kicking off. You get troublemakers in every walk of life and the Navy is no different.'

'Booze is usually behind it,' says Marie, '. . . not to mention youth and male testosterone!'

'I don't know about that,' interrupts Scouse. 'Sometimes the girls get stuck in as well.'

'You're right,' says Marie. 'Some of the toughest fights I've seen have been between girls – not just Navy but generally. That's unusual though – it's normally the lads having a go.'

'Often problems arise with the civvies because they can get jealous of Jacks' money,' says Scouse. 'Sailors earn quite a lot compared to many of the youngsters around here, and if they are too flash people react, don't they Marie?'

'Yeah, and also there can be a view that sailors are preying on the civvies' women as well.'

'Yeah, it's usually about booze or birds . . .' grins Scouse, 'and if we don't get there quick, it can escalate. Sailors will always stick up for each other, so if one of them is in trouble his buddies will all step in.'

'I guess it's how they have been trained,' I say.

'Well that's it,' laughs Scouse. 'We always look after our own. That's good in a war situation, but not always so good on Union Street on a Friday night!'*

The van patrols the whole of the town centre, but continuously changes its route so that people can never tell where it might be at any one time.

'As a visible presence we are a deterrence,' says Marie. 'People need to know we are around.'

We tour all the side streets off Union Street itself, including a particularly seedy and badly lit road which prompts Scouse to shout out to me, 'Choose a number between one and six, quick!'

'Four,' I say immediately, without understanding why.

'Six!' says Marie.

'Three!' says Scouse.

We proceed slowly down the dark street whilst Scouse and Marie peer into the shadows.

'There's one!' shouts Scouse.

'There's another!' says Marie. 'And another!'

'Another what?' I enquire.

'Prostitute,' says Scouse. 'This is the red light district. We always guess how many might be out when we drive down. The loser has to make the tea.'

I look into the shadows of the street again and, sure enough, begin to make out the silhouetted figures hiding in the darkened doorways, shivering in the chill night air as they wait for their custom to arrive.

'There's another on the corner,' says Marie, 'and two more crossing the road. That's six. I win!'

The headlights pick out a man, clearly the worse for drink, urinating in a doorway. 'Oi, you!' shouts Marie sternly. 'Stop that now or you will be nicked. Move on!'

The man, shocked but confused, turns to face the lights.

'And put it away, sir. Not that impressive.'

*By all accounts, it used to be an awful lot worse in the past – it was a virtual war zone in Union Street up to the late seventies, at least at the weekends. Fights would frequently break out, often between sailors and marines who have nursed a deeply held enmity for each other since the eighteenth century. This was when the primary duty of the Royal Marine was to protect naval officers from the sailors – many of whom had been press-ganged and so held understandable grudges. Sailors, always referred to generically as 'Jack', and marines, always known as 'Bootnecks', have 'fought the good fight' ever since but, whilst there is still a real sense of 'us' and 'them' between the two, evidently relations warmed considerably after the Falklands War when they found a new respect for each other.

The man nods his head vigorously, adjusts his dress and wobbles up the road.

'He was a civvy,' says Marie. 'You can tell from the haircut. If he had been a serviceman, he would have been in trouble because, as it says in the book, he would have been behaving "in a disorderly manner likely to bring discredit on Her Majesty's Service".'

We move back into Union Street, and then head east towards the more prosperous Barbican area which is speckled with pubs and wine bars.

'A lot of sailors start off drinking in the Barbican but the pubs close at eleven over there, so then they start to wander over here where everything stays open longer. We always check they behave themselves on the way.'

We pass a police van parked up at the side of the road. Scouse waves to the policemen who are questioning a man with blood gushing from his mouth and nose.

'We work very closely with the Devon and Cornwall Constabulary,' says Scouse, '. . . and whilst we mostly concentrate on servicemen, we do sometimes pull in civvies if the local police are not around to deal with a situation. We don't take 'em back to our base of course – just hand 'em over to the local nick.'

Our van has returned to Union Street where people are beginning to leave the pubs on their way to the clubs. Hundreds are emerging from the Two Trees, the Clipper, the Union Rooms and the Reflex and are heading over to the Dance Academy, Jesters, Koolaroos, Flairs and the Hackney. Everybody is in high spirits, but there is no sign of any trouble. Just to our left as we drive by, a group of raucously singing and well-muscled men are emerging from the Two Trees. All are dressed as schoolgirls, complete with pigtails, short pleated skirts and black suspenders for good measure.

'Hello,' says Scouse, 'Royal Marines in their preferred civilian garb I would say.'

At that moment the short wave radio spurts out a burst of static followed by a measured but urgent message: 'Disturbance at the Walkabout in Union Street . . .'

Even before the message has finished the van is accelerating down Union Street towards the Australian-themed pub. Within minutes we are outside the Walkabout, where a young man, obviously the worse for wear, is shouting and screaming abuse at one of the bouncers on the door. As he sees the regulators advancing towards him, he does his best to run away but is no match for the pace of the naval law keepers. He is quickly apprehended and, despite a great deal of swearing and struggling, he is marched back to the van and put into the lock-up at the back.

'Not one of ours,' says Scouse. 'A civvy with a skinful, but apparently he was facing up to a sailor who did the right thing and walked away. We'll take him up to the nick and hand him over. Probably just needs a couple of hours in the cell to cool down. *They* can do all the paper work!'

Location: Plymouth Hoe
Time: 01.15

I am back on the Hoe overlooking Plymouth Sound where this morning I was watching seagulls. Right now, below me, I can see the silhouetted shape of HMS *Cumberland*, which arrived back earlier this evening and is now anchored safely in the lee of Bovisand Hill. Deep in the bowels of the ship, the party to mark the end of a long deployment is probably still in full swing. Some sailors on the upper deck are flashing torches in the direction of Bovisand car park, because that is where wives, husbands, girlfriends, boyfriends, sons and daughters are also sending torchlight messages of welcome. Tomorrow morning she will sail proudly into Devonport dockyard and deliver an emotional crew safely back to their delighted and equally emotional families, in plenty of time for the Christmas holidays.

Meanwhile, no more than a mile away, HMS *Chatham*, tied up along-side, is guarded by armed sailors. She is now only days from deploying to the Gulf in what will undoubtedly be a sad and tear-stained departure.

It occurs to me again that HMS *Cumberland* and HMS *Chatham*, currently both within the confines of Plymouth's harbour, are at opposite ends of the emotional spectrum that pervades life in the Royal Navy. One is about to enjoy the 'big hello', as Mike Brotherton would call it, whilst the other is bracing itself for the 'big goodbye'.

The incoming tide pushes *Cumberland* symbolically towards the coastline, but she is restrained by her heavy anchor cable. The same rising tide lifts *Chatham* higher in her berth and the angle of the gangway from the ship to the quayside increases dramatically. As it does so it creaks noisily, disturbing the seagulls resting on her superstructure, but they do not fly. They have done a lot of flying today and will be doing a lot more tomorrow.

The regulators are still on patrol and will remain on duty until about three o'clock in the morning when the last of the Union Street clubs closes. Right now they are probably taking the chance for a quick cup of coffee and a sandwich from one of the street kiosks, but remain ready to respond to any call.

On the other side of the harbour, at HMS *Raleigh,* the new recruits are in bed on their first night away from home – their first night in the Navy. How many are asleep? How many are still awake, thinking of tomorrow; thinking about the rest of their lives?

CHAPTER TWO

Hello – Goodbye

The Following Day
Location: Wharf 15
Time: 08.00

The Royal Marine Band marches impressively down the quayside. The colour sergeant leading it raises his ceremonial mace high above his head then points it to his right. Instantaneously the band wheels smoothly, and on the next order strikes up with 'We Are Sailing'. The crowd of families that has been building for the last two hours turns to look and bursts into delighted applause. Everywhere there are Union Flags, Ensigns and every conceivable type of banner bearing a 'welcome home' message – the most common being 'Welcome home Daddy' and signed with a child's name.

The band draws level with the crowd and is halted by the colour sergeant, but it never stops playing. Piccolos, trumpets, trombones, clarinets, euphoniums, French horns, marching drums and a big bass drum now launch into 'A Life on the Ocean Wave'.

'There she is!' shouts a man at the end of the quay. All eyes swivel and the crowd gasps at the distant sight of HMS *Cumberland*, flanked by two tugboats, cutting resolutely through the grey harbour waters towards them. Hundreds of flags and banners start to wave in the chill November wind as the Marine band changes tempo with 'I'm Dreaming of a White Christmas'. Young mothers are pointing towards the ship, showing small children where to look.

'Daddy's on that big ship.'

'Where? Where's my Daddy?' shouts one small girl in a festive red dress with white fur on the collar and at the hem. 'Where Mummy? I can't see him!'

As the frigate gets closer and grows in stature, the lines of sailors along her upper decks are clearly visible. Up on the bridge wings officers are waving their hats. Slowly she draws level with the wharf and the tugs start to coax her into the quayside. Now, for the first time, families are able to spot 'their' sailor. Hankies and tissues are being pulled out of pockets and handbags to dab at increasingly moist eyes.

'Where's my Daddy?' screams the little Christmas girl. 'Where's my Daddy?'

The battleship-grey frigate is home after six long months. As riggers catch the ropes hurled from the ship and start to secure her on quayside bollards, a female sailor pulls a rope on the bow jackstay to release a Union Jack that unfurls proudly in the now rain-bearing wind, but nothing is going to dampen the emotion of the moment. The band, now playing 'Auld Lang Syne', tweaks that emotion to breaking point as the gangway is dropped into position by a shoreside crane. As soon as it is secured, the sailors are released and they surge down the gangway and into the arms of their waiting loved ones.

'There's my Daddy!' screams the little girl, but her mother can't speak for her own sobbing. Soon the quayside is a mass of hugging, crying, laughing people.

'Hellos' do not come much bigger than this at the end of a long deployment . . .

Location: Weston Mill Lake. Wharf 11
Time: 09.00

HMS *Chatham*, just three days from deploying to the Gulf herself, is starting the long process of taking on food stores. Huge pallets of boxes, sacks and tins are swinging on to the ship's forward missile deck from mobile cranes on the quayside. As soon as they touch the deck, sailors descend on them to unload: rice, flour, cooking oil, huge jars of Marmite, catering cartons of HP Sauce, cake mix, jam, curry powder, pasta, mayonnaise, cornflakes . . . it just keeps coming. The Vertiflow lift down to the storage spaces is broken, so a human chain of men and women in blue working rig stretches from the upper deck all the way into the ship: all along One Deck and then down the ladders into Two Deck and then down further into Three Deck, well below the waterline. There Ginge Grieveson is frantically directing the storage of goods as they arrive in seemingly endless fashion.

'Get that lot over here,' he shouts at the final man in the human chain. 'Come on, Shippers [Shipmates] – stack the rice flat. Pack it down. We gotta lot to get in here.'

'Do you remember where you put everything, Ginge?' I enquire.

'In theory,' he laughs. 'I pretend to anyway, but I tell you what – whatever it is we want, from a spud to a glacé cherry, it'll always be right at the back of somewhere so we have to go potholing for it!'

'Sod's law,' I laugh.

'No mate – that's Pusser's law. Pusser made that law up long before Sod did!'

Pusser, by the way, is a generic word that refers to anything that is officially 'Navy'.

A frigate is not a large ship and space is at an absolute premium so it was impressive to see Ginge supervise the storage of so much food.

'Yeah, well, sailors are good at making the most of small spaces,' he says, wrestling with a bag of cake mix. 'You should see where we have to sleep!'

'Oi Ginge,' comes a shout from the human chain. 'Branston Pickle coming next – where do you want it?'

'Under the Tommy sauce, far left, second shelf down,' says Ginge instantly, then turns back to me. 'We got the frozen food on yesterday, and by the end of today we'll have all dry stores stowed – enough for sixty to seventy days, but we would never let stores go under twenty days.' He puts his shoulder to a huge catering bag of self-raising flour, urging it into an unyielding gap between the dried peas and the porridge oats. 'We replenish whenever we can – especially fresh food of course. It was always a bit dodgy getting good stuff in the Middle East, but it's much better now. We've got reputable suppliers, but we still have to check everything out – Jack's not ready for camel kebabs just yet.'

'Christmas puds, Ginge! Inbound. Hundreds of 'em . . .'

On a six month deployment HMS *Chatham*'s ship's company of 246 will consume:
36,360 eggs
22,960 rashers of bacon (21 miles)
27,220 sausages (17 miles)
8,000 litres of milk
21 tonnes of potatoes
4,600 toilet rolls (18 each)

Location: HMS *Raleigh*. Main class room
Time: 11.00

The recruits are well into their second day and waiting for a class on Discipline. Suddenly, the door bursts open and a Royal Marine officer strides in, perfectly turned out and ramrod straight.

'Sit to attention! Do not be slovenly. Do not be sloppy.'

The recruits jump. 'Standing to attention' they have done but 'sitting to attention' is a new concept altogether. The Marine officer twitches his perfectly groomed moustache whilst surveying the new recruits in front of him.

'You are in the Navy now,' he barks, 'and there are three things you MUST learn: discipline, turnout and bearing.'

The day-old recruits look on, stony-faced but wide-eyed. The marine twitches his moustache again – a sign, clearly, that he is about to say something of great import.

'Discipline. This means you will do as you are told – that is, obey orders from any superior rank. That does not mean think about it. That means do it.

'Turnout. It will be immaculate at all times. One crease in the trousers top to bottom at the back and front and no Irish pennants – that means no labels sticking out – ever. No rings unless you are married persons and no chewing of gum at any time.

'Bearing. You will carry yourself proudly. We will teach you this through drill – marching, turning, saluting and then with SA 80 rifles…'

The recruits glance at each other. They now know without any doubt they are in the military – good and proper.

'We are transforming you from civilians into Royal Navy sailors. The next eight weeks will not be easy. They will be difficult – but remember, if it was not difficult everybody would be doing it.'

The Marine officer softens his tone and eases back on the moustache twitching.

'There will be times when you will have regrets. You will be tired, wet and miserable – push through it people – you won't regret it!'

Location: Wharf 15, Weston Mill Lake
Time: 13.00

All morning Mike Brotherton has been transforming his chapel on HMS *Ocean*. It had been a dirty green colour, but now he is painting it pure white and adding a blue rope-design motif to all the vertical struts on the bulkheads.

'I've had enough of painting for a while,' he says. 'I need a break. Come on, I'll show you my favourite place on the ship.'

We walk for miles – or that is what it feels like, because this ship is immense. Its passageways seem infinite, but eventually we get to the stern of the ship and open a huge metal door into an airlock, and then another door out to an open area at the stern of the ship, just above the propellers but underneath the main deck.

'This is the quarterdeck,' says Mike. 'I love to come here when we are at sea because it is so exhilarating when the props are spinning at full throttle – the water is just so churned up, like it is boiling with anger. But then, when we are stationary in the water or just moving slowly, this can be a place of great peace.'

'You prefer being at sea don't you, Mike,' I say, as we look over Weston Mill Lake to where HMS *Chatham*, just a couple of hundred yards away, is still taking on stores.

'Every time. Absolutely. No doubt about it. I mean, I miss my Mum and Dad of course and my friends, but the sea is where most sailors feel at home. I do. At the moment we are alongside for refit and maintenance, but I tell you, I envy that lot over there on *Chatham*, about to go on deployment.'

'Is it simply a sailor thing for you, though, Mike, or is it a God thing too?'

'Well, I reckon God wants me to do his ministry in ships with these sailors. That's for sure. I'll tell you something else – it is only at sea that I can find what I call the spirit of a ship.'

'How do you mean?'

'Well, a ship has a spirit, an identity if you like, and I think that that spirit only really comes alive when the ship becomes a community and that only happens when we are at sea. It becomes home to all those it carries. People refer to a ship at sea as an iron village, and that is just what it becomes – or for me, an iron parish.'

'Is it also to do with going into the unknown?'

'Yes. It is. *Chatham* over there is off to the Gulf in a few days, but nobody knows exactly what she is going to face over the next six months. That's why it is such a strange life in the Navy – you go from one extreme to another. One day you are here, and the next it is all change and you are being sent somewhere else. As a single man I don't mind, I love the adventure, but it can get very difficult for married people.'

We both watch as a crane swings another gigantic pallet of boxes on to *Chatham*'s foredeck.

'I liken serving in the Navy to the weather sometimes,' Mike adds thoughtfully. 'I mean, it can all be lovely and placid one moment, and then it can turn. Suddenly it is stormy and threatening and this affects our emotions – of course it does. Sometimes emotions on board are in turmoil just like the sea, as restless as the sea.'

'It's very different from being in the Army or the Air Force then?'

'Oh yes. They can get away from it. We have to live on our ships 24/7 when we are away. We can't get off. And even when we come home to port, we know it is only a matter of time before we are going to return to the sea. The sea is our master. It controls our whole existence and we respect it. I know it is the master of "I". I am not the master of it.'

'So, you are frustrated when you are alongside like this?'

'To an extent, yes I am – but then, the shore base has its own charm. It is still a naval community with naval people. We are still combined by our "navalness" and I love that too. So much goes on here, so many lives are played out here, and in so many ways. People think this is just a place where ships are tied up, but it is so much more than that. Guzz is a world unto itself . . .'

Mike, the Mad Bish, with his passion for Charlie Chaplin, Dr Who (at his home in Wales he has a full-size Dalek) and motor scooters (he is a self-professed Mod) is in a philosophical and contemplative mood today, but soon his trademark grin returns to brighten both his face and the mood of the moment. 'Come on, let's go to the wardroom for tea and biscuits. I think I have some Chocolate Hobnobs hidden away somewhere . . .'

Location: HMS *Raleigh*. Main parade ground
Time: 15.00

The Forty-Sixers are out on the parade ground on drill practice. Chief Petty Officer Chris Lewis is their instructor and he is teaching them from scratch, as he has taught hundreds if not thousands before them.

'At the end of eight weeks, people, I will 'ave you marching like you would never believe you could – but that will mean some graft from you . . .'

He stops what he is saying and looks up with a start.

'No talkin'! I find anyone talkin' and that will mean press-ups. Not just for the one talkin' but for everyone else. Get it? Then you can all take it out on the culprit later – that's psychology that is.'

Chris Lewis is strict but fair and is known for a laconic wit.

'Oi, you!' he shouts at Paul Ferris. ''Ow old are you then?'

'Thirty-two, Chief.'

'What the 'ell are you doin' here?' Chris Lewis says in mock shock. 'Did you get on the wrong bus or somethin'?'

'No, Chief,' says Paul with a smile. 'I meant to come here.'

'Bloody 'ell,' comes the rejoinder. 'I'm about to leave the mob after twenty years at the age of thirty-six, and you are just comin' in at thirty-two? What do you wanna do?'

'Cheffing, Chief.'

'Right. Is that what you did in Civvy Street?'

'No, Chief. I did all sorts. Mainly social work, childcare work.'

'Oh ideal!' says the chief, genuinely impressed. 'Well, good luck to you mate.'

Chris Lewis is a hard taskmaster, but, like most chiefs that I have met, has a soft human streak running through him. The chief, along with the warrant officer, is the interface rank between the rating and the commissioned officer, and to be effective in this position not only has to apply the rules effectively but also read people well and command the respect of everybody above and below them. These people are the solid spine of the Royal Navy and, whilst they are just another cog in the machine that is one huge hierarchical team, these senior ratings all but run the show – at least on a day to day basis. They make things happen, even if it is the officers that plan the wider strategies and issue the orders.

CHIEF PETTY OFFICER CHRIS LEWIS SHOWS HOW TO SALUTE

'OK! Drill. Lesson One. Standing at ease!' shouts Chris Lewis to the fifty-two recruits starting to shiver in the Plymouth drizzle. 'Your feet should be at 45-degree angles, and you should have them apart by twelve inches – no more, no less. Let's see it, come on. Parade, parade – stand at ease!'

The recruits adopt the position, but do so in a range of styles from the 'almost at attention' to the near splits.

'Now listen to me, people!' shouts Chris Lewis, slapping his forehead. 'I said twelve inches didn't I? The ONLY time in your lives – gentlemen AND ladies – you will ever 'ave twelve inches between your legs will be when you are standin' at ease. If any of you can truthfully tell me otherwise, then you should not be here anyway. You should be in America makin' bleedin' porn movies. Right, one more time . . .'

Location: HMS *Drake*. Wyvern Sports Centre
Time: 17.30

For the next two days this will be the venue for the Royal Navy Inter Command Novice Boxing Championships, which is a sort of legalised punch-up between the four Royal Navy Commands – Portsmouth, Plymouth, Scotland and the Fleet Air Arm, with the Royal Marines thrown in for good measure. Every boxer is fighting for the honour of his Command, his commanding officer and his shipmates and, if allowed, would probably fight to the death. Chief Petty Officer Natasha Pulley, a physical training instructor, is organising the event. Forget the stereotype. Forget the chromosomally challenged demi-woman with bulging

CHIEF PETTY OFFICER
NATASHA PULLEY AND ME

biceps and five o'clock shadow. Natasha, or Tasha as everyone calls her, is a petite, demure, pretty mother of two, as bouncy as a kangaroo on a trampoline, and in a constant state of excitement and/or panic.

'Oh my God! Oh my God!' she says excitedly. 'I've got so much to do. The Inter-Commands is one of the biggest nights of the year for us, and I have to get the hall ready. We have to get the ring up, the flags up, the tables set up and I have to arrange the music too. Every boxer's entrance has to have a different tune. I'll never do it all. Look at my list of things to do. It's endless – and we don't know about the boxers yet. I mean if we are going to have enough. Oh my God . . . this is turning into a nightmare!'

'What do you mean you may not have enough boxers?' I enquire. 'Surely the squads have been worked out by now.'

'Oh yes, of course!' she says with mock impatience. 'But the boxers are all working sailors and are coming from all over the country and from all sorts of ships – some on deployment abroad. Loads are having to travel a long way to get here in time. We have the preliminaries tomorrow night and then the finals the night after. Right, now, what do you reckon to Robbie Williams's 'Let Me Entertain You' for one of the boxer's entrance and then we can have Queen's 'We Will Rock You' for another and . . . oh, excuse me, I must go and check on the flags they're putting up over there . . .'

Tasha continues to rush around like a crazed banshee – issuing orders about the precise placing of White Ensigns all around the gym, the positioning of tables for the VIP guests, and the catering arrangements.

THE WYVERN GYM IS TRANSFORMED FOR THE INTER-COMMAND BOXING CHAMPIONSHIPS

'Jock' Eastern, the lieutenant commander in charge of the Wyvern, comes into the gym to see how things are going.

'Are you winning, Tash?' he shouts with a broad smile from the other side of the hall.

'Er, yes, sir. In a manner of speaking,' replies Tasha, walking towards the genial Scotsman. 'Organised chaos at the moment, sir.'

'The hall's coming along,' he says, surveying the walls that are being hung with White Ensigns. 'You're not having the Marine trumpeters to bring in the fighters are you?'

'No, sir. Thought we would have more modern music blasting out – and smoke machines, lights, the works! It'll make it a bit less military – more . . . more . . .'

'*Rocky*?' suggests her boss.

'Exactly! Well I hope that's as in Sylvester Stallone you mean, sir, not as in *Horror Show*?'

'Well, we'll have to wait and see won't we?' says Jock Eastern with a smile as he walks out of the gym.

'Oh God!' says Tasha. 'I couldn't show him my list of things to do. He would have exploded. Look at it!'

She holds up a typewritten sheet with a neat list of tasks written in one organised column.

'Looks good that, doesn't it?' she says. 'Well, look at the other side!'

She turns over the sheet to reveal a mass of scribbled notes, with crossings out, numerous arrows and frantic exclamation marks indicating a frenzy of changed plans, timings and ideas.

'Madness!' she says. 'Every year I do this and it's always the same. Total madness!'

'But you still do it,' I observe.

'Yes, I do. The thing is, it's worth it for the sake of the boxers. These young lads are putting themselves on the line in order to represent their Commands, their ships and their mates. Some of them have never boxed competitively before, and it takes a lot of guts to get into that ring. I admire that and want to make it the best possible evening for them … Oh look! That's fantastic!'

One of the smoke machines by one of the doors has been turned on and is billowing white clouds backlit by a spotlight.

'Brilliant!' says Tasha. 'The boxers will enter through that smoke. Big music . . . applause . . . crowd screaming. It'll make the boys feel really important, you see. I love it!'

At that moment a large and looming shape appears through the smoke. The silhouetted figure gradually takes form as it enters the gym.

'Bleedin' smoke machines!' says Rab Butler, putting on a mock coughing fit. 'Thought a fuckin' bomb 'ad gone off!'

'Button it, Butler,' replies Tasha good humouredly. 'Thought you were meant to be sailing away on your ship!'

'I am. In a couple of days,' replies Rab. 'Just got back from storing ship. It's like a floatin' Tesco's. Never seen so many flamin' cornflakes, and hundreds of Christmas puds. Don't even like the bloody things!'

'You just missed the boss!'

'Oo-er,' says Rab. 'Is he still around?'

'Probably.'

'Mmmm, well, that's all water through the bilge-pump, ain't it?'

'Err, yes . . .' says Tash, widening her big brown eyes, '. . . as long as you got rid of those cards saying you were the most important man in the world of boxing!'

'Ha, ha. Very funny,' grins Rab. 'Go an' sort out yer smoke machines…!'

'Yeah, actually I will. We need to get another one on the other side of the hall. See you guys!'

Rab looks over to me. 'She's a good girl, Tash. Might steer clear of the boss though – don't want to rake up the past do I? I'm goin' over to the boxing gym next door to see the Plymouth squad sparring – want to come over . . .?'

Right across the road from the Wyvern Sports Centre is a small gym called the Randolph Turpin, named after the great British middleweight who became world champion in 1951 and who was himself a chef at HMS *Raleigh*. As we walk in, I notice a series of telling boxing epithets written all over the walls and windows like: 'To be the best you have to beat the best', 'You are now entering an excuse-free zone', 'Train hard, fight easy' and 'Fail to prepare – prepare to fail'. At the far end of the long room is a boxing ring with a group of men around it and two inside it.

'Keep your gloves up, Sam!' shouts Paul Ransley, the Plymouth Command's boxing coach, as he watches two of his team facing up to each other in the ring. 'Chilly, you're standing too square. Keep your weight on your back foot!'

'Not too hard now. Don't kill each other!' shouts a young Scottish PTI called 'Lily' Savage.

'That's right,' adds Paul. 'Keep all that aggression for tonight.'

'How are the squad shaping up?' I ask Paul, as he continues to watch the sparring pugilists.

'Not bad. Not bad. It's been difficult getting the squad together. Two of them only arrived back from deployment last night, so they're not going to get much of a build-up. We have another on his way from Gibraltar who is going to be knackered when he gets here. More

importantly, it is difficult to get a squad spirit going when half your people are still on the way.'

'Have you got a full squad?'

'Well, yes. Some of our best fighters are away on ships and can't get back anyway, but we've got some talent around. Chilly Jenkins in the ring now is a good prospect as a light-heavyweight. Natural fighter. And Sam Yarnold in there with him is a good boy. Heavyweight, but needs to be more aggressive. Actually, he's only a few pounds short of being a super-heavyweight, and I reckon we might put him in at that weight if

PAUL RANSLEY THE PLYMOUTH COMMAND COACH

we can get him to eat a few extra pies and stickies.'

I make a mental note that in naval parlance cakes and buns are 'stickies' and then ask, 'Do we know much about the other guy?'

'He's a big marine, but he's never fought in competition before, apparently, so he won't have the ring craft and probably not the fitness either.'

'He's a bleedin' marine,' retorts Rab. 'They're all as fit as butcher's friggin' dogs!'

'Yes. Marine fit. Obstacle course fit. Yomping fit. But that's not the same as boxing fit. Anyway, if Sam enters as a heavyweight, he will have to fight a preliminary bout tonight, which he will have to win if he wants to get to the final. Then, even if he gets through, he will be knackered, because there are some useful fighters in that category. As there's only one super-heavyweight contender, he could get straight into the final, and if he stays light on his feet he could tire the bugger out and win on points.'

'Yes . . .' agrees Rab, 'if his head's still attached to his fuckin' body after the Booty lands his first punch.'

'Well, we're not going to take any risks, but first we need to see if Sam's up for it,' says Paul. 'I'm going to have a word with him in a minute, when he's finished in there with Chilly. Listen, Rab, do you want to work behind the scenes for the prelims and the finals? Warming the lads up with the pads?'

'You don't want me in the corner then?' says Rab, looking a little crestfallen.

'No, 'cos I'll be there with Lily. We need someone to warm 'em up, and I reckon the boss would prefer it that way – if you get my drift.'

'OK, mate,' says Rab. 'Say no more . . . I don't want no more aggro.'

'I think they've had enough right now,' says Lily Savage, looking at the two fighters sparring in the ring. 'They'll pulverise each other in a minute.'

'Yeah, you're right,' says Paul. 'OK Sam and Chilly – that'll do! Sam, a minute of your time please, shipmate.'

Whilst Paul chats to Sam about the prospect of him fighting at super-heavyweight, Rab takes me over to meet a young protégé of his from HMS *Chatham* who is attacking a punch bag at the other end of the room. We watch for a moment whilst the boxer continues with what has clearly been a punishing workout.

'Look at that balance . . .!' says Rab admiringly, 'and the power and speed. Beautiful style. Pound for pound one of the best fighters we got I reckon.'

I see what Rab means. The punch bag is shuddering with the blows raining down on it: hooks, left and right in quick succession, then a constant, metronomic jab, as powerful with one hand as the other, followed by crunching uppercuts that thud into the dead leather. The punches are perfectly timed and lightning fast. After about five minutes, this highly impressive athlete decides to take a rest and wanders over to us.

'This is Amy,' says Rab, introducing me to a small, attractive, but clearly deadly, young woman.

'Hello,' she says in a gentle voice that takes me by surprise.

'Hello,' I reply. 'Are you fighting in the Commands?'

'No,' she replies shyly. 'There's no opposition.'

'That's right,' interrupts Rab. 'No other women boxers eligible I'm afraid. There are a couple over in Pompey, but they ain't eighteen yet, so can't compete. Bloody pity that, 'cos Amy 'ere is a very good little fighter. Strong and very intelligent. And I'll tell you somink else – she's got a lot more balls than a lot of blokes I know.'

Rab is clearly very proud of Amy, and takes a lot of satisfaction in training her.

'Go and towel down, Amy,' he says, 'and get some water inside you before you start to cramp up. Good girl!'

Amy walks off to her rucksack and reaches for a huge two-litre bottle of water.

'Jeez!' exclaims Rab. 'Ten years ago I would never have imagined I would be trainin' a bird to box. Didn't agree with it, but you gotta move wiv the times aven't ya? Bugger me, I didn't 'ave a lot of time for women comin' to sea either, come to that, but I reckon they're OK now. Don't really think about it to be honest. Just accept it really.'

'You didn't like it at first, though?' I press him.

'Well, we were all set in our ways, I suppose. You know – us blokes. It was a male world. A male bastion. We didn't want a load of Dorises comin' on board, upsettin' everythin' and makin' everythin' all pink and fluffy. But they've come along and got on wiv it, and even old bastard sea dogs like me 'ave got used to them bein' around. Yeah, funny old world . . .'

'Does everybody feel the same about women at sea now, then?'

'Yeah, pretty much. I mean there are still some who yearn for the old days, and they would always prefer to serve on stag ships – that's all-male ships – if they could. But that's their view, know what I mean? Opinions is like arseholes, everybody's got one!'

Rab goes over to the punch bag and dances around it for a moment, performing a few jabs.

'You know how I got into boxing?' he asks, and continues to answer in the same breath, 'Got into a street fight some years ago. I didn't lose and I didn't win, but I thought to myself after that: "Right! That ain't never gonna happen again. If I ever have to face up to someone again I'm gonna win." So I 'ave to thank that bastard that bashed my nose in, all those years ago, 'cos he made me into a fighter. Thing is, I never have had to fight anyone ever since – 'cept in the ring.'

'Sam's going to fight super-heavyweight,' calls over Paul Ransley from the ringside. We all look at Sam who smiles sheepishly and shrugs his broad shoulders.

'Good luck, big man!' says Rab encouragingly.

'I'll give it a go,' says Sam, 'as long as I make the weight.'

'When's the weigh-in?' asks Rab.

'Tomorrow morning, 09.00,' replies Lily Savage.

Paul, Lily, Rab, Sam and I wander back over to the Wyvern, to see how the hall is coming along.

'Higher!' shouts Tasha. 'Higher on the left side.'

'Like this?' shouts back a male PTI, hanging precariously from ropes near the top of the gymnasium's climbing wall.

'Yes. Perfect. Tie it off there!' yells Tasha, with a big thumbs-up.

The PTI takes the corner of the large White Ensign that he is holding with his teeth and proceeds to fix it to the wall.

'Hello, Sex Kitten,' says Paul Ransley to Tasha. 'Did you want to talk about music or something?'

'Yes. Need to get the music sorted for the boxers' entrances. Got Robbie Williams, Queen, Usher and House of Pain. What do you reckon?'

'Personally I would like a nice bit of Dean Martin or Bing Crosby,' says Paul wryly, 'but I don't suppose that would go down too well, would it?'

'No, Granddad, it would not!' laughs Tasha. 'Do you want to see the smoke machines working?'

'Do I have a choice . . .?'

'No!'

Sam, the newly appointed super-heavyweight for the Plymouth Command, walks over to the boxing ring still being erected in the middle of the hall. He is looking pensive.

'Sam's a submariner,' says Lily Savage. 'Works on HMS *Torbay*. Good boxer, fast around the ring and has quick hands, but he has one overriding problem as a boxer.'

'What's that?'

'He doesn't like hitting people.'

'Yes,' I say, nodding my head. 'I can see that that would put him at something of a disadvantage.'

'He's very mild-mannered,' agrees Rab. 'Softly spoken, gentle sort of bloke. A real nice guy, actually. Need to get him riled up for the fight.'

'OK, big man?' Rab shouts over to the tall submariner.

'Yup,' Sam calls back. 'Just getting a feel for the place.'

'Don't forget the weigh-in tomorrow morning, Sam,' says Paul. '09.00 hours – on the dot!'

The Following Day
Location: HMS *Drake*. Wyvern Sports Centre
Time: 09.00

Dozens of boxers are lining up in one of the corridors of the sports centre, waiting to be weighed for tonight's preliminaries. One by one they enter the weighing room where they strip and climb on the scales. There are featherweights, lightweights, light-welterweights, welterweights, middleweights, light-heavyweights, heavyweights and, of course, just two super-heavyweights to get through.

A gigantic marine comes into the room and pulls off his tracksuit to reveal the well-muscled body of an obvious athlete. Judging by the extra ballast around the midriff and the distinctly crooked nose, he is or has been a rugby prop or second-row forward.

SAM PUTTING ON WEIGHT

'On the scales,' orders an official. The marine obeys.

'One hundred and two kilograms! Super-heavyweight,' affirms another official.

'Fuck me!' whispers Rab Butler, who is standing in the corner. 'He's a bleedin' giant!'

Sam is next. He strips down to his shorts.

'He's got to weigh in at least ninety-one,' says Rab.

Sam steps on to the scales.

'Eighty-nine kilograms. Heavyweight,' says the official.

'Bugger!' says Rab. 'Two kilograms short – that's five pounds in old money. The boy's got some eating to do.'

Paul and Lily take Sam aside. 'Sam, do you reckon you can put on two Ks in twenty-four hours? If you can weigh in at ninety-one by tomorrow morning you'll be OK.'

'Two Ks eh?' says Sam. 'Yeah, I guess I could do that.'

'Right,' says Paul. 'Start now. Get yourself over to the NAAFI for some more breakfast. Get that plate piled high, Sam!'

We all go over to the NAAFI with Sam, to give him support and encourage his appetite. He starts off with a huge dish of muesli, yoghurt and fruit, accompanied by a large glass of orange juice.

'Go on Sam! You can do it!'

'Get it down you, mate.'

'That's good eating, Sam. Go for it!'

Sam goes up to the canteen counter and comes back with a tray laden with a fuller than full English breakfast: four fried eggs, four sausages, fried bread, tomatoes, bacon, black pudding, fried potatoes and mushrooms.

'Good boy, Sam, get it down you, mate!'

'Not too fast, Sam. Chew it properly, then you can get more in.'

Sam mops up with four croissants and a pint of milk, followed by two rounds of toast and marmalade.

'That's good going, Sam. Just four hours to lunch . . . !'

Location: HMS *Ocean*
Time: 10.00

Mike Brotherton is in his cabin, sitting with a young rating who has come in for a chat.

'Life's not so good at the moment, then, Simon?'

'No, Bish. Can't say it is.'

'What is it? You're unhappy on the ship?'

'No, it's not that. It's the bird back home. She chucked me last night.'

Mike Brotherton nods gently and looks at the young sailor with sympathetic eyes. As chaplain he holds no rank, so can step outside the rank structure on which the Navy is otherwise built. He can thus all the more easily provide not only spiritual support but moral support, or just plain sympathy, to anyone who needs the attention, whether it be a four-ring captain or, as in this case, an able seaman stores accountant.

'I'm sorry, Simon. Did you see it coming?'

'Well, we've been arguing a bit recently. Just niggles really. Well that's what I thought . . .'

'What were you arguing about?'

'Well, towards the end it was just about anything, but it all started with me being in the Mob . . .'

'She couldn't handle the going away – the separation?'

'Well, that's the strange thing, Bish. The time apart wasn't the problem. It was the time spent at home. Here in Guzz. She had a problem
with my mates.'

'Your shipmates?'

'Yeah. Not just from this ship, but others from previous ships.'

'Do you mean she didn't like them as people?'

'No. She knew most of them and liked them I think. They're good
lads. She got sort of . . . jealous I think. Thought I was too close to them.
Spent too much time with them.'

'Did you, do you think?'

'Well, obviously I could spend months with them at sea, and then
we would meet up sometimes at home – for a drink, darts, a bit of football . . .'

'I think it can be very difficult sometimes, Simon, for people outside
the Navy to understand the way we are in the service. We spend a lot of
time together because we have to, but it creates a need in us, I think, to
remain with each other even when we don't have to. Serving at sea com-
bines us in a funny way. It's camaraderie, and you can't always just
switch it off. Maybe it was difficult for . . . er . . .'

'Suzy, Bish.'

'. . . yes . . . for Suzy to understand that. Do you think so?'

'Yeah, maybe. She always said I was different when I was around
Navy lads.'

'Why don't you leave her be for a few days? Let her calm down. Then
ask if she would see you for a drink or something. Then talk to her.'

'And say what?'

'Let her into your world, Simon. Our world. Explain what it is like –
the dependency on each other – and maybe she will understand. When
people join the Navy, they don't always realise just how much it is going
to rule their lives . . .'

Location: HMS *Raleigh*. AstroTurf games field
Time: 11.30

The recruits, dressed in their naval games kit, run in ranks of three on to
the AstroTurf and line up in front of four determined-looking PTIs.

'No talking!' shouts out one of the instructors. 'Unless you want to
do press-ups – and lots of them!'

'Stand up straight!' shouts another. 'You're in the military now – remember? No slouching!'

The recruits pull their shoulders back and visibly tighten their lips.

'Right, listen up!' says a female PTI, stepping forward to face the now upright and silent ranks. 'You are going to do your one and a half mile fitness test. Males must achieve a time of eleven minutes, and females a time of thirteen minutes. You MUST achieve these standards if you are going to pass into the Navy. If you should fail to meet these standards today, you will have another go next week. If you fail again, you will be put on to remedial training, after which you will be allowed to try it one more time. If you persist in failing this test, you will not be allowed to proceed with your naval career. Is that clear?'

'Yes, Staff!' comes the collective response from the ranks.

'I said, is that clear!'

'YES, STAFF!' comes back the amplified response.

'That's better. OK, follow me for a warm-up, and then you will start. You will run five times around this field, and every time you pass me at

RECRUITS DO THEIR MILE
AND A HALF FITNESS TEST

this point you will shout out your lap number: Lap One, Staff, Lap Two, Staff, and so on. Do not cheat, because we are watching you, and if you try it you will be in serious trouble.'

The PTI leads the recruits on a jog around the field and then proceeds to go through some stretching exercises prior to their fitness test. She is strict, grim-faced and ready to pounce on any wrongdoer. The recruits are careful not to aggravate her, or any of the other PTIs, because they know they will pay for any misdemeanour with a multitude of press-ups, pull-ups or sit-ups. It is interesting to consider these PTIs at HMS *Raleigh*, and the way they are treating the recruits, because, watching them, it would be easy to assume that they are typical of PTIs throughout the Navy. However, they are not – far from it. Indeed, these very PTIs would behave very differently in the Navy proper – especially on ships, where their duty is not only to maintain levels of fitness but also to maintain high levels of morale and good spirits. PTIs are invariably extrovert characters who are able to encourage and cajole everybody from the lowliest rating to the commanding officer, and normally this is done with great good humour. The PTIs at *Raleigh*, however, have a duty to help prepare these young recruits for life in a disciplined environment, as well as make sure they achieve at least a minimum degree of fitness. To be able to do that, they have to adopt a manner that will guarantee respect. They are firm but fair and, although they no longer apply some of the extreme 'beasting' sessions that were typical of training regimes in the past, they ensure that new recruits will never toy with the sensitivities of a PTI.

'Are you ready?'

'YES, STAFF!'

'Then, get set . . . GO!'

The recruits surge forward as one, but within a few yards the line of young but reddening faces begins to stretch out. The natural athletes strike out on a fierce competition of their own. The less gifted runners either stick in bunches for mutual support or else tuck in behind on their own.

'Lap One, Staff!' comes the first shout, as a stringy but accomplished runner passes the PTI who will call out the lap times.

'Lap One, Staff!' comes the next shout, and the next, and the next.

A minute later the front runners are shouting, 'Lap Two, Staff!' They have already passed the tail-end Charlies who have yet to shout out the end of their first lap.

Eight minutes after that, the front runners are coming in. 'Lap Five, Staff!' shouts the stringy athlete, who dips for the line even though he is fifty metres clear of the second-place runner. The rest of the field, however, is now very stretched out, and there are a number of suffering runners bringing up the rear. They are not going to achieve the required time and will have to try again next week. Amy, Sharon and Jenny achieve good times and pass the test. Paul Ferris, the 32-year-old wannabe chef, just makes the grade, with a time of ten minutes and fifty seconds. He is delighted.

'Fantastic!' he splutters, still fighting for breath. 'I was really worried about that, because I had to work really hard to get my weight down before I joined up. I was eighteen stone and got myself down to thirteen stone, but I didn't know how fit I was.'

'How did you get your weight off, Paul?' asks Sharon, before taking a long drink from her water bottle.

'Dieting and exercise, but my partner made it really hard at first,' replies Paul, breathing a little easier now. 'She wasn't keen on me joining up, and knew I wouldn't be accepted if I was so overweight, so she used to encourage me to eat cakes and puddings all the time. But I managed it, and she's proud now. Ten minutes fifty – bloody fantastic!'

It occurs to me that Paul Ferris's partner might be a good person to help beef Sam up for his weigh-in tomorrow morning.

The Following Day
Location: HMS *Drake*. Wyvern Sports Centre
Time: 09.00

Sam waits in the corridor outside the weighing room. Rab is sitting next to him. Both are looking morose.

Last night was not a good one for the Plymouth Command boxing team in the preliminary bouts. Although Chilly got through on points, with an impressive display of combination punching, four Plymouth boxers were stopped – one on points, one through exhaustion and two were counted out.

'Yeah, disappointing that . . .' says Paul Ransley. 'A couple of them just didn't have time to prepare and another just did not drink enough water – got dehydrated. I felt terrible for them. They've got the hearts of lions these young chaps, and you hate to see them hurt. I wish sometimes I could get in the ring for them. Anyway, that means we've only got two in the finals tonight. Chilly and Sam. As long as Sam makes the weight . . .'

Half an hour later we are in the weighing room. Sam has stripped off and is waiting for the moment of truth. 'Step up,' says the official. Sam tentatively mounts the electronic scales, and when he is steady the official activates them.

'Oh bugger!' whispers Sam.

'Fuck it!' exclaims Rab.

Paul Ransley purses his lips.

'Ninety point five kilograms,' says the official.

'Half a bloody K short,' says Rab through clenched teeth.

'OK,' says the official, sensing the disappointment. 'Look, I'm here for another hour or so. The NAAFI's still open. I will weigh him again before I go.'

Paul nods in gratitude. 'Right, Sam. Hop off. Rab, get him over to the NAAFI. Sam, eat!! Rab, make him eat! Then get back here pronto!'

Sam has a glazed look in his eyes as he pushes a second pork sausage into his mouth. He has eaten four Weetabix, muesli, yoghurt and is forcing himself through another full English breakfast.

'Go on, my son!' says Rab encouragingly. 'Wash it down with some tea. More toast.'

'That's it, mate!' says Sam despondently. 'I can't eat another . . .'

'Sam!' interrupts Rab. 'When I said "More toast" it was not a bleedin' invitation, mate, it was an order. Now eat – you have a snorker left on the plate.'

Sam groans, but obediently sinks his fork into a third sausage . . .

'Step up!' says the official. Once again Sam steps forward, and all eyes are on the scale display.

'Ninety . . . two kilograms! Super-heavyweight.'

'Thank God for that,' says Sam. 'I'm stuffed!'

'That's good, Sam,' says Paul. 'Now, just relax. A little bit of light training this afternoon, otherwise just get your head together.'

Sam gets dressed and heads off to his submarine, to chill out and watch DVDs for the day. I suspect he will be skipping lunch.

Back in the gym, Tasha is having the first of her day's kittens.

'It's all collapsing around my ears!' she says. 'Six marines have pulled out, or *been* pulled out, I should say. At this rate, we're not going to have anyone to fight tonight!'

'What do you mean, the marines have been pulled out?' I ask. 'They'd got through the prelims, hadn't they?'

'Yes, they were all finalists,' says Natasha, walking towards the other side of the gym hall faster than most people sprint, 'but this is the Navy, remember?'

'Sorry?'

'Never depend on anything – any plan, any arrangement at all – because it will always change. We had a full complement of boxers this morning. Now we don't. Six marine commandos have disappeared.'

'Sorry?' I say again.

'Disappeared! Gone! Kaput! HMS *Albion*, which was out near southern Europe on trials, has been called down to the Ivory Coast because there is some trouble brewing, and they might need to go in and bring out the Brits living there. They wanted more marines, so they sent for them first thing this morning. Typical!'

'That'll hit the rugby teams hard as well,' says Rab despondently.

'Course it will. It makes it next to impossible sometimes to get any teams, let alone squads, sorted out. Football, hockey, rugby – you name it. And now it's boxing. I don't know how many bouts we're going to have now . . .'

In the old days, the Navy was large enough to be able to sustain large sporting squads, provide strong teams in many sports and convene large sporting competitions without any trouble at all. Today's Royal Navy, however, is a lean service – just 38,191 strong compared to 76,200 in 1975, 81,000 in 1960 and 492,800 in 1945. Of course, it is no argument that we need a bigger Navy so that better sporting teams can be generated, but it is true, none the less, that sport, and particularly sporting success, is good for morale. Again, in the old days – that is, up to 2001 – the Navy's Field Gun Competition was a hotly contested inter-command battle between finely honed and superbly trained teams of naval athletes. Budget cuts and streamlining measures killed the Field Gun Competition, because the Navy could no longer afford for one-hundred-plus sailors to be taken out of service for six or seven months at a time for training. This makes perfect sense in strictly budgetary terms, but rather less sense, I think, when measured by the tape measures of morale and team spirit within the Navy. I know, even today, the annual confrontation between the Navy and the Army rugby teams at Twickenham is watched by everybody in the Mob. Thousands go to Twickenham itself, but only if duties allow it. Others, on ships all over the world, wait eagerly for a signal with the result, unless they are somewhere where they can watch it live through Sky Television and BFBS (British Forces Broadcasting Service).

It is six o'clock, and everybody is arriving at the Wyvern Centre. Coaches and cars are disgorging hundreds of boxing supporters from all the

NATASHA PULLEY AT THE INTER-COMMAND BOXING CHAMPIONSHIPS

Commands, as well as civilian fans from Plymouth, Portsmouth and London. Tasha has changed into her Number Ones, and is running around, making sure the bar is properly staffed as the first comers are already queuing for beer. Rab is dressed in his red Plymouth Boxing Command T-shirt, and is preparing to take his place in the changing rooms where he will help with the warming-up.

'Bleedin' 'ell,' he says. 'Tasha never stops, does she? Doin' a very passable impersonation of a chicken minus head at the moment – mind you, if we could plug her into the national grid we would 'ave unlimited power I reckon!'

Slowly the massive hall fills. The atmosphere is palpable.

Sam is in the changing room, looking relaxed. I ask him how he is feeling.

'Good, thanks. Yeah, looking forward to it now.'

'Feeling aggressive?'

'Yes!' he laughs. 'I am working on that 'cos I'm a bit too laid back sometimes. I need to find my inner monster!'

'You've seen your opposition?'

'Yes. Massive Marine – but did you notice he has a big head, I mean literally an enormous head?'

'Good target,' I say.

'Exactly! Bloody great target. Let's hope he has small hands. Big head, small hands – that's the way I like 'em!'

'Ladies and Gentlemen,' says the master of ceremonies, from the centre of the ring. 'Welcome to the Royal Navy Inter Command Novice Boxing Championships. We have a slight change to the order of fights tonight . . .'

Back in the dressing rooms, Rab is warming up Chilly Jenkins on the pads, and Paul is talking to Sam, beginning to psych him up, prepare him mentally for the fight.

Tasha has been running round the hall, seeing that people with allocated tables are finding their places.

'How's it going?' I ask.

'It's a huge crowd,' she replies, 'but we have lost at least three fights from the original line-up of nine. So that's only six fights left, but we've managed to get two of the best boxers from the Navy's senior team to do an exhibition bout for us, which will fill a bit of time, and then we just have to get everybody filled up with alcohol so they won't notice the lack of boxing! Excuse me, must talk to the judges.'

Tasha rushes over as the judges take their positions next to the ring. At the doorways the people in charge of the smoke machines are standing by, and up on the balcony the sailor put in charge of playing the CDs for the boxers' entrances is making sure he has the right order.

'You'll love this!' says Tasha, coming over from the ring.

'What's happened?' says Jock Eastern.

'I just met Tommy Goodwin. He's one of the Navy chaplains, and has come along because he says he has never seen boxing before and just wants to see what it is like. He couldn't find a place at the tables, so look where he's sitting! Right next to the doctor at ringside! Look! You have the timekeeper, judges, doctor, doctor's assistant – and then the padre. It's as if he's there to give the last rites!'

The lights lower, the smoke machines make smoke and the music blasts out. The two exhibition boxers stride out to the ring to start the evening off. Back in the changing room, Sam is now looking nervous. He is pacing up and down and no doubt summoning his inner monster. Paul is making sure Chilly's hands are properly taped and Rab is giving him a shoulder massage.

By 7.30 the exhibition fight has finished, and so too has a comic spoof fight put on by two PTIs to help fill the evening.

'Oh my God!' says Tasha, rushing over now with her head in her hands. 'I didn't think things could get worse. Someone in the audience has just had a suspected heart attack. The doctor's rushing off to hospital with him. Now we can't have any boxing till he has returned. Nightmare!'

'Bleedin' 'ell,' says Rab who has come out to see some of his mates from HMS *Chatham*. 'Is the bloke all right?'

'Yes, thank goodness,' says Tasha, 'but he looked a bit shocked, and he has to be checked at hospital, obviously. We'll have to serve dinner earlier, and we could hold the raffle now as well. We've not had one proper fight yet!'

Dinner and the raffle are over. It is already nine o'clock, but the doctor is now back in place and we have had the middleweight bout. Chilly Jenkins stands at the doorway, waiting for his entrance. Paul Ransley is at his side looking concerned – he is feeling the nerves he says he always feels, and is wishing, as always, that he could go in the ring for his boxer. He puts his hand on Chilly's shoulder.

'. . . Ladies and Gentlemen. Please welcome the boxers for the light-heavyweight category – Marine Ford and O M Jenkins.'

Operator Mechanic Chilly Jenkins walks through the smoke to the strains of Robbie Williams, looking for all the world like a true champion. A great cheer goes up in the hall and the boxers climb into the ring.

It is a hard fight and neither boxer gives quarter. Chilly is caught several times by Ford's right hook. However, although they are scoring punches they are not hurting the young sailor. Chilly responds with some pounding jabs that continually pierce the defence of the marine, who then counterattacks with more hooks and uppercuts. In the second and third round Chilly is warned about hitting with the back of the glove, but he maintains the pace with flurries of punches in fast combinations. At the end of it all, the referee raises Chilly's arm in glorious victory. The Plymouth supporters are ecstatic.

Tasha is now, at last, looking more relaxed. The crowd are enjoying the evening and nobody is feeling they have been short-changed with the boxing.

My watch shows ten o'clock, and at last it is time for Sam to face his destiny. He is in the doorway, waiting to make his entrance. Rab is

SAM YARNOLD PREPARES
TO FIGHT

massaging his biceps. Lily is whispering encouraging words into his ear
whilst Paul, once again, places a morale-boosting hand on his young
warrior's shoulder. Queen's 'We Will Rock You' blasts out of the speak-
ers. The smoke billows and Sam takes the long walk . . .

Sam is back in the changing room and the hands on my watch have moved but a few minutes.

'Why did the referee stop the fight? I never went down . . . I was landing shots . . . I was defending . . .'

'No Sam, the ref was right,' says Paul, unwrapping the tape from the despondent boxer's fists. 'At the end of the day the other bloke was too big and we could not take the risk. You might have got him with a lucky punch, or you might even have taken him on points if it had gone the distance, but we could not take the risk of him landing a sledgehammer and doing you damage.'

'But . . .'

'No "buts", mate. You did well. You got through two good rounds. In the end he was a monster and you're not.'

The fact is, Sam had found his monster: not the one within, unfortunately, but one outside – the guy in the opposite corner, the guy with a punch like a rocket-propelled grenade. Sam did not know it, but Paul Ransley had already spoken to the referee before the fight, asking him to stop it the moment it looked like serious damage could be inflicted. For Paul it was the next best thing to getting in the ring and fighting himself. Sam, like the rest, was still a novice and had to be looked after. Fighting him at super-heavyweight had seemed like a good way to get to the final quickly – but, in the end, it was a gamble that he was not prepared to see through.

Even without a full team the Royal Marines won the championships and, although Sam was deeply disappointed, everybody thought the evening went well. Tasha, particularly, is relieved.

'The heart attack guy is fine, we've heard, so that's a relief,' she says. 'We managed to fill the evening with boxing and everyone had a good time.'

'Bloody shame about old Sam,' says Rab. 'He's a good boxer, but you can't box against a human tank. Chilly did well. Great win that. Bloody Marines won the Championship though, even without a full-strength team. Anyway, that's over now and I'm just glad I could be here before pissing off on deployment. Happy days!'

The Following Evening.
Location: East Plymouth. Rab's house
Time: 19.00

Rab and his wife Mel are getting his last-minute packing sorted out. All over the floor in their living room are the extras he is taking on the ship for Christmas – nuts, crisps, biscuits and chocolate, loads of chocolate, including two gigantic tins of Quality Street.

'I don't care where you are in the world. You gotta have Quality Street for Christmas,' says Rab. 'I could be personally chasin' Osama Bin Laden around the Gulf in a bleedin' canoe on Christmas Day but I will have me Quality Street with me, that's for sure, an' I won't be givin' 'im one neither. Well, he can 'ave the marzipan ones – I hate them!'

Rab is what you might call a 'geezer' – a cross between Del Boy, Arthur Daley and Blackadder. He has been in the Navy for twenty-five years and adores it, even though he seems to thrive on mishap and calamity. He loves to complain, or 'drip' as sailors call it, but is full of wit and has a heart of gold. He is as typical a 'Jack Tar' as

SOMETHING FOR RAB'S
JOURNEY

you could meet. Mel has been a long-suffering navy wife for eleven years, and knows exactly how to deal with the pressures and problems of marrying into the Navy.

'The goodbyes are hard, but you have to get on with life,' she says, as she packs the Quality Street into a large carrier bag. 'There is no point in moping around.'

'Will you see him off, the day after tomorrow?' I ask.

'Oh yes. I will go down to Devil's Point to wave them off. I will cry. Then I will dry my eyes and get on with things.'

'How about you, Rab?' I say. 'Do you just get on with life as well?'

'Yeah, of course. You gotta. If you can't, you shouldn't be in the Navy.'

'Yes, but it's easier for you, Rab,' says Mel. 'You have your shipmates. It's like another family, a "ship family", and you all look after each other. I'm on my own. You live in a mess of fifty men.'

'True,' concedes Rab.

'And so, whilst the goodbyes are hard, the hellos can be hard too,' adds Mel.

'You mean because he's got used to being with his other family?' I say.

'Exactly,' says Mel with a laugh, whilst Rab nods his head. 'So when he does get home, I always give him a warning. I say, "You've got three days to wind your neck in and mind your language, or you get back on the ship!"'

'Is his language bad when he gets off a ship?' I enquire, with a glance towards Rab.

'No, it's "bad" at the best of times. When he gets off a ship it is "industrial strength" filthy!'

'Oi! That's quite enough of that, thank you very much. Or you don't get a Christmas present,' laughs Rab, studiously trying not to insinuate a swear word into the sentence.

'How much longer have you got in the Navy?' I ask Rab.

'About another five years, I reckon. Maybe ten if I make petty officer.'

'Are you ready to leave?' I ask.

'No, not really. I like it. Anyway, I'm not sure what to do in Civvy Street. I mean, I would like to do social work with deprived kids I think – but I'm not really sure yet.'

'That's the trouble,' breaks in Mel. 'I feel sorry for some of these sailors coming out after 25-years-plus inside. I mean, they've learned how to fire missiles or torpedoes or something, and then suddenly they are outside and queuing at the job centre. Missile expert. Very useful qualification that!'

'Oh, put a sock in it, woman!' Rab says with a laugh. 'I'll put the kettle on for a cup o'tea, and then I want to carry on packin' my goodies. Is this all the chocolate, or have you hidden some away?'

'Here, you'd better pack this somewhere,' says Mel, passing Rab a package in Christmas wrapping.

'What's that?'

'Your Christmas present . . .'

The Following Day
Location: Devonport dockyard
Time: 10.00

HMS *Chatham* is being pulled gently from the quayside by two tugboats
– one at her stern and one at her bow. Officers are lined up on the bridge
wings and all other ranks are lined up on the upper deck, the flight deck
and the fo'c'sle. Once she is clear, the frigate's own engines kick in and
she begins to glide towards Plymouth Sound, from which she will head
for the open sea.

As the ship gains momentum, the men and women of *Chatham* look
out over Devonport dockyard and see everything that is familiar pass
them by. Most are excited, because foreign deployments are by their
nature exciting, but those who are leaving loved ones and families are
still dealing inwardly with the goodbyes said this morning – some in
cars at the naval entrance, others on doorsteps all around Plymouth.
Many will still have that sick feeling in their stomachs that only final
farewells before a long deployment can instil.

The ship nears Devil's Point – the nearest piece of land to any ship
passing out of the harbour. It is here some families choose to come and
wave to a departing ship, stretching that moment of final leave-taking to
its limit. Sailors all over *Chatham* begin to crane their heads as the rocky
promontory gets nearer. A few banners at the Point flutter in the wind:
'Miss you Steve' says one, 'Love you Micky' says another and, inevitably,
one saying 'Goodbye Daddy' is held at either end by two small children
waving frantically.

HMS *Chatham* raises her pennant as part of her own farewell salute
to the families at Devil's Point. The turquoise rectangle waves proudly
in a freshening westerly wind, showing the ship's mascot – Mighty
Mouse holding a trident – and of course, the ship's motto: 'Up and
At'Em'.

Rab's wife Mel is at the base of Devil's Point with her friend Tracey.
They are both waving. Rab, on the flight deck, spots them and waves
back. Tracey puts her arm around Mel who is dabbing at her eyes with a
hankie.

'Gets you every time, this does,' says Rab with a shake of the head.
He waves again.

Down the line from Rab, a young sailor is in tears. Flushed and sobbing, he tries to wipe his eyes with the back of his hand. A female sailor

nearby passes him a tissue and the sailor next to him pats him gently on the back. Already, the 'ship family' is looking after its own.

Down below, Ginge Grieveson sits in his store room.

'You're not going up on deck?' I ask him.

'No. I've said my goodbyes. I shed my tears when I left home. Amanda and the kids won't come down to see the ship off, either. It's too painful for all of us.'

'So you're already counting the days?'

'Absolutely, and the hours!'

'Why do you it?' I ask him. 'Why do you put yourself through this?'

'Good question,' he says with a self-mocking laugh. 'Because I'm a sailor and it's what I do, I suppose. Nobody likes leaving the family, but it's what I do for my job. I don't really understand why I do, but I carry on doing it, don't I?'

MEL WAVING GOODBYE
TO RAB

RAB WAVING GOODBYE
TO MEL

'What does Amanda think about it?'

'Well, she doesn't make a thing of it, but when it gets near the time for me to go away, I know we get niggly with each other. Subconsciously, she blames me for abandoning her, I think. And I get grumpy too, because I don't want her to feel that way. She's my soulmate . . .'

'Fire! Fire! Fire!' Ginge jumps as the central broadcast system inter-rupts our conversation. 'This is not an exercise. Fire! Fire! Fire!'

'Bloody hell! This does not augur well,' he says, as he moves quickly to the passage outside his office. Sailors appear from everywhere – some changing immediately into fire-fighting gear, some, like Ginge, helping them with their breathing apparatus, whilst others start to unroll large red hoses.

No sooner have the fire-fighting teams readied themselves than the tannoy rings out again: 'A fire occurred in one of the Tyne engines. It has been extinguished.'

'Nice one!' says Ginge. 'Half an hour after we leave the wall and we get a fire in the engine. And we're trying to get to the Arabian sodding Gulf!'

'Break out the oars,' says another sailor, struggling out of his fire-fighting suit.

'We train for this sort of thing all the time,' Ginge says to me. 'Fire is one of the worst things that can happen on a ship.'

'Yeah, sinking's none too clever either,' chortles a petty officer, rolling up one of the hoses.

'. . . or running out of bog rolls!' The rejoinder brings the weighty subject safely back to the lavatorial.

'. . . or your bloody cooking Grieveson!' Going for the personal dig is a favourite form of amusement on the high seas.

'Bloody hell,' says Ginge, shaking his head. 'Six months of this . . .!'

The central broadcast system speaks again. 'Hands to flying stations! Hands to flying stations!' The flight deck is closed up and the flight team prepares to receive the ship's Lynx helicopter, coming in from its base in Yeovilton where it has been fully serviced and readied for deployment.

Ten minutes later, the Lynx lands on the flight deck where it is secured before the engines are closed down. Soon after this the flight commander, Lieutenant Toby Clay, and his flight observer, Lieutenant John Turner, known to everyone as JT, walk into the hangar. Both are carrying a large number of Christmas presents in their arms.

'Presents from the family,' says JT with a smile.

'And strict instructions not to open them till Christmas Day!' adds Toby, with a stern look to his flight observer.

HMS *Chatham*, engine room intact and helicopter stowed, continues her journey into the English Channel. From here she will set course for Gibraltar, and then on to the Suez Canal which she will transit on her way to the Arabian Gulf. She is heading for the most volatile region in the world, and nobody knows what lies before her in the months to come. She will not see the coast of Britain again until May of next year – that's in 180 days.

Ginge Grieveson pins up a calendar above his desk in the catering office and next to it a picture of Amanda.

'I'm going to cross off every bleeding day as it passes,' says Ginge. 'Just another seven hours and that'll be the first day gone!'

FACING PAGE:
HMS *CHATHAM* HEADS
FOR THE GULF

CHAPTER THREE

Oxtail Soup, a Clip Round the Ear and a Kiss on the Quarterdeck

Location: HMS *Bulwark*
Date: 23 November 2004
Time: 14.00

I am going to a village fête. This fête, however, is not in a village, it is on a ship – and, furthermore, it is not even a fête, at least not the sort you would expect in Civvy Street. Specifically, it is billed on its publicity poster as 'The *Bulwark* Village Fête to be opened by our very own Mayor and Lady Mayoress', but the small print at the bottom reads: 'Guaranteed: No screaming kids, no push chairs, no bric-a-brac, no dodgy ethnic products, no wicker, no stinking portaloos and no car-parking problems. Just a bunch of matelots trying to persuade you to part with your hard-earned cash . . .' The poster also draws attention to some of the main attractions and stalls, such as the Condom Challenge, the Bum Face Game, Human Skittles, the Slave Auction and the 'Gobble my Sausage' hot-dog van. It also points out that 'The Women's Institute have kindly agreed to show us their buns on their cake stall!'

This suspect event is to take place on the vehicle deck of one of the navy's largest state-of-the-art warships.

HMS *Bulwark*, as sailors say, 'is straight out of her box'. In other words, she is brand spanking new. Described as a Landing Platform Dock or an LPD, this gargantuan ship is not only to act as a floating command platform for an amphibious task force, but also to embark, transport, deploy and recover, by helicopter and landing craft, up to 710 troops with their equipment, vehicles and whatever other cargo of war they may require. She is in fact the tenth HMS *Bulwark* to enter service in the Royal Navy and so has inherited the *Bulwark* motto – 'Under Thy Wings I Will Trust', although this is popularly adjusted to 'Under Thy Wings I Will Rust'.

Captain Jerry Stanford, the first commanding officer of the latest *Bulwark*, has invited me to follow the progress of his new charge for the first year of her life. It is an extraordinary opportunity for me to witness, if not the birth of a ship exactly, then certainly her first tentative steps towards being a grown-up ship of war with all the attendant teething problems that that will no doubt entail.

Jerry Stanford is the original officer and gentleman. Like Tony Johnstone-Burt on HMS *Ocean*, he is a career naval officer of the highest calibre, but also, to coin a phrase, a thoroughly nice bloke. I am once again fascinated by the naval style of command – his easy way with people of all ranks and yet his obvious ability to command respect.

Anyway, back to the fête. All ships have village fêtes at some time or another – it has become as much a naval tradition as Splicing the Mainbrace and dancing the Hornpipe.

Simply put, the village fête is a ship's way of having fun (as well as making money for the ship's charity), but it also provides a breath of fresh air that helps to oxygenate the ship's company and reinvigorate relationships that could wither in the permanent shade of a rank structure. Rig for today's fête, for example, is specifically detailed as Civvies or Banyan (fancy dress), which means no uniforms and therefore, of course, no outward sign of rank.

Even before the fête starts I am ushered down to the female mess to witness a remarkable sight. Two Royal Marines – hombres as tough as they make them – are being carefully made-up by one of the girls. One Marine is to be the Mayoress, and the other, Merv, is being made-up – well, for the hell of it really! Mascara, lipstick, blusher, powder, eyeliner – everything is being applied very liberally.

'OK!' says Merv, 'that'll do for the slap. Now for the tits!' Whereupon he blows up two condoms and shoves them down the top of a tight floral swimsuit so tight in the crotch that it barely contains the manhood that otherwise he is trying so earnestly to conceal.

ROYAL MARINE COMMANDOS IN DEEP COVER!

HUMAN SKITTLES AT THE *BULWARK* VILLAGE FÊTE

Jerry Stanford has turned up more tastefully in a sports jacket and flannels, and other officers are dressed in Hawaiian shirts, various types of sports gear and even the odd exotic sarong. Otherwise, the general rig is jeans and T-shirts, apart, that is, from the cross-dressing Royal Marine Commandos. The Mayoress, whose right breast tragically seems to have burst as she was adjusting her bra strap, has duly joined the Mayor, aka the marine engineering officer, to open the *Bulwark* Fête. Arm in arm they walk the length of the vehicle deck, waving and smiling their way through the hoots of derision, wolf whistles and cat calls that are being hurled from the general populace. They reach a red ribbon stretched out before them which, after a few choice words of welcome, they cut with a pair of scissors. The fête is officially open.

One of the favourite stalls is Human Skittles. Eight officers stand precariously on square plastic containers in skittle formation. They face a huge sandbag suspended from a long rope. The contestants, having paid 50p each, walk forward one by one, grab the sandbag, pull it back as far as they can and then launch it with all their might to dislodge the wobbly officers. CRUNCH! A well-directed shot can dent a lot of officers. Another great favourite is the Bum Face Game – consisting of about twenty enlarged photographs of bare bottoms and twenty more photos of faces. For 50p you attempt to pair the bums with the faces. Condom Challenge is a simple matter of hurling water-filled condoms at some unfortunate sailor's face sticking through a hole in a piece of cardboard.

At one point in the afternoon a bunch of marines manage to gather together several condom water-bombs and, without warning, launch a mammoth missile attack on a whole crowd of unsuspecting sailors. The marines, for whom Jack is always fair game, whoop with delight before making a tactical retreat to the beer stall.

At the same time as all this is happening, Dave Harris, the master at arms, is attempting a world indoor rowing record on an ergo machine. He is going for the 100,000 metres. Dave already has a collection of indoor records, and is well-known for his prowess on the rowing machine – although today, as he puts his customary zeal into the challenge, the extraordinary display of sup-

MASTER AT ARMS DAVE HARRIS GOES FOR ANOTHER WORLD RECORD

port from the howling and applauding crowd seems to have less to do with Dave's heroic attempt on the record than the fact that one wayward testicle has escaped the confines of his tighter-than-tight shorts.

As everybody is intently watching the master at arms – who, judging from the troubled look on his face, is beginning to realise the real reason for all the attention he is getting – a gaggle of about five stealthy female sailors creep silently over the gantry above the vehicle deck. Each is carrying a large bucket. They masterfully position themselves immediately above the Royal Marine condom bombers and, counting to three, simultaneously tip the buckets of cold water all over them. To everyone's delight the marines are counter-drenched and Jack's honour is restored.

The afternoon is well attended and well enjoyed. Beer is consumed in moderate quantities. A female steward successfully pairs up all the bums and faces – and no questions are asked! The master at arms breaks the world record and promptly adjusts his dress. Merv the Marine unfortunately smudges his lipstick. Money is made for charity. Above all, Jerry Stanford is delighted. *Bulwark* has successfully hosted her first village fête and, in so doing, has started to consolidate her newly assembled and, indeed, first-ever, ship's company. It has been a small but significant step towards forging them into an efficient team and, ultimately, an effective fighting force.

Location: HMS *Raleigh*
Date: 24 November 2004
Time: 12.00

The recruits, continuing their Phase One training, have had a busy week. They have been attending lectures on kit maintenance, history of the naval uniform, naval law, ship's safety and team building. Today they have been learning about the mechanism of the rifle, and now they are on the rifle range for the first time. Petty Officer George Peart is in charge.

'Listen to me very carefully!' he shouts in a broad Geordie accent. 'These rifles fire live bullets. Live bullets travel fast. Live bullets can kill you. That's the point of them – but not here! Safety is important at all times. You will do exactly what I tell you at all times – is that understood?'

'Yes, Staff!'

'Right, you will start with prone firing at twenty-five yards . . .'

*These are recruits who have completed their initial training, and are now beginning to specialise in their chosen branch.

Half a mile away, in the catering school, Leading Chef George Hebron is teaching Phase Two* recruits to make apple pie. As he describes the method for shortcrust pastry, the sharp report of gunfire from the rifle range comes through the open window.

'So, that's the way to mix the pastry and that's the way to roll it out – now you try it. But remember, it's easy in here. Just imagine that one day you will be having to do this on a rolling ocean in a hot galley when you are sweating your tits off and about to spew your guts out. Think on it!'

George Hebron, another Geordie, has been in the Navy for sixteen years and is a committed submariner, but he loves to teach as well.

'It can be very satisfying teaching,' he tells me, surveying his students as they roll out their pastry. 'Cooking at sea is not like your namby-pamby cooking in Civvy Street. Gordon Ramsay wouldn't stand a chance on a warship! Besides,' he adds with a laugh, 'I reckon we drink more than him and we definitely swear more than him!'

GEORGE HEBRON

'Does it take a particular type of person to be a Navy cook?' I ask.

'Yes. Definitely. And it's not about the cooking either. You have to be "gobby" – that is, have a big mouth on you. People on ships are always ready to complain about the food. No matter how good the scran is, sailors will always complain – it's in their nature – so you have to be ready to stand up for yourself. I teach my lot how to cook, but I also teach them how to be gobby and stand up for themselves!'

'Were you taught to be gobby when you joined?'

'Yes, but it was very different in those days. It was more disciplined.'

'You mean it was better?'

'Well, when I joined up I was literally knocked into shape. If I fucked up, I got a belt round the ear, but you can't hit them today. I mean, it is probably good that we don't resort to physical violence – I suppose – but the discipline has taken a tumble.'

'Does that make your job more difficult?'

'Yes. These recruits are coming from a society which doesn't have any discipline either, and they are full of ideas about their rights – all pink and fluffy political correctness. Sometimes, if we shout at these people, we get a bollocking for giving them a bollocking. If someone is late they are in trouble as far as I am concerned but then we are told, "Go easy, they probably have some underlying problem." Sorry, they are late – *that* is their underlying problem!'

George Hebron is a larger-than-life character who speaks his mind, but he reflects an attitude that I have noticed is quite common amongst seasoned leading hands and some petty and chief petty officers.

'It's all very well being lenient and understanding, but what about when we go to war? That is when you need rigid discipline – or else you sink!'

Despite his apparent sternness, he is a great favourite with the recruits, who respond well to his brash nature, knock-about sense of humour and what they call his 'Old Navy' opinions.

'I hate "skimmers".* I love submarines,' he says categorically. 'I like the people on submarines, and cooking on a sub is special. On a long deployment, most of it under water, all they have to look forward to is their scran, so cooks are well respected and we make it special for them. I tell my students to join the submarine service if they can – except the women of course.'

'They're still not allowed to serve on submarines, are they?'

'No! And if they ever were, I would leave the Navy!'

'Why's that?'

'Bad luck! It is an old superstition. Women are Jonahs – just like oxtail soup!'

'Oxtail soup?'

'Yes. Very bad luck. You would never make oxtail soup on a submarine.'

'Is there a reason for that?' I ask.

'Well, I think a sub sunk once and they found out they had been eating oxtail soup, so it just became a superstition. Women have always been regarded as bad luck though, and a lot of people think they would be dangerous anyway. The Netherlands Navy has a woman submarine captain who is in charge of some very powerful missiles – what happens at her time of the month when she gets a bit unstable?'

George Hebron smiles and winks mischievously.

'OK class! That's the pastry done. Now for the filling. Start peeling and coring your cooking apples . . .'

Back on the rifle range the Forty-Sixers have finished their rifle practice. George Peart is making sure all live rounds are accounted for, and asks each recruit in turn if they have any ammunition on them. Everyone says no, but is then told to check the soles of their boots, in case a round

*Surface ships

has become lodged in the tread. Only when the gruff Petty Officer is satisfied does he tell the recruits they can prepare to leave. He brings them
to attention and gives them the order to march off, as they are due in a
classroom for a lecture on naval discipline.

I think to myself how much George Hebron would like to deliver
that particular lecture.

Location: The North Sea
Date: 25 November 2004
Time: 14.30

I have joined HMS *Bulwark* again, but this time we are at sea on a two-
day trip to Newcastle upon Tyne. The reason for this trip is three-fold:
first, she is going to carry out some ship safety exercises on the way;
second, she is going on an official visit to her affiliated county – County
Durham; and third, her ship's company is going to enjoy their first-ever
run ashore together. It is a fact that, of all the places in the world where
sailors run ashore, one of the top favourites is Newcastle.

'I don't know why that is,' says Jerry Stanford. 'I think it is a combination of things, but I would guess that the main reason is the people in
the North East. Always friendly and welcoming. The beer is good too,
and cheap!'

'Are you worried?' I ask.

'Well, about a quarter of the ship's company are new to the Navy –
and have come straight from training – so this run ashore will be the
first they have experienced. In one way that is very exciting, because running ashore is an essential part of Navy life, but I am slightly apprehen-
sive for them as well, because they're going to be let loose in one of
Europe's busier and more boisterous cities.'

'You're concerned there might be one or two wobbly sailors coming
back up the gangway at the end of the night?'

'I would be very disappointed, actually, if there weren't any wobbly
sailors coming back to the ship because, inevitably, that's part of having
a good time. Alcohol will be consumed, of course, but my main fear is
that over-indulgence could lead to personal difficulties and danger. As
long as they can have a few drinks, enjoy themselves and wobble back
safely, then I will be happy.'

HMS *Bulwark* is a remarkable ship, and reflects the changing role of

HMS *BULWARK*

the Navy in the world. As the nucleus of the UK amphibious capability, her primary role will be to provide what is called C4 ISTAR – that is Command and Control, Communications, Computers, Intelligence, Surveillance, Targeting, Acquisition and Reconnaissance. These are essential facilities for both naval and military commanders during amphibious and joint operations. HMS *Bulwark* is a very complicated ship and will spend the best part of a year being prepared for deployment. A lot of people have a lot to learn about operating the ship to the maximum of her efficiency and effectiveness and, again, this is partly why we are sailing to Newcastle.

We are due to start a fire exercise. There is always a risk of fire at sea – as we saw when HMS *Chatham* left Plymouth on her way to the Gulf – and everyone has to be fully trained up to deal with it, wherever and whenever it may occur. Clearly it is impossible to train with real fire, but the simulated exercise is made as realistic as possible – although everyone knows an exercise is due, they don't know where the 'fire' will break out.

'For exercise! For exercise! For exercise!' proclaims the ship's central broadcast system. This is followed by the deafening noise of the alarm siren. 'Fire! Fire! Fire! There is a fire in the main galley! Attack party close up at the scene of the fire! Support party close up at the scene of the fire. Close all smoke curtains! Crash stop ventilation!'

Action is immediate. Speed is of the essence – more so on a ship than anywhere. The attack party go straight to the galley, where a smoke canister has been detonated to simulate the fire. The first two fire-fighters do their best to get through the billowing smoke to the source of the fire, armed only with fire extinguishers as an initial action. Meanwhile, the next two fire-fighters in the attack party pull on their breathing apparatus and, as soon as they are ready, take over from the first two. During this time the support party have climbed into their 'Fearnought' suits, so called because these thick woollen padded suits, treated with fire-retarding chemicals, provide maximum protection to their wearers. The support party moves in and takes over from the attack party.

The air-conditioning system has been closed down immediately, and smoke curtains are pulled across passageways, so that smoke is not spread around the ship.

Even before the support party have extinguished the galley fire, there is an announcement that another 'fire' has broken out in the gash* compacting room. Another attack party and support party react immediately . . .

*gash – rubbish.

'How are the exercises going?' I ask Jerry Stanford, later in the afternoon.

'Good. People have responded very well, although there is always room for improvement. We have to maintain training all the time because you never know when you will have to face the real thing.'

'And the new sailors who have just joined the ship – are you pleased with them?' I am thinking back to what George Hebron was saying at HMS *Raleigh* about the modern generation coming into the Navy.

'I am. Enormously.'

'Some people say the modern sailor is not what he used to be,' I suggest.

'I think every generation of sailors ends up saying that about the generations that follow. We have to recognise that we will always reflect the society we recruit from – and I think we have to recognise what we are asking of our young sailors as well, because joining the Navy can be a very real shock to the system.'

He looks out over the North Sea that stretches before us, and then over to a couple of young ratings doing some painting on the bridge wings.

'It is all so new to them, a completely different way of life – and the disciplined nature of the life can be the biggest shock of all. We do expect enormous things of them in such a short space of time. For most of them it has probably only been a matter of months since they were at school or college – where they had total freedom, where they could behave exactly as they wanted. In a heartbeat we expect a totally different form of behaviour – so that if it was acceptable for them in their normal life to go out, get blind drunk and wake up in the gutter, it certainly isn't now. Before, they could just go home and sleep off the hangover. Here, there is no allowance for hangovers – we want them back on board by a certain time, ready for duty. That's hard if you're not used to it, and I do not underestimate that.'

As I wander around this massive ship and get frequently lost, I bump into many sailors, many of them very young as they are straight from training. Around twenty-five per cent of them are female, so it is inevitable to consider the obvious potential problems. There is a strict No Touch rule on ships, which is designed to prevent contact of a physical or sexual nature. But then, when you consider that some of these young sailors are no more than seventeen or eighteen, and in the grip of their own powerful and raging hormones urging them to do what is, after all, only natural, one wonders how effective the No Touch rule really is. Of course, it is impossible to know. If anyone is caught redhanded, so to speak, they are charged and 'Tabled' – that is, disciplined – whatever rank they are. Just how much goes on that nobody ever sees is anyone's guess, as people attempting to contravene the No Touch rule would presumably go to considerable lengths to conceal their actions.

This is not to say that male and female sailors living on the same ship cannot have relationships, or, come to that, males or females cannot have homosexual relationships, but they have to be pursued off the ship. The No Touch rule does not apply once a sailor is off the gangway, is off duty and out of uniform. Ashore, he or she can do what they want, within the realms of common decency, just so long as it is not brought back on the ship. The rule is simple and complicated all at the same time.

Location: Newcastle
Date: 26 November 2004
Time: 10.30

As soon as HMS *Bulwark* comes alongside in Newcastle, the ship prepares for a busy schedule of events that will spread over the next two days. The ship's rugby team will be playing the Durham police in the city of Durham, whilst the ship's football team will play a local college. Tomorrow the ship will be opened to the public and Master at Arms Dave Harris will be attempting yet another rowing record aiming to beat his own 100,000 metres time. Tonight, there will be an official cocktail party on the massive vehicle deck for two hundred guests from the ship's affiliated county. The galley, therefore, is called on to provide some delicate finger food for the event. As I look at the vol au vents, cheese and pineapple squares, baby sausages on sticks and mini lemon tarts being carefully arranged on silver trays, I immediately recall the words of George Hebron back at HMS *Raleigh*, and his insistence that 'cooking in a ship is not like your namby-pamby cooking in Civvy Street'. At the moment, *Bulwark* is proving him wrong.

It is 20.00, and the cocktail party is in full swing. The guests are being entertained by members of the Royal Marine Corps of Drums, who have come down from Scotland for the event. Stewards are moving around the crowd, offering wine and the snacks made in the galley.

Down on the quarterdeck, 'libertymen' are starting to go ashore. Dressed in their party clothes, they walk off the gangway and head for the long row of taxis waiting to take them towards the bright lights of the city centre. The pubs and clubs beckon and, understandably, spirits are high.

At the head of the gangway, the ship's armed guards look on with envy, cursing the duty rota but looking forward to tomorrow, when they will be released to raise a little hell for themselves.

Two hours later, the distinguished and honoured guests begin to leave the ship. They have clearly had a great time and one or two of them are not walking quite as straight as when they came aboard. Carefully, they negotiate the tricky route from the vehicle deck to the gangway and cheerfully bid the armed guards goodnight.

'It might be a good night for them,' says one of the guards. 'We have to wait here for the return of the bleedin' natives – and I wonder what sort of state they will be in. No I don't. I know exactly what they will be like . . . out of their friggin' heads!'

They first start to come back from town about one o'clock in the morning, and they continue to trickle in over the next three or four hours. Some are wobbly, some are very wobbly, but nobody has to be carried. (It is an offence if you cannot make your own way back on board.) Just after three o'clock, one young marine lurches on to the ship with one of the female sailors. Both are in a fairly advanced stage of inebriation, and both are well decorated around the neck and shoulders with a series of freshly delivered love bites.

'Oh, look at Sprog and Tracey!' laughs another sailor, also the worse for wear. 'How did you get those marks you two? Is this a love story unfolding before us?'

'No, mate!' slurs Tracey. 'Had a session with a Hoover, didn't I?'

'Oi, Sprog! Tracey's been having it off with a Hoover. Howd'ya like that?'

'It wasn't a bleedin' Hoover pal. That was me!'

Whereupon Marine Sprog seizes the giggling Tracey and gives her a long and passionate kiss. If he had delivered this a few yards away on the jetty, it would have been perfectly legal. As it happens, he has done it right in front of the officer of the watch. Even before Sprog unclamps his lips from the female sailor's, they are both on a charge, having blatantly flouted the Navy's code of social conduct – the No Touch rule. They might have become an 'item' ashore, but as soon as they step on the gangway they must revert to being shipmates and nothing more. The charge is likely to be 'conduct prejudicial to good order and discipline'.

CHAPTER FOUR

Heading Out

Location: Eastern Mediterranean
Date: 3 December 2004
Time: 10.00

Ship's Daily Orders. Weekly Objective: 'Timely passage to Suez'
Notes: Be careful about who you release the ship's programme to,
including other military establishments. As a guide, if people do
not strictly need to know where we are going, do not let them
know. There is no point compromising ourselves unnecessarily.
Lightweight fatigues will be issued to upperdeck crew at 14.00.

HMS *Chatham* is slicing through the gleaming waters of the eastern
Mediterranean on her way to the Suez Canal. Riding the pressure waves
at her bow are four dolphins that periodically leap high out of the water,
apparently for the sheer, unbridled fun of it. The sun, so cold and pale
when the ship left Plymouth, has transformed into a fiery yellow orb
that now beats down hard on the upper deck of the British frigate.

'Bugger this for a lark!' says Rab Butler, keeping watch on the port
bridge wing. 'I know all about mad dogs and bleedin' Englishmen, but
this is takin' the piss this is. Number Fours,* body armour and a fuckin'
helmet. Sweating me bollocks off here I am.'

'Oh shut up Rab, you big girl's blouse!' says fellow gunner Alex Her-
riot, adjusting his Rayban sunglasses. 'I like the sun!'

'Yeah? Well, I reckon you've got a touch of it, mate. Me flamin'
head's meltin' under this tin lid.'

'Quit moaning. They're issuing lightweight desert gear later. After
scran I think – it was on Daily Orders.'

'Roll on!' says Rab. 'I'm dressed for the flamin' Arctic at the
moment.'

*No. Fours (formerly
known as No. Eights).
Blue, thick-cottoned, fire-
retardant trousers and
shirt. Everyday working rig
at sea.

'And they'll be giving us those camel pack things.'

'You what?'

'Those water pouches you carry on your back, with a rubber tube you suck through. Stops you getting dehydrated.'

'Livin' the dream, we are!' says Rab, sweltering under his helmet. 'Livin' the bleedin' dream!'

RAB BUTLER ON THE
UPPER DECK

At eleven o'clock, the ship's main broadcast system delivers an urgent message: 'D'you hear this? Clear lower deck. All hands will muster on the flight deck in five minutes.' Immediately everybody on the ship – except dutymen in the engine room, the operations room and the bridge – files down passageways towards the stern of the ship. There they congregate on the flight deck and wait.

A few minutes later Captain Steve Chick, the commanding officer, walks out. The ship's company comes smartly to attention, and they are immediately stood at ease.

'Gather round!' says the captain. 'Right. As you all know we will soon be in our operational area, the Arabian Gulf, where we will be patrolling for the next six months as part of what is called Operation Calash. We will be stopping and searching merchantmen fairly continuously, as part of the attempt to suppress terrorism and bring some stability to the region at this troubled time. Clearly, we are looking out for suspect shipping that might be transporting contraband – arms, drugs, people. I can't pretend that there is no threat. There is. The threat is there – but we need to keep it in perspective.'

Steve Chick is a sailor's captain. He is firm but very fair and has the gift of the common touch. I know already from my time on *Chatham* that he is well liked and highly respected – the sort of captain that most sailors would want to have in charge if they were heading into any sort of danger.

'Tomorrow,' he continues, 'we will transit Suez, and once we are through the business really starts. I am confident you are up to it. We need to keep ourselves safe, so what I need from everybody for the next six months is complete commitment to the task – whether you are engineers, logistics – keeping us fed and watered – or involved in warfare. Complacency is the slippery slope downward.'

Everybody is listening intently to their captain. Few notice that at the stern of the ship an entire school of pilot whales has risen to the surface. Breathing noisily from their blow holes, the glistening mammals all turn towards the ship, giving the distinct impression they too want to hear what Steve Chick has to say.

THE SHARP END OF HMS *CHATHAM*!

'Our plans must be very fluid, so don't pin too many hopes on particular runs ashore. Christmas Day will be at sea. It is an emotional time of the year, and none of us asked to be away at such a time, so let's do our best to enjoy this time together as the community that we are. Let's try and enjoy ourselves. No own goals please.'

He pauses briefly to survey his audience.

'That leads me nicely I think to the subject of a run ashore. Anybody who knows me realises that I'll probably be leading it, but let's remember that we are coming to a part of the world with a very different culture. Respect that. Let's get it right. Don't drink to excess and don't wear ladies' underwear unless you are a lady . . .'

The captain looks up with a half grin and fixes the few smirking faces with a long stare. Sailors, and particularly marines, have a long and proud tradition of donning women's undergarments, or even entire women's wardrobes, for runs ashore. This might go down well in New-castle or Glasgow, but it is unlikely to be appreciated in the United Arab Emirates.

The ship is being primed for entering theatre in Operation Calash. The Royal Marines and naval boarding parties are now constantly practising their procedures: climbing down rope ladders, fully armed, into small,

A ROYAL MARINE COMMANDO – ONE OF THE NAVY'S SEA SOLDIERS

high-powered rubber boats for rapid transfer to prospective vessels that might need questioning or inspecting. Every day, guns are being methodically dismantled, cleaned and tested all over the ship. The General Purpose Machine Guns mounted on the bridge wings, the fo'c'sle and the flight deck are all loaded with live rounds and test-fired in long and short bursts. So too are the brand new Mini Guns mounted on the port and starboard waists – at the press of a button 3,000 vicious rounds a minute rip into the blue Mediterranean waters that instantly boil with indignation. The Sea Wolf missiles, stowed in their magazines back in Plymouth, are carefully taken out, inserted into the loaders at either end of the ship and made live. Toby Clay and John Turner take off in the Lynx helicopter to test out the newly fitted heavy-duty machine gun. Finally, every man and woman in the ship practises firing rifles from the stern – with and without gas masks.

HMS *Chatham* is in a high state of readiness to 'Up and At'Em', and, ladies' underwear notwithstanding, clearly means business.

Down below on Two Deck lightweight hot-weather gear is being unpacked and distributed. Shirts, trousers and sun hats, all in desert colours, as well as camel packs are being issued to all members of the ship's company who spend time on the upper deck – notably gunners, weapons engineering mechanics and other operator-maintainers.

Leading Seaman Ratz Rackliff, a twenty-stone hulk of a man, with a flat-top haircut on which you could land a Hercules Transporter, is struggling to stretch a camouflaged shirt across his massive shoulders. 'Have you got a bigger one?' he says pleadingly.

ACTION LYNX

I think that's the largest we have,' says a flustered-looking sailor, searching through a small mountain of camouflage clothing.

Ginge Grieveson comes out of his catering office to watch the proceedings.

'The Ratz Rackliff fashion show. Excellent!' he says with a laugh.

'This shirt's minuscule,' replies Ratz. 'I'm getting a bigger one.'

'I doubt you are, mate,' says Ginge, looking at the label. 'This one is XXL.'

'Can't be!' says Ratz. 'Look, the buttons don't reach at the front.'

'Hang around,' says the flustered sailor. 'Here's one that says it's XXXL.'

'Bloody hell!' says Ginge. 'That looks like a camouflaged circus tent!'

'Do you ever get to wear this sort of stuff, Ginge?' I ask the leading chef.

'No mate! That's only for people who go up top and see the sunlight – and get shot at!'

'Perfect,' says Ratz, having pulled on the shirt. 'A little snug under the arms, but otherwise just right. Where's the trousers?'

RIFLE PRACTICE AS WE
ENTER THE GULF

'Here we go,' says Ginge, picking up a voluminous pair. 'These look about right for your magnificent girth, Ratz.'

'Excellent,' replies Ratz as he climbs into them. 'Yup, they'll do.' He tucks in the shirt and poses proudly in his new outfit.

'Oh no, don't tuck it in!' exclaims Ginge. 'That's *so* "last deployment"!'

'Rackliff – man of steel!' says Ratz, flexing his muscles. 'The enemy will shiver when they see me coming!'

'But they won't see you, will they?' says Ginge. 'I thought that was the point! Here, put the hat on – to complete the ensemble.'

Ratz dons the floppy sun hat.

'Oh yeah!' says Ginge. 'Look at that – barely perceptible. Just a face floating in the air. Practically invisible.'

'So my bum doesn't look big in this, then?' rejoins Ratz.

'Ratz?' says Ginge. 'I can hear you but I can't see you . . .!'

Date: 4 December 2004
Time: 09.00

* goofing – watching, spectating

† OOW – Officer of the Watch

Ship's Daily Orders. Weekly Objective: 'Safe passage through the Suez Canal'
Notes: Smoking and goofing* may take place at all times from the quarterdeck. If the bridge is quiet, the OOW† may allow goofing from the bridge.

We are heading directly towards Port Said. The minarets of some of the coastal mosques are clearly visible and numerous ships are stretched out in a long line in front of us – all heading south to the entrance of the Suez Canal. We are the only warship in a queue of merchantmen: oil tankers, car transporters, livestock carriers, grain carriers and massive container ships.

Eventually it is our turn to enter the canal. We reduce our speed to seven knots and commence our passage through one of the most extraordinary manmade wonders of the world – a massive 101-mile trench, dug virtually by hand in 1869, that, by linking the Mediterranean to the Red Sea, became the 'Crossroads of Europe, Africa and Asia'.

A short stone's throw away, on either side of us, are the sandy banks of the desert through which the canal was dug a century and a half ago. In places they are lined with palm trees, under which shepherds and

RAB BUTLER EXPLAINS!

goat herders are seeking some welcome shade from an angry Egyptian sun. Camels wander languorously amid the grazing sheep and bleating goats. Half-naked children, skimming stones on the flat water, scream and wave excitedly as our frigate glides past.

'It's like goin' back in time, ain't it?' says Rab, waving back at the urchins.

'Biblical like.'

Rab is on watch on the flight deck. He is carrying a fully loaded SA 80 rifle, wearing upper-body armour and his new lightweight summer fatigues, camouflaged in desert colours. This is 'reverse camouflage' because clearly it does not blend in very effectively with the battleship-grey of the warship – but that is the point. It actually makes the wearer more conspicuous, and emphasises the visible presence of upper-deck sentries.

'We 'ave to repel all comers so need to keep a good look-out,' says Rab, pointing to the high-powered binoculars around his neck, 'and we 'ave to be armed to the 'ilt, because you never know when some silly bugger's goin' to come along and try and ruin our day. I don't mean other warships, but the suicide bomber bearing down on us in a bleedin' pedalo or somink. That's the sort of thing we 'ave to be ready for these days.'

OVERLEAF:
THE DEADLY MINI-GUN IS
MANNED AS CHATHAM
TRANSITS THE SUEZ CANAL

'Are you missing home yet?' I ask, as he scans the banks with his binoculars.

'Yeah, but I don't think about it. I'm getting into the deployment now and 'er indoors is OK, I reckon, accordin' to an e-mail she sent. Just got to get on with it now. Get through Christmas on the briny and then into Dubai for a New Year's knees-up. No point in clock-watchin'. Countin' the days just makes the time go all the more slowly.'

RAB BUTLER STILL
EXPLAINING

'Thirty-one days and fifteen hours gone!' says Ginge Grieveson in the caterer's office. 'That's one hundred and forty-eight days and nine hours to go.'

'Still marking off the calendar then, Ginge?' I say to him.

'Oh yes! Every day, as soon as I get into the office. High point of the day for me.'

'You're not enjoying it at all?'

'I try to make the best of it, but it gets harder, not easier, as I get older. It's my son's birthday today – he's ten – so I'm feeling it a bit more than usual, I suppose.'

Ginge reaches for his laptop.

'E-mailing helps. Didn't have that in the old days – just had to depend on intermittent mail drops. Look at this.'

He opens up an e-mail he received this morning. It is a picture of his son playing rugby.

'Just burns me up sometimes that I am missing things like that . . .'

Ratz Rackliff is sitting in the shade on the starboard waist, stripping a machine gun prior to cleaning it.

'I hate the sun,' he says from underneath his newly acquired floppy hat. 'Bit of a vampire, me – the Prince of Darkness – but this canal's amazing, isn't it?'

'Is this your first Suez transit?' I ask.

'No, this is my sixth time to the Gulf,' he says. 'The Navy's still the best way to see the world. I couldn't stand working in an office – send me barmy looking out of the window and seeing the same tree every day. On a ship the view changes minute by minute.'

'You don't get bored then, Ratz?'

'No. Deployments are what you make them. You got your mates. Biggest social club in the world – the Royal Navy. I could join any ship in the fleet and I reckon I would know ten to fifteen per cent of those on board.'

'You're married?'

'Yes, and I miss Theresa like mad, but we've got used to separation. Mind you . . .' he adds emphatically, 'things are about to change. She's pregnant with our first!'

'When's she due?'

'A week before we get back, but I've put in for advanced leave so I can be with her for the birth. Can't miss that!'

HMS *Chatham* continues her journey through the Suez Canal, carrying on board a community of 246 men and women towards the troubled and risky waters that lead to the hotspots of the Middle East. The ship's company, comprising individuals distinct in personality, attitude, life experience, humour and aspiration, is none the less united by purpose, duty and allegiance.

Date: 6 December 2004
Time: 08.30

**Daily Orders. Weekly Objective: 'Effective handover with HMS
*Campbeltown'***
**Notes: Scrooges Corner. The proliferation of Christmas
decorations is to be curtailed until at least after we have passed
Aqaba on 13 Dec – bah humbug!**

We are now well into the Red Sea and about to rendezvous with HMS
Campbeltown – the ship HMS *Chatham* is replacing in Operation Calash.
Campbeltown has come out of theatre and is on her way home. She will
be back in Plymouth just in time for Christmas.

Campbeltown comes level with us about three hundred metres off
our port side and we proceed to sail in parallel. The Lynx transfers
Captain Chick to *Campbeltown* for discussions with her captain, at
which time there is an exchange of top-secret and highly classified
information.

Two hours later the official business is complete, and it is time for
the sailpast – a naval tradition that symbolically puts the seal on a handover at sea.

The two ships take positions some four or five hundred metres apart,
and then proceed to steam towards each other at top speed – the *Campbeltown* heading north towards the Suez Canal and home and the
Chatham heading south towards the Arabian Sea. As we draw level and
pass each other, with only about a hundred metres between us, all hell
lets loose. Everybody from both ships has gathered on the upper decks
to scream, shout and throw general abuse at each other; orange smoke,
generated from the ships, billows into the sky; deafening music is
played on the ships' broadcast systems, and powerful hoses on both
ships aim great plumes of sea water. The *Campbeltown*'s Lynx does a fast
and low flypast, and all the time everybody is trying to outdo everyone
else in the screaming stakes. *Campbeltown* gets the last word, however,
by waving a huge banner with a festive farewell message – Navy style:
'GUESS WHO'S STUFFING YOUR BIRD THIS CHRISTMAS!!'

CHAPTER FIVE

I Saw Three Ships A'Sailing

Location: Devonport dockyard. Camel's Head Gate
Date: 7 December 2004
Time: 08.30

A figure on a motor scooter approaches Camel's Head Gate – the most westerly entrance to Devonport dockyard. The scooter is no ordinary scooter. It is a classic 1960s Lambretta, resplendent with a dozen silver mirrors splaying from the front fender, and a Union Jack design on the engine casing with 'Boy About Town' written across it in big white letters. The rider is no ordinary rider either. It is the Reverend Michael Brotherton, aka The Mad Bish, on his way to work. He is wearing a huge green helmet and an authentic khaki 'Mod' Parka with The Who written across the back in massive black and white letters. He shows his naval ID to the Ministry of Defence policeman at the gate and then drives through to his ship, HMS *Ocean*, tied up at Wharf 15 in Weston Mill Lake.

Mike has a busy morning – he still has to finish painting the ship's chapel.

Before he does that he goes to the wardroom to make a cup of tea which he then takes to the quarter deck for a few moments of peace and quiet.

'I've always been into scooters,' he confides. 'They are one of my hobbies. Sometimes I get together with other scooter enthusiasts and we go on mass rallies.'

Mike Brotherton has many interests and quite a few of them, it has to be said, are on the eccentric side. Charlie Chaplin, of course, is his great hero and he has been known occasionally to appear dressed as the great man – complete with bowler hat, moustache and cane. That is the way he was dressed when he turned up to join HMS *Ark Royal* in 1993. He is fascinated by the *Titanic*, and has decorated his front room at home in Wales in the style of the great liner. One of his other great passions, Dr Who, has resulted in his buying the full-size, ex-BBC Dalek which he keeps at home, but which he has in the past brought along to play a part in his church services.

'It's true!' he exclaims. 'I always try to perk up my services – especially my sermons. When I was chaplain at HMS *Raleigh* I had a very young congregation – recruits – and I really wanted to capture their imagination. There was no point just throwing all the traditional religious stuff at them because they were never going to relate to it. I needed to tap into their youth and their way of seeing the world. They like zany stuff – so do I. That was our connection.'

The Bish is undoubtedly larger than life, but it is important to understand that his brand of eccentricity is not a simple case of being crazy for the sake of it. He is the way he is because that is the way he expresses his deep spirituality. A boundless sense of fun is not only his way of rejoicing in life but also the way he reaches out to people and connects with

MIKE BROTHERTON ON HIS
BELOVED LAMBRETTA

them. At forty-eight, he claims to have mellowed a little, and so no longer brandishes the Mad Bish label as he used to in the past.

'"Mad Bish" is a nickname given to me by others but, these days, I prefer it to be more in brackets than something I would underline. However, it is an image that continues to help me to relate to young people and that is something I have to do in this job – constantly.'

He sips from his steaming mug of tea and looks out across Frigate Alley to a group of sailors, laughing and joking as they walk down the jetty towards Camel's Head Gate.

'The Navy is full of young people. Fifty or sixty recruits join every week and they need guidance as they progress on to ships and shipboard life – not necessarily spiritual guidance per se, but a sense of support. They, and indeed everybody in the service, want to know there is somebody they can go and talk to if they need to. Sailors have their divisional officers to confide in, and that is great, but as chaplains we can provide a very different type of contact. I always say to people coming into my cabin: "Abandon rank all ye who enter here."

'When we go into a danger zone, of course, people call on me and God a lot more. That's human nature because people are confronting their ultimate fear. So I always feel I need to talk to the new recruits who have just come from *Raleigh* about the fact that they are joining a ship of war. I point out that our aim is never primarily to wage war, because our main purpose in the Navy today is to preserve peace. Nevertheless, I stress that we are a military organisation and, by definition, that means they could well have to place themselves in danger's way at some point.'

Location: Dartmoor National Park
Date: 8 December 2004
Time: 07.00

'OK, you lot! It's too cold to hang around so get fell in – on the double! NO talking – unless you want to do some press-ups. Right, listen up!'

The recruits from HMS *Raleigh* are now into week five of their Phase One training.

'This weekend is going to be hard – make no mistake about it. Be prepared for the worst . . .'

Normally the eight-week course is uninterrupted, but the Forty-Sixers are lucky because Christmas will mean a welcome two-week break in which they will be able to go home and replenish their internal batteries. Before that, however, the recruits face their greatest challenge yet.

'There will be discomfort. There will be blisters. You will be exposed to the elements, so take no chances . . .'

They are about to start a rigorous survival weekend on Dartmoor to practise map-reading, leadership skills . . . and being frozen to the absolute marrow.

Lieutenant Commander Chris Trotter is briefing them. He is stern because he needs them to listen and, above all, take this exercise very seriously. He knows that Dartmoor in the 'bleak mid-winter' can be savage – even life threatening – if you do not know what you are doing.

'You will be camping, so be neat and tidy at all times. That means you will be organised. Eat and drink your victuals because you will need energy. Pack those calories in . . .'

Sharon looks on without expression, but is clearly not impressed; Paul looks uneasy, but manages a nervous smile at Jenny whose face seems to have turned a light shade of blue. Amy, devoid of her beloved make-up, and with her blonde hair screwed up in a bun, pulls a woolly hat over her freezing ears before thrusting her hands deep into her pockets.

'No hands in pockets, people, or else you will pay with press-ups – remember!'

Amy extracts her hands and bites her lip. She is not looking forward to this weekend.

'I want one hundred per cent effort, folks. If you give it everything, you may even enjoy it.'

Amid the sound of chattering teeth there is a ripple of nervous and disbelieving laughter.

Lieutenant Commander Trotter attempts to sugar the bitter pill.

'It's nearly Christmas, so if you do well, we might have time one evening for a few Christmas carols . . .'

Unimpressed, the recruits shift uneasily on their frozen feet.

'. . . and on Sunday, after a fourteen-mile hike you should end up in Princetown. There is a pub in Princetown called the Plume of Feathers. If you make it, if you don't get lost, you will be allowed a pint and a plate of steak and chips!'

Now, very much more impressed, the recruits nod their heads, and some even manage to summon a smile.

'OK, folks – get those tents up. At the double!'

After the campsite is established, all recruits gather behind a wind-break where they are to be taught how to prepare and cook the contents of their emergency 24-hour ration packs – all they will have to live on until that prospective steak and chips tomorrow evening.

'In this 'ere box . . .' says a hearty chief petty officer with more than a hint of Jamie Oliver about his manner, '. . . you 'ave all you need for a lovely five-course meal. Watch and learn!'

He proceeds to illustrate his point in double-quick time. It is like watching a film that has been speeded up.

'First . . .' he says, pulling out a small tin. 'Pâté – not sure what type, but it's lovely!'

He rips the ringpull lid off the tin and turns out a gelatinous globule of meat-like substance on to a tin plate.

The recruits groan loudly.

'Second course . . .' he continues, throwing a food bag into a can of water boiling on a portable solid-fuel burner. 'Beans, sausages and broken-up biscuits – delicious!'

After a few minutes, he extracts the bag, tears it open and turns out its contents.

Groan!

'Don't be down-hearted shipmates! It's all in the presentation . . .'

He prods the sausage and beans, heaping them into a small mountain on the plate before sprinkling crushed biscuits over the top.

'This is fusion cooking guys . . . you'd pay a fortune for this in a fancy London eaterie! Third course – suet pudding and treacle!'

Another bag is thrust into the boiling water. When it is properly heated, he extracts it and once again turns the contents on to a dish. Truth be told, it looks remarkably similar to the sausage and beans that preceded it.

The recruits do not even bother to groan now. They seem to have given up the will to live.

'Lovely grub!' says the chief, licking his lips. 'Fourth course!'

He pulls out a bar of plain chocolate, breaks it up and throws it into a mess-tin on the fire. When the chocolate has melted, he breaks some more biscuits into it and mixes it up.

'There you go – a sort of chocolate pudding thing! Right, fifth and final course . . .'

He takes a small packet of processed cheese, tears it open and then smears the yellow-orange contents over one remaining biscuit.

'Cheese and biscuits – ideal!'

Amy looks at Sharon and screws up her face. Sharon does the same. Jenny sits there in a trance – quite possibly thinking that spam and pickle sandwiches are not so bad after all. Paul sits there with unblinking eyes, looking as if he might be contemplating his future as a naval chef.

'That's how and what you will be eating tonight, people. It's designed to fill you up and then clean you out. Packed with calories it is, and you'll be burning them up like good 'uns, so eat it all up, there's good sailors. Ladies – forget the diet. Stuff yourselves. OK – off you go. You have a nice ten-mile hike across the Moors now, as a practice for tomorrow and to build up an appetite.'

The recruits, looking a little shell-shocked, wander down to the tents to collect their waterproofs. As they move off the chief shouts after them, 'And remember, people! Tomorrow morning we start at the crack. Happy days!'

The Following Day
Location: Dartmoor National Park
Time: 05.00

The recruits start to crawl out of their tents, even though it still pitch-black outside. If they thought it was cold yesterday, they will think today is positively Arctic.

'Oh my God!' says Amy, watching her breath condense instantly on the chill morning air.

'I could have got a job stacking shelves at Tesco!' says the voice of a girl hidden in the darkness. 'A lovely job stacking baked beans in a nice warm supermarket in Wolverhampton . . .'

'Dream on sunshine!' says another voice, still inside a tent.

At last all the recruits have emerged from their canvas sanctuaries, and make their way to the windbreak for breakfast – porridge and hot sweet tea.

'I hope the porridge tastes better than last night's meal,' says Sharon.

'I didn't think it was so bad, actually,' says Paul. 'The treacle pud was half-decent.'

'Steak and chips at the Plume of Feathers is all I can think about,' says Jenny, ladling some porridge into her mess-tin.

'As for the carols last night . . .' says Amy, sipping at a mug of steaming tea. '. . . what a racket! I'm glad we're not being tested for our singing!'

A dozen or so recruits have gone straight to the first-aid post to have their blisters tended to. Yesterday's practice hike has taken its toll on a lot of young and untested feet.

'Blisters?' enquires the medic, rather unnecessarily, to the first in the queue.

'Yes. Both feet. All over!' says Richard Patterson, the boy with impressively sticky-out ears.

'OK, get the shoes off. Name?'

'Wingnut.'

'What!?' says the medic looking up. 'Oh I see – because of the lugs? I actually meant your real name.'

'Oh, sorry. Patterson,' says Wingnut, pulling off his socks.

'Excellent, you've got some beauties there! Right, keep still whilst I clean them up and dress them. It will sting a bit.'

The medic sets about the reddened and blistered skin with the confidence and certainty of someone who has tended to a thousand such feet.

'So you got that name since you came to *Raleigh*?' he enquires.

'Yes. Some call me Teapot. Others Jugs. But most call me Wingnut.'

'Typical Navy that,' says the medic. 'Everybody gets nicknames. I know a "Sticky" Stamp, a "Bunny" Warren, a "Tommy" Cooper, a "Dutchy" Holland, a "Jack" Russell, a "Grassy" Meadows, and I know one submariner called Potter. Everybody calls him "Trains".'

'See that bloke over there?' says Wingnut, warming to the subject. 'The one with red hair and a big conk.'

'Yes,' says the medic, looking across to a serious-looking recruit methodically packing his rucksack.

'Well, he was made a squad leader after two weeks of training 'cos they thought he had leadership skills, but it's gone to his head a bit, so we call him "Thrush".'

'Why's that?'

'Because he's an irritating cu – OUCH!! That hurt!'

The coal-black sky, diluted by the dawn, is transforming into a deep, dark blue that stretches to the distant horizon. Threatening dark clouds race each other above our heads and, just in front of us, a tangle of trees, just half an hour ago as one with the night, is emerging as a ghostly silhouette waving in the bitter wind blowing off the moors. The recruits, with rucksacks on their backs and maps and compasses in hand, have been split into groups of ten. Each group will have a different route to follow, according to plots drawn on their maps. They will have to hike to each plot in turn by use of the compass, and they will have to measure distance by pacing. One after another each group is given the signal to start.

'Remember everyone . . .' says Lieutenant Commander Trotter, 'you are only as fast as your weakest or slowest member. Don't surge ahead and leave team members behind – work as a team, and apply your individual strengths to helping the team. That's the Navy way. Good luck!'

The vision of a pint of beer and a sizzling steak at the end of it all is the only thing that beckons the groups into the bleakness that is Dartmoor in December.

Amy, Sharon and Jenny are in the same group. They set off at a brisk pace with everybody taking it in turns to pace the distance. They also take it in turns to be leader and to do the compass work. At first all goes well, and the first plot is quickly reached. The second plot is also quickly found, but then it all goes badly wrong.

'This is definitely the way,' says the current leader.

'Well, we only had five hundred metres to pace out . . .' says Sharon, 'which we've done, and we're not there yet, so I reckon we got the direction wrong. The ground is getting very wet around here!'

'I think we should go on another hundred metres, just in case we didn't pace it properly. Come on!'

We trudge on through the saturated grass. Five minutes later we are up to our shins in wet turf. Seven minutes later we are waist high in Dartmoor bog and some are sinking.

'Hang on!' shout the ones still on semi-solid ground. 'Here, reach out for our hands!'

One by one the sinking recruits (and one attendant film maker) are dragged out of the mire. Eventually, we are all on dry land, but we are soaking and our boots are full of water.

'Great!' says Amy. 'I actually thought it couldn't get worse. Now we've got the whole day in wet clothes.'

Progress is slow, wet and cold. Gradually, however, one plot mark after another is reached and the group takes heart. Jenny is finding the going tough with the heavy rucksack, so some of the stronger ones take it in turn to support her load as they walk along. We have a near setback when Amy tries to take a compass bearing on some distant Dartmoor ponies, but then realises it is always advisable to choose something that does not wander around – such as a rock or a tree.

'Sorry!' she says. 'I was having a blonde moment there!'

'You're telling us!' says Sharon. 'Do you want me to take the bearings?'

'No!'

'OK! But just so you know, those fluffy white things over there are sheep.'

Location: Princetown. The Plume of Feathers
Time: 17.00

One by one the groups arrive – bedraggled, wet, cold but delighted.

'I never *ever* want to do that again!' says Amy. 'But I'm pleased I've done it. I feel quite proud, actually, but now I just want to get these wet clothes off!'

Hot showers are available at the Plume – a favourite for hikers and Outward Bound enthusiasts – so all the recruits take it in turns to luxuriate in the streaming, steaming water before changing into the civvies they have all been carrying in their rucksacks. Amy, scrubbed, dried, powdered, mascara'd, and lipsticked, lets down her hair and dons a clinging pink top and white flared trousers.

'I'm a girl again!' she shouts delightedly, and then joins the others in a long but happy queue of recruits, lining up in front of a bar about to do booming trade. Beer, lager and cider are ordered en masse. So too are numerous steak platters – which arrive stacked high with best sirloin, chips, peas, mushrooms and fried onions.

This is the first evening the recruits have had off since arriving at Plymouth station. Soon, they will all be home again, enjoying the Christmas break. Right now, with Dartmoor behind them, life couldn't be much better.

That evening, as I drive back from Dartmoor, I hear the news on the radio that a naval helicopter has apparently crashed into the sea during a search and rescue mission just off the Cornish coast, and that four crew are missing. A major search is underway for the Lynx helicopter, exactly the same type of aircraft, I think to myself, as that flown by Toby and JT on HMS *Chatham*. Apparently, it had been dispatched from its base at the Royal Navy air station at Yeovilton, Somerset, after two sailors on board HMS *Montrose* heard cries for help from the sea, but just after 7 p.m., contact with the helicopter was lost, nineteen miles off Lizard Point.

From the edge of the moors I can see the lights of Plymouth in front of me, and beyond them the dark and forbidding Channel that may, once again, have claimed the lives of Royal Navy aviators. I think of the recruits in the Plume of Feathers, laughing, joking and looking forward to Christmas, and then I think of the four young men somewhere out there in the blackness. I console myself that it may have been a controlled ditching and that they are all safe in their liferaft waiting to be rescued . . .

The following day the news is released that the mangled parts of the missing helicopter have been found in eighty-five metres of water by an unmanned submarine. An underwater television camera, sent to examine the wreckage further, had discovered four bodies in and around the wreckage itself. It is further announced that the original SOS call to which the Lynx helicopter was responding was a false alarm. The Christmas tragedy for the family of the four airmen and, indeed, the entire naval aviation community, is complete.

Flags are being flown at half mast throughout the Plymouth Command.

Location: HMS *Ocean*
Date: 14 December 2004
Time: 10.00

Mike Brotherton is in a state of controlled frenzy. This morning he is hosting the ships' companies from HMS *Albion* and HMS *Bulwark* for a massive carol concert on board HMS *Ocean*, and there is still much left to organise.

'I have no idea how many will turn up,' says Mike, half running, half walking down one of *Ocean*'s massively long passageways. 'We are going to hold the carol service in the main hangar. Normally it would be full of helicopters and equipment, but it's empty at the moment so, for today anyway, it will be my church . . . cathedral even!'

We move down a huge and very wide ladder that takes us deep into the belly of the gigantic ship. Arrowed signs on the bulkheads say 'Assault', indicating that these stairs are designed to be used by fully armed marines making their way to be transported to battle – either by air or by landing craft. Today the only marines we pass are carrying a huge Christmas tree.

'Excellent!' Mike says to them. 'Have you got a bucket or something to put it in?'

'Yes, Bish,' says one of the marines. 'Nabbed one from the Buffer* and got some quick-drying cement to plant it in, so it won't fall over.'

> *Buffer – Chief Bosun's Mate. Senior rating in charge of all matters relating to seamanship.

'And we've found a whole bunch of decorations too, Bish,' says the other marine with a wink. 'Don't ask where.'

'Oh dear. Have you ransacked a mess?'

'Adapt and overcome, Bish. It's the marine way!'

At last we reach the cavernous hangar, which is a hive of festive activity. On one side a dozen stewards are putting up trestle tables and laying them with paper tablecloths decorated with holly and Robin Redbreasts. Others are putting out huge plates of mince pies and large bowls for the mulled wine being heated in large urns nearby. On the other side of the hangar, the Salvation Army band are taking their instruments out of their cases and organising their chairs in three rows. Just in front of them the marines have placed the Christmas tree in its bucket of cement, and are beginning to sort out the nefariously obtained decorations.

An hour later, Mike Brotherton welcomes his great friend Angela Thomas to HMS *Ocean*. Angela is landlady of one of the best and most well-known pubs on the Cornish coast, the Helzephron, and is also an amateur opera singer who is going to perform a solo at today's concert.

'Mike! Dear Mike. How are you?' she says theatrically but sincerely, as she gives him a hug that takes his breath away.

'Hello Angela,' gasps Mike, flashing his broadest and most boyish smile. 'Thanks so much for coming. We are thrilled you are going to sing . . . oh dear what's the time? I must see if the sound system is working . . . are you all right by yourself for a minute? . . . I just have to . . . oh goodness . . . I hope the Sally Army band are OK . . .'

Mike's panic tickles Angela's funny bone. 'Oh Mike, dear Mike . . .' she says, and then bursts into laughter. Did I say bursts? Let me rephrase

MIKE AND ANGELA

that. Her laugh does not burst. It does not explode either. These are small, puny words to describe the laugh of Angela Thomas. It is more akin to the sound of a thermonuclear blast, and the energy released is of the same proportion. It is high-pitched but with great body and astounding resonance, and I swear the sides of HMS *Ocean* shudder in response.

Mike leaves Angela in his cabin to practise her scales whilst he returns to the hangar.

'Ah, it's filling up nicely,' he says, watching sailors and officers pour in from the gangway entrance. 'These are all from *Bulwark* and *Albion*. Excellent. Good turnout. They don't know it, but at the end of the service we are going to sing "I Saw Three Ships A'Sailing" and the companies from all three ships are going to take it in turn to sing a verse. Adds a nice competitive element to the proceedings!'

The service commences at midday. Mike, standing at the lectern in front of the Christmas tree, now permanently embedded in the Buffer's bucket, welcomes everybody to HMS *Ocean*. Then, flanked by his opposite numbers from the other ships – a trinity of Bishes – Mike invites everybody to sing 'Jingle Bells'.

As the massed congregation of sailors, officers and marines sings about the joys of riding in one-horse open sleighs, Mike looks over at

Angela who is leading her section of the hangar by great and loud example. He smiles and then surveys the whole assembly with great satisfaction.

'Jingle Bells' is followed by 'Rudolph the Red Nosed Reindeer' which is followed by 'Once in Royal David's City', with the first verse sung as a solo by Angela. Then comes the 'Calypso Carol', 'Away in a Manger', 'Good King Wenceslas' and 'Silent Night'. During the last verse, Mike turns to the Revd Michael Meachin, the chaplain of HMS *Albion*. They speak seriously and intently for a few moments, after which Mike nods and grasps his arm in an affirming sort of way.

When 'Silent Night' is finished *Albion*'s chaplain steps up to the lectern. Mike's head is already bowed.

'We must now spend a few moments thinking of others at this special time of the year,' the chaplain says gently. 'This Christmas is going to be very difficult for some people – the homeless, children in need, those for whom Christmas is an anniversary of the death of a loved one who is now with God. This is particularly true for us in the Royal Navy as we remember those who died last week in the helicopter crash. Let us observe a moment's silence as we remember them, and as we pray for their families at this Christmas time and for all those who loved them and continue to love them . . .'

The hangar is shrouded in silence and every man and woman in it stands to respectful attention with head bowed. Quietly the names of their lost comrades are read out: 'Lieutenant David Cole . . . Lieutenant Robert Dunn . . . Lieutenant James Mitchell . . . LAEM* Richard Darnell.'

*LAEM – Leading Aircraft Engineering Mechanic.

There is a further silence. Some in the congregation unashamedly wipe away tears.

'Father, rest eternal grant unto them. May light perpetual shine upon them. May they rest in peace and rise in glory. Amen.'

There is another brief period of silence before Mike Brotherton takes the lectern.

'Right!' he says, summoning a smile, '. . . the last carol is "I Saw Three Ships A'Sailing" and we are going to do this in a slightly different way . . .'

CHAPTER SIX

Hands to Reindeer Stations

Location: HMS *Chatham*, Straits of Hormuz
Date: 24 December 2004
Time: 09.00

Ship's Daily Orders. Our Mission: 'To detect, disrupt and destroy terrorist elements operating in the region'

Toby Clay lines up his Lynx astern of HMS *Chatham* and edges towards the mothership's flight deck. The flight controller on deck is waving him in with beckoning arm movements and six flight-deck crew stand by, extinguishers and hoses at the ready, in case of an emergency. Take-offs and landings from a moving warship are the most hazardous tasks a helicopter pilot has to perform. One mistake, one slip and the spinning rotors could make catastrophic contact with the ship's superstructure.

Toby brings the aircraft level with the flight deck which is now below him to his right. He brings the Lynx to a hover, adjusts the trim and checks his instruments – particularly his automatic horizon. The aircraft is no more than fifty feet above the water, and its enormous down-draught throws a cloud of spray high into the air. Penetrated by the sun's rays, it forms a small but perfect rainbow.

When the Lynx is straight and stable, the flight-deck controller waves Toby across. The young flight commander eases his aircraft slowly to the right until it is directly over the flight deck. Allowing for the up and down movement of the ship in the gentle to medium ocean swell, he lowers the roaring helicopter slowly, ever so slowly, until finally its wheels make contact with the deck. There is the slightest lurch, the smallest bounce, but then the Lynx is home – safe from yet another patrol over the Straits of Hormuz, just south of Iran.

Toby Clay and his flight observer, JT, shut down the Lynx and proceed to the hangar to take off their helmets and radio equipment. They exchange the usual banter with the flight-deck crew and share a mug of tea with them before returning to their cabins.

They know about the lost Lynx back in Britain, and the death of the four aviators – all of whom they knew.

'We heard about it soon after it happened,' says Toby Clay. 'It's difficult to know how to react when these things happen, to be honest. So many thoughts fly around your head.'

'Knowing them must have made it worse for you?' I say to him.

'Yes. Of course,' he affirms emotionally. 'Both JT and I shared an office with three of them for a while, but the Fleet Air Arm is like a family anyway. We nearly all know each other to a degree. It's the game we are in. These things happen – tragic for the families – but the rest have to get on with the job.'

'But does it make you think more about the danger?'

TOBY CLAY AND ME AFTER
A FLIGHT IN THE LYNX

He purses his lips and pauses for thought.

'To be honest . . . yes. Of course it does. You have your moment of "it could have been me", but you have to put it behind you. As flight commander, I could not let it affect the morale of the team – I don't just mean JT and me but the whole flight-deck crew as well, because they felt the loss too.'

'What did you do, then?'

'Well, JT and I were having a talk about it after we heard, and getting pretty morose. Suddenly, I just jumped up, gave him a big hug and said, "Look, we are bloody brilliant, so come on, let's go flying!" We needed to do it. Everybody needed to see the Lynx flying, and we have been flying constantly ever since, because we need to patrol these waters. We've been sent out here to do a job, so we have just got on with it.'

THE LYNX TAKES OFF FOR ANOTHER PATROL

HMS *Chatham* is in theatre. For the past couple of weeks she has been engaged in Operation Calash – patrolling the Arabian Sea in the search for suspect shipping. Every day she tracks down any vessels in the area, either through her own radar or through helicopter searches, and then, in some cases, intercepts them and boards them by fast seaboat carrying armed marines, in order to check their papers and, if necessary, their cargo. It is routine work and very monotonous for most of the ship's company, but it is an essential part of the policing of these waters at this crucial time for the region, as Iraq prepares for its first democratic elections.

Mid-morning, Ratz Rackliff is in his mess, hammering pieces of wood together and constructing a sort of canopy in one corner of the room.

'This magnificent structure,' he says, 'will be our mess's Santa's Grotto. Gotta make the best of Christmas at sea, haven't we, and sailors are good at adapting – it's what we do.'

The mess, like all the messes in the ship, is already decorated with tinsel, plastic holly and coloured streamers. Everybody is lending a hand to get the grotto built, but Ratz, as mess leader, is in charge. He calls the shots.

'Obviously we don't have a Santa's Grotto stowed away, so we have to construct it from nothing. Beg a bit here, borrow a bit there, nick a bit – it's the sailor's way.'

Gradually the grotto takes shape – not a cheap approximation but the proper thing – red walls topped with snow, icicles, and coloured flashing lights.

The ship is being readied for Christmas Day. Although we are on patrol in the narrow stretch of water between Iran and the United Arab Emirates, the ship is being turned into everybody's living room back home in Wolverhampton, Glasgow, Manchester, Liverpool, Newcastle or Bristol. The fact that a Royal Navy warship on deployment is only ever a little piece of Britain cast out on the high seas has never been truer than it is now, with HMS *Chatham* preparing for her Christmas patrol.

RATZ RACKLIFF IN HIS CHRISTMAS GROTTO

At 17.50, Chief Petty Officer Jim Wharton walks into the ship's darkened operations room, the nerve centre of the ship. It contains a dozen warfare operatives peering at radar screens.

'Excuse me, sir,' he says to Lieutenant Chris Saunders, one of the principal warfare officers. 'Permission to use the main broadcast?'

'Carry on, Chief,' comes the reply.

Jim Wharton takes the black handset and presses the transmit button.

'Do you hear there!' he says with urgency. 'All ship's company – hands to reindeer stations! Hands to reindeer stations! That's all!'

He replaces the handset.

'Thank you, sir.'

'That's OK, CPO Wharton. Nice costume!'

'Thank you very much, sir,' replies Jim Wharton, adjusting his thick cottonwool beard. 'I am a bit of a traditionalist when it comes to Christmas, so I always break out the Santa cossi. I hardly dare imagine what some of the others will be wearing!'

It only takes ten minutes for the ship's company to start flooding on to the flight deck. There are numerous Elvis Presleys, a lot of pixies, a handful of assorted fairies, a couple of Hell's Angels, a hippie, several punks, various animals, an astronaut, a Mr T, three Supermen, two people in gas masks and thongs, and numerous hookers – every one with an Adam's apple – in the most garish make-up, mini-skirts and tight but well-filled blouses.

'Bloody hell, Simmo, I almost fancy you in that dress,' says 'Sweeney' Todd, the physical training instructor, to Chief Petty Officer Simpson. 'And I love the lipstick. So very you!'

'Thanks Clubs,'* replies Simmo Simpson. 'Very sweet of you, mate!

'And what the hell are you dressed as, Clubs?' enquires a nearby 'elephant', looking at the tall muscular PTI in his tight turquoise shorts, black leather chaps and white crash helmet.

'Gay Biker, mate!'

Where everybody got their costumes from is anybody's guess, but it is well known that sailors love to dress up and, it has to be said, are very good at it – combining imagination, initiative and, very often, a highly suspect but very naval sense of humour.

Rab Butler, tonight dressed as the skinhead he once used to be, with bovver boots and little black trilby, watches as a fellow gunner and a stoker adjust their stockings and hitch up their skirts.

'Friggin' 'ell,' he says, loud enough for them to hear. 'Matelots who can produce frocks from their personal kit bags that fit them perfectly, is a bit fuckin' suspect if you ask me!'

*Clubs is short for clubswinger – a traditional naval method of keeping fit.

I GO NATIVE!

THE CHIEF PETTY OFFICERS!

'Bog off, Butler!' they laugh, blowing him a kiss.

'So ladylike . . .!'

Reindeer racing is another great naval tradition. Actually, it is normally called 'horse racing', but this is Christmas Eve. The race track consists of thirty squares, each about a metre in length, laid out on the flight deck.

AND THEY'RE OFF!

The horses, differently coloured wooden cut-out figures with jockeys (tonight transformed into little reindeer with Santa riders) are lined up at one end. The reindeer are moved across the track by throwing two enormous dice, about a foot square, which have been knocked up in the workshop. One is painted a different colour on each of its sides to coincide with the colours of the reindeer. The other dice is numbered. The coloured dice is thrown first to determine which reindeer will move, and then the numbered dice is thrown to determine how many squares it will advance. The track has various obstacles like water jumps that, if landed on, deliver a penalty such as going back some squares or missing a go.

REINDEER RACING ON THE FLIGHT DECK

The racing is taken very seriously because the stakes can be quite high. Before each race, the reindeer are auctioned. Bids are invited for each reindeer in turn, and the highest bidder will own that reindeer for that particular race. Once the last reindeer is sold, all the money is totalled. Ten per cent is taken off for charity and the rest is given to the owner of the winning reindeer. The 'owner' could be a syndicate such as an entire mess and can, therefore, involve many hundreds of pounds. Also, of course, it is possible for regular punters to bet on a particular reindeer. Once all the reindeer are auctioned, bets can be placed as multiples of £1 and run on a tote basis. Once all bets are in, the odds are displayed on a board and the race is run.

'You can win a bundle if you are lucky and a bit clever,' says Rab Butler with relish. 'The trick is to watch the coloured dice for a while, because it's bleedin' impossible to make those things perfectly square. There's bound to be a tendency for it to go to one colour more than the others – a dodgy dice we call it – so once you work that out, you can clean up – in theory.'

The races start. Frantic auctions are followed by even more frantic dice-throwing. The yellow, blue, black, red, green and silver reindeer advance to the raucous cheering of an increasingly excitable crowd. Beer flows freely and soon the flight deck is transformed into a sort of manic street party crossed with the Cheltenham Gold Cup.

Able Seaman (Store Accountant) Becky Nobbs tours the deck with a sprig of mistletoe and official permission that she can relax the strict No Touch rule between men and women.

'The XO says I can give everyone a Christmas kiss!' she chirrups, 'but he said no kiss must be more than two seconds, and absolutely no tongues!'

'And the next race,' shouts race official Warrant Officer Steve Price 'is "The Beef Stakes" sponsored by Shergar. It is over thirty squares with water jumps. We have running as the red reindeer "Pocket rocket" out of "His Trousers" and trained by the galley – should win by a good length. Green is "Filthy Mare", out of "Bed", trained by the stokers' mess . . .'

Race after race is run, much to the delight of everyone here. Captain Chick puts in an appearance and shares a beer with some of his sailors, who are delighted to see him on deck with them.

'This was always the plan for Christmas Eve,' he explains to me. 'It could be a time for homesickness to set in, so we all need to join in together and have some fun, even though we are still in our patrol area.

Everybody's been working very hard since we left Plymouth, so they deserve this. It is still a while before they get their next run ashore in Dubai, so I want to take the pressure off them a little, both tonight and tomorrow, if I can.'

Halfway through the evening there is an interval in the racing, at which point the ship's band 'Bovisand' make their debut appearance, and immediately the all-purpose flight deck becomes a dance floor. Two lead singers – one male, one female – one bass guitarist, one lead guitarist and a drummer strut their stuff with impressive energy and even more impressive volume, but at least there are no neighbours to disturb out here.

Add rock concert to Cheltenham Gold Cup and manic street party, and you have a sense of the atmosphere that has kicked in. Most people seem to have forgotten, for the moment anyway, that they are on a warship, let alone one that is floating just outside the territorial waters of the Islamic Republic of Iran.

RATZ RACKLIFF AND I AT THE REINDEER RACING

On the bridge, however, the officer of the watch and his duty team of navigators peer into the night and guide the frigate slowly forward. In the ops room, dutymen continue to scour their radar screens and sonar screens for anything out of the ordinary. There might be Christmas cheer on the flight deck, but the warship is still primed and ready to react, should she need to.

Just after midnight the urgent voice of a radar operator shatters the silence in the ops room.

'Unknown aircraft approaching ship from the north!'

'Issue air threat warning One!' responds Chris Saunders, the duty principal warfare officer, immediately.

'Unknown aircraft,' says the radarman over his radio. 'This is Royal Navy warship *Chatham*. You are approaching us in a threatening manner. Please answer our call and turn away. I repeat, please answer our call and turn away . . .'

Minutes later, the ship's main broadcast system bursts into voice.

'Hear this!' says the principal warfare officer. 'We have just been monitoring an unknown aircraft that was closing the ship. We issued air threat warnings and were about to prime the Sea Wolf missiles . . . but then we heard the sound of sleigh bells and a deep resonant laugh far above us. Happy Christmas everybody!'

Location: Straits of Hormuz
Date: 25 December 2004
Time: 08.00

Ship's Daily Orders: Message from the XO: 'Have a relaxing and enjoyable day. Merry Christmas!'

The wake-up pipe, a long series of blasts on the bosun's 'call' or whistle over the main broadcast system, signals the start of the day. Today HMS *Chatham* is the only Royal Navy ship at sea anywhere in the world and, whilst she is on official patrol and, as always, on the look-out for suspect shipping, the daily routine will be more relaxed than usual. 'Call the Hands' is usually piped at 07.00. Today everyone gets an extra hour in bed.

After breakfast Christmas unfolds in a traditionally naval way. First of all the youngest member of the ship's company is made captain for the day. A seventeen-year-old steward is given Captain Steve Chick's four-ring epaulettes to wear, and the run of his cabin including his bathroom. Whilst she is not actually allowed to command the ship, she is allowed to throw her weight around a bit. The first thing she does is call three of her messmates to her new cabin and order them to sing her Christmas songs, make her a cup of tea and run her a bath.

Elsewhere, people are generally relaxing and opening up the presents they have brought from home. The galley is the busiest place on the ship as the cooks put dozens of turkeys into the ovens, along with potatoes, sausages, bacon, carrots, and parsnips. Sprouts are washed and prepared, and Christmas puddings are lined up ready for boiling.

STEWARD SIAN SUGDEN – CAPTAIN FOR THE DAY!

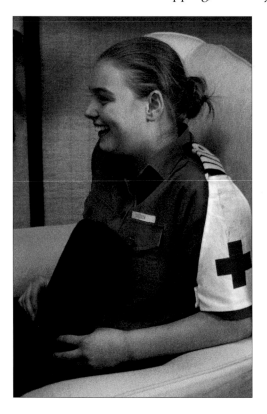

At 10.15, about fifty people muster on the flight deck for a church and carol service.

'Brothers and sisters,' says Tommy Goodwin, the ship's chaplain. 'We are all members of HMS *Chatham*, a community and a special family within the Navy, and together we share this Christmas morning. Let us pray for all those not with us today. Let us think of our wives and husbands, boyfriends, girlfriends, mums and dads, children, brothers and sisters . . .'

CHRISTMAS SERVICE ON THE FLIGHT DECK

Despite a savage Middle Eastern sun, most of the congregation are wearing Santa Claus hats, and one midshipman, determined to capture the flavour of a British Christmas, is wearing a long, woollen winter scarf. Tommy Goodwin nods towards Lieutenant Kenny Dalgleish, the deputy weapons engineering officer, who sits in front of a portable electric organ.

'Let us now sing "We Three Kings of Orient Are".'

Tommy Goodwin, an ever-smiling Scot from Glasgow, is responsible for three frigates – HMS *Chatham*, HMS *Norfolk* and HMS *Monmouth*, and moves from one to the other on a rota basis. When he realised *Chatham* was going to be at sea for Christmas, he made sure he would be with her for the period, so he flew out and joined the ship from

Aqaba in Jordan after she had transited the Suez Canal. Like Mike Brotherton back in Plymouth, Tommy is both a deeply devout man and also a man of great character, who imbues his pastoral duties with a delightful sense of fun. This morning, however, his mood is thoughtful and melancholic.

'Today we will all be thinking of those we love and care for at home. So, Lord, we pray that this Christmas time our love may reach them, and also that we may know your love today. And grant that this day may be a joyful one.'

Intercessions are followed by 'Away in a Manger' and 'Good Christian Men Rejoice'.

After the service, the congregation disperses, most returning to their mess decks, but a few stay on the upper deck, leaning on the guard rails and looking thoughtfully out to sea, coming to terms with their own longings and heartaches. One of them is Ginge Grieveson.

'It just gets harder and harder,' he says, shielding his eyes from the glare of the sun. 'This is not Christmas. I mean Christmas is all about being with the kids and watching John Wayne films, isn't it?'

'Won't you enjoy anything about Christmas on board?' I ask.

'Yeah, up to a point, but I do feel a bit Grinch like. I would just like to paint myself green and humbug about all day to be honest.'

He looks down at the gentle swell of the Arabian Gulf.

'You know that old saying?'

'Which one's that, Ginge?'

'We joined the Navy to see the world. And what did we see? We saw the sea!'

Everybody is going to get a present today from someone in their mess – though they don't know who. Some weeks ago, everyone in a particular mess would have put their names on a piece of paper, folded it and put it in a hat. Then each member of the mess would have picked out one piece of paper, and whoever's name was on it was the person they had to buy a present for. Nobody is left out, and this is typical of the inclusive nature of shipboard life. Inevitably the presents are cheap, but they are always very cheerful and invariably extremely rude – at least in the male messes. Blow-up dolls, plastic breasts and girlie calendars are stock favourites. Rab Butler grimaces when he unwraps an enormous black dildo from a nameless messmate.

'Oh thanks a bleedin' bunch,' he says, making a suitably obscene gesture with his new toy. 'Just what I always wanted!' Rab's embarrassment, however, is soon compounded when he makes the mistake of opening one of the presents he brought out with him from his wife Mel in full view of everyone in the mess.

'Jesus H Christ!' he exclaims. 'What the bleedin' 'ell 'ave I got 'ere?'

There is an explosion of laughter round the mess.

'It's a fuckin' handbag!' says Rab. 'A black, patent soddin' handbag!'

It transpires that Rab inadvertently picked up the wrong parcel when he left his house, and that the black, patent handbag was actually a present to his wife from one of her friends, but such a prosaic explanation was never going to do for Rab's unforgiving shipmates, who leap at the chance to twist the knife.

'Oh yes, Rab! Of *course*, shipmate! *We* believe you!'

'Come on Rab – come out the closet. Don't be shy, sweetie!'

'You are so in touch with your feminine side, ducky!'

'Give us a kiss, big boy!'

In the girls' mess the Secret Santa ritual is underway as well, but here it is an entirely different affair. There is not a rude or distasteful gift in sight, just make-up, cuddly toys, scented stationery, soaps, and perfumes.

'Girls are always much nicer to each other,' says Becky Nobbs, wearing a flashing Rudolph the Rednosed Reindeer nose. 'We are pink and fluffy, but the boys always have to take the piss. It comes naturally to them. They can't do any different!'

The wardroom are also unwrapping presents, and here again there is a very different style to the gift giving. The vast majority of the officers unwrap some sort of toy. There are space guns, Spiderman outfits, model aeroplanes, board games and, in one instance – for the doctor, Alison Dewynter – a gigantic Scalextric set. For two hours the officers revert to childhood, racing cars, assembling model planes and shooting each other with Star Wars laser guns.

Lunch is served at twelve, and with it another naval tradition is observed. The captain and his officers leave the comfort of their cabins and the wardroom and come down to the main galley on Two Deck, where they pull on aprons and dish out the food to the rest of the ship's company. The Captain carves turkey, the XO is in charge of roast potatoes, the mechanical engineering officer spoons out the sprouts, the weapons engineering officer serves the sausages, the logistics officer allocates the parsnips and the principal warfare officers pour the gravy and the bread sauce.

THE WARDROOM OPEN
THEIR PRESENTS

THE OFFICERS PLAY WITH
THEIR TOYS

Whilst the lower-deck ratings attack their heaped plates of roast turkey and all the trimmings, Captain Chick and his highly trained team of officers take command of the Christmas puddings, custard and brandy sauce and prepare them for imminent distribution.

Meanwhile, at the tables crowded with stokers, gunners, writers, stewards, store accountants, weapons engineers and flight-deck handlers, paper hats are donned and everyone joins in the ritual chorus of groans as people read out the jokes and riddles that came out of the Christmas crackers.

Although the ship has been on standby to board suspect shipping, no such vessels have so far been found. There could still be a call to boarding stations, but until that time people are settling down to watch television, because the British Forces Broadcasting Service has sent out a recording of the Queen's speech. At seven o'clock, the officers in the wardroom pull their chairs round the TV and listen attentively to their monarch's message, which this year is very relevant to HMS *Chatham*. Her Majesty bids her subjects to remember all those who, for whatever reason, cannot be with their loved ones today, and then she alludes to the spectre of terrorism in an increasingly uncertain world.

The officers watch silently and respectfully.

After the Queen, the wardroom puts up the big screen to watch two DVD films. The first is Nick Park's Wallace and Grommit adventure *A Close Shave*, and the second is the classic war adventure *The Guns of Navarone*, starring Gregory Peck, David Niven, Anthony Quayle, Anthony Quinn and James Robertson Justice.

Later that evening, the XO makes a general pipe.

'I would just like to thank the warrant officers' and chief petty officers' messes for organising the reindeer racing on Christmas Eve, and on their behalf I would like to thank everyone who attended the event, and in the process raised £1,331 for charity. That's all.'

And so ends 25 December in the Straits of Hormuz. We might be two thousand miles from home, but our Christmas, in the end, has been as traditional as any in Britain and probably more so than most.

Location: Straits of Hormuz
Date: 26 December 2004
Time: Midday

Ship's Daily Orders: 'To continue to conduct successful patrol of area'

Today it is back to work in no uncertain way. Two dhows are boarded virtually back to back, but the sea state is deteriorating and the weather has suddenly become unseasonably stormy. The Royal Marines have a hard time getting to the dhows in their high-powered seaboats and come back looking decidedly queasy.

'Appropriate!' laughs Rab Butler. 'Green faces for the Green Berets!'

Later, the news starts to spread round the ship that a massive earthquake has struck Indonesia, and that a fearsome tsunami has been unleashed. Immediately, there are concerns that the current sea state

OVERLEAF:
THE ROYAL MARINE
BOARDING PARTY

THE ROYAL MARINES BOARD
A FISHING DHOW

and unusually dark skies are signs that things might be about to get an awful lot worse.

Later in the day, the XO makes a general pipe.

'Some of you have had very natural concerns that we may be in the path of the tsunami. Geographically, we are, and quite possibly the deteriorated sea state is connected to this event, but rest assured that we are in sufficiently deep water for the main energy of the wave to pass harmlessly beneath us.'

'Bloody 'ell!' remarks Rab Butler. 'Friggin' monster wave on the loose. Bet that's gonna do a bit of damage.'

CHAPTER SEVEN

Doobers

Location: Persian Gulf
Date: 28 December 2004
Time: 07.30

Ship's Daily Orders. Our Mission: 'Enjoy Dubai!'

Over the last few days we have followed the news of the tsunami as best we can, but the sea has calmed and the weather has settled, so life on board has returned to normal. Our world, at least, is safe and undamaged. It just goes to show how insular a ship's company can be because, whilst Tommy Goodwin prays daily for the victims of the tsunami in his morning services, the rest of us just get on with shipboard life – the extent of our immediate horizons and concerns.

At last, the current patrol period has come to an end and the ship is heading for the port of Dubai in the United Arab Emirates, where the ship's company will be able to enjoy a few days' rest and recuperation to recharge the batteries. Everybody made the best of Christmas but, in the end, no amount of tinsel and plastic holly could change the fact that we were on a grey warship in foreign waters. The New Year promises to be a very different affair, because Dubai is a traditional favourite with the British sailor.

'Yeah – Crimbo at sea's tough-titty for sure,' says Rab Butler cheerfully, as he surveys a hazy horizon with his binoculars, 'but we'll be in Doobers soon. Crackin' watering-hole that, so we'll be threaders till we leave!'

He refocuses his binoculars.

'There she is! Skyscrapers ahoy! Four days of Doobers, and don't we need it? Bring it on!'

FACING PAGE:
DOOBERS AHOY!

The prospect of Doobers has actually sustained the ship's company for weeks – and now it is in sight, its distinctive skyline shimmering in the far distance.

'I don't know what I'll be doin' on New Year's Eve,' says Rab with a chuckle, 'cept that I'll be drunk. I warned you about that back in Guzz, didn't I, Chris?'

'Warned me about what?'

'Coming out on a bender – Navy style. Your time has come, shipmate!'

I do indeed recall that morning in Plymouth, when Rab promised me 'a knees up of which legends are made' in some foreign port.

'I can hardly wait, Rab,' I say with inner trepidation. I am due to fly home on New Year's Day so at least I will be able to recuperate on a nice long flight.

The XO, expecting Dubai to be a very popular run ashore, has posted a notice on Daily Orders:

Notes: Have a great time ashore and enjoy yourselves. Please note, however, that certain of the entertainment establishments are out of bounds to all Royal Navy personnel as they are identified as possible terrorist targets (the names of these will be posted separately). Alcohol is readily available in Dubai, but it remains a sensitive issue amongst locals so please be sensitive to this. There is a lot to do here from golf to tennis to belly-dancing. However, remember that Dubai lies in the Gulf and the terrorist threat is very real. Do not unnecessarily advertise your nationality or job and DO NOT discuss the ship's programme.

For many, New Year's Eve promises to become a beer-fuelled celebration in a city which, though technically 'dry', boasts a multitude of hotels, clubs and discos where alcohol is freely available. Others, however, who are flying out their wives and girlfriends for a few days, are no doubt planning to spend much of their time in the blessed solitude of a hotel room. The female ratings intend to party hard and have already declared their intention to go out en masse – dress code 'ultra-posh'. Otherwise, gaggles of matelots will no doubt split up into groups and see what they can find in the main streets and back streets of festive Dubai.

One way or another, terrorist warnings apart, everybody is preparing for four glorious days of fun, hangovers and general light-hearted excess before resuming the patrol in the southern Gulf.

As we approach the port all hands go to harbour stations. Rab is in his usual position on the bridge wing, looking out for any small craft venturing too close – the threat of the suicide bomber is always felt more keenly as we approach or depart ports and harbours. Ratz Rackliff is in the ops room, monitoring pictures coming to him from external cameras on the ship's superstructure.

'Just another way to see what is approaching,' he says. 'The upper-deck watches see most things, but I can scan 360 degrees around the ship and pick up anything suspicious. It's infra-red, so I can see at night too. Useful bit of kit.'

'Looking forward to Dubai?' I ask.

'Oh yes! We all need a breather. Get some solid ground under our feet. I want to get straight down to the Gold Souk to get Theresa an eternity ring. Gold is cheap as chips in Doobers.'

Ratz pauses as he zooms his camera towards a distant jet ski.

'It's OK, he's going away from us.'

'Hey Ratz,' says a radarman sitting nearby, 'how long to go before your missus drops the sprog?'

'Five months and then I will be flying home in time for the birth. Roll on. Have you seen my book?'

He pulls out a large book from under his desk. It is The *Haynes Baby Owner's Workshop Manual* and is subtitled *From conception to two years – all makes, shapes and colours.*

'It's good,' says Ratz, 'though I skipped straight to Chapter Two because the first chapter is all about conception – and I reckon I've pretty well got that one weighed off!'

'Don't speak too soon, mate,' says the radarman. 'It might look like the milkman!'

Spirits are high on HMS *Chatham* as we tie up at Port Rashid's Jetty 74. Even the immediate need to store ship with fresh food supplies does not dampen spirits, and the long human chains cheerfully pass bags of potatoes, carrots, cabbages, swedes, tomatoes, apples, oranges and lemons through the ship to Ginge Grieveson and his team of stackers and stowers. Some of the girls are actually dancing as they pass huge sacks of potatoes to each other, imagining they are already boogying on the strobe-lit dance floor at Rock Bottom – Dubai's premier night club. Once the ship is stored, the first wave of libertymen prepare to depart the ship to go down-town, whilst others call up their wives and girl-friends, making sure they have arrived in their hotels.

It is now, however, that most of us see the terrifying images of the tsunami for the first time. In the wardroom, TV signal restored, every-body watches in stunned silence as the latest bulletin brings the news that the death toll is now approaching 150,000 and counting. The extraordinary footage of the wave blasting its way through coastal settle-ments and destroying everything in its path seems strangely unreal – almost as if it is from a Hollywood disaster movie – but of course it is all too tragically factual.

It is now that reality catches up with us, in no uncertain terms. Even before anybody steps off the gangway, a shock announcement is made: 'All leave is cancelled!'

'Oh fuck!' says Rab Butler, neatly summarising the reaction of the entire ship.

The tsunami which passed underneath our hull so harmlessly on Boxing Day, but which we can now see has devastated a massive swathe of the earth's surface from Indonesia to Somalia, is now touching our life again – but this time in a very different way. The British government has decided that HMS *Chatham*, the nearest Royal Naval asset to the dis-aster zone, should be despatched immediately to the southern Indian Ocean to assess the situation and provide assistance in any way she can.

'Frankly, I'm not surprised,' says Ginge Grieveson. 'I read in the paper that the earthquake that caused the wave was so powerful that it actually jolted the earth in its orbit.'

'Fuck me!' repeats Rab, only more forcefully.

'I reckon we should be going,' says Ginge.

'I agree,' says Rab immediately. 'I mean, we can only be three or four days' sailing from them poor blighters what's been tsunamied down in Indonesia and everywhere. They'll need help and fast. I don't deny 'em that – but I'm gonna miss my beer fest in Doobers.'

Certainly, it seems inconceivable that an earthquake so powerful that it might momentarily have knocked the world off its axis would not somehow affect Rab Butler's plans to get drunk on New Years' Eve.

And so it has proved. In fact, even before we came into Dubai, Captain Chick had already been contacted by the MoD in Whitehall and told to stand by, whilst an idea of the needs in the disaster area became clearer, but he had kept that close to his chest. Now, the official decision made, we are to stay in Dubai just long enough to complete some basic maintenance and take on fresh water for the trip south, but the ship will depart tomorrow afternoon. The promised days in Dubai have turned into mere hours.

Some, like Ratz, immediately rush down to the Gold Souk to buy jewellery for their other halves. Rab, on the other hand, needing some high-protein powdered drink for muscle growth, heads to the Central Shopping Mall in the Deira district of the city. All around Dubai, sailors are frantically choosing presents, haggling for gold, grabbing burgers, buying CDs and phoning home.

As for myself, I have already moved off the ship and am on the way to the hotel in which I am booked to stay till the New Year. My plan is then to return to the UK, to carry on filming with the recruits at HMS *Raleigh*. It is now, however, that I receive a phone call from the ship. It is Lieutenant Commander 'Peter' Sellers who, as well as being the ship's weapons engineering officer is also the public relations officer.

'Chris, I know you are meant to be flying home, but we thought you might like to stay on board for this one. Can you come with us? We need you to help us with the news angle, TV coverage etc. All eyes will be on us I reckon.'

'Peter, I'm on my way back to the ship right now!' I say, tapping the cab driver on the back to tell him to return immediately to Port Rashid, Jetty 74.

On the one hand, of course, I am responding to this opportunity as a journalist and documentarian – it is a terrific chance to witness the aftermath of one of the worst natural disasters the world has ever seen, and be in the thick of the human drama that is bound to unfold once *Chatham* arrives on the scene. This is no training exercise – it is the real thing, and an amazing opportunity for a film maker and writer such as myself.

There is, however, another reason I want to go. By now I feel very much at home on *Chatham*. I have made friends and become, in part anyway, absorbed by the very special community that a ship's company invariably is. I want to be with everybody for this journey, as well as for the challenge at the end of it – not as a mere observer, not a hanger-on, but as an integral part of HMS *Chatham*. If they want someone to report on the ship's progress to a watching world, I am happy to be that person. It's my chance to give something back, my chance to contribute to the ship and its crew that up to now I have, in a sense, been feeding off for my own ends. I also realise that if I do not go with the ship, the Ministry of Defence and the Admiralty will have to let other media on to cover the story. That is the way of the world in the information age, but I am damned if I will give up 'my' ship to some other hack or news cameraman. I feel possessive of HMS *Chatham*, and I freely admit it.

Location: Dubai Port. Jetty 74
Date: 29 December 2004
Time 16.00

Ship's Daily Orders. Our Mission: 'Prepare for disaster relief operations'
Notes: <u>Weight Trainers</u>. All users of the 01J weight training facility are to ensure that they stow all weights and bars correctly in the ATU. This means: weightdiscs on the poles, dumbbells in the rack and straight bars in the frame of the dumbbell rack. If the ATU continues to be left unsecured and in a mess, it will be locked, and the weight training facility will be removed for a 24-hour period.

Nearly everyone is on board – leave cut short and wives and girlfriends bidden farewell. Only Toby Clay, the flight commander, is still on the quayside saying a lingering goodbye to his wife Rachel, who has flown in all the way from Sydney in Australia to see her husband. A number of the wives and girlfriends who have come to Dubai to see their men for the New Year, but who are now deprived of that possibility, have evidently agreed to stay on and see in 2005 together. One suspects they are well aware of the vicissitudes of Navy life, but feel the need to show solidarity with each other and, quite possibly, drown their sorrows together.

Usually, it is said, the British sailor is only happy if he has got something to 'drip' about, and foreshortened leave is always guaranteed to get his or her gander up, but on this occasion there has not been a single word of complaint from anyone. By now everyone has seen the graphic news of the death and the destruction wrought by the tsunami – the wrecked towns, the razed villages and the shattered lives of millions. On the deployment so far, the routine patrols and boarding operations have been monotonous for many, and it has been difficult always to keep a clear perspective of how important the ship's role has been, because the enemy has been an invisible one and therefore hard to

STORING SHIP IN DUBAI

identify. Now, in the face of raw nature and its terrible awesome power, every man and woman in the ship's company seems gripped by a determination to get back to work – no longer on a military tasking but a mission of mercy.

The ship is still taking on stores – emergency supplies of bottled water, not for disaster victims, but for the ship's company itself. If any of us are going to spend any time ashore in the disaster-affected areas, we are likely to find the local water supplies badly polluted. Everyone forms a huge human chain to help get on board hundreds of heavy boxes full of bottles. There is not the exuberance or cheeriness that typified yesterday's human chain, but nevertheless everybody just gets on with it. No moaning. No griping. No dripping.

Lieutenant Surgeon Alison Dewynter, whose husband was one of the spouses who had come out to Dubai for the New Year, has gone straight to her cabin to start reading up on infectious diseases like cholera and typhoid. She has downloaded an information sheet from Fleet headquarters: 'How to Manage Dead Bodies in Disaster Situations'.

'You never know with this job what you are going to be called to do,' she says. 'One day it's dealing with a sore throat, the next day it's appendicitis, and then it's something like this – but until we get there I don't know what we will be required to do.'

She leafs through a book called *Refugee Health*, issued by Médecins Sans Frontières.

'One thing is for certain though, we need to keep very adaptable in our operations. Flexible is too rigid. We need to be fluid. Very. I just hope we can make some sort of difference . . .'

Reverend Tommy Goodwin is gearing up as well. He is here to look after the spiritual health of the ship's company, so he has got his work cut out for him now.

'They are likely to see some terrible things and deal with true tragedy,' he says, clutching a book called *Coping With Catastrophe*. 'Some of them are very young, and most have never seen a dead body before, but sailors intuitively look after each other – they would not call it pastoral care, but they practise it daily without even thinking about it. It's the sailor's way. I will be there for them, but they will be there for me too.'

Ratz Rackliff, eternity ring in his pocket, is man-handling boxes of water down the gangway.

'This is when the Navy comes into its own,' he states firmly. 'We don't just do wars, you know. Nobody will complain about this. We can't. At least we are still alive. Not like the thousands down there who will never come up for air again. Bring it on, I say.'

At 18.00 precisely, we leave Dubai and set course for the southern Indian Ocean and the chaos that presides there – precise destination as yet unknown.

Location: Arabian Sea
Date: 30 December 2004
Time: 10.00

Ship's Daily Orders. Our Mission: 'Prepare for disaster relief operations'
Notes: <u>Armed Forces Pay Review Body</u>. We will receive a 3% pay rise with w.e.f. 1 April 05. Details on Ship's Company Notice Board.

HMS *Chatham* is heading south at speed. She is also undergoing a remarkable transformation. A lethal, front-line warship is starting to metamorphose into a benign ship of mercy. A ship designed to do damage, and lots of it, is being turned into one that we hope will repair, build and save life. The Sea Wolf guided missiles are being taken out of their loaders and stowed below; the powerful Mini Guns on the port and starboard waists are being dismantled, as are the machine guns on the fo'c'sle, the bridge wings and the flight deck. The Lynx helicopter machine gun is being replaced with a winch. The ops room, the nerve centre of the ship, from where war would normally be waged, is reconfigured. It will now be the planning HQ for a major disaster relief operation and the principal warfare officers will co-ordinate everything. This is not just the transformation of a warship, it is the radical transformation of everybody's mindset – but this is what the modern Navy knows it may have to do, and it trains for it.

Back in Plymouth, within the shore base, there is an entire disaster-struck village built into a hillside. Ships are constantly being put through their paces by having to respond to simulated situations. Volunteers take on the roles of disaster victims and countless scenarios are acted out. Ships are assessed on everything from evacuation procedures, riot control and fire-fighting to first aid, reconstruction and the counselling of distraught civilians.

But that is on a hillside in Plymouth.

What we are facing now is no simulation. It is the biggest natural disaster in living memory with 200,000 now reported dead – a figure that rises daily. All around the ship, ratings and officers are variously adapting their conventional roles. Weapons specialists, gunners and stokers may now be wanted for rebuilding water storage units or reconnecting electricity supplies, radar and sonar operators may now be needed to re-establish telephone lines, chefs, stewards and writers may be required for first aid or for burial parties. At this stage nobody knows what to expect – so everything is prepared for. Even I, the only civilian on board, am drafted into duty. As a journalist and cameraman, I have been asked by the captain to supply news on a pool basis to broadcasters throughout the world, as well as copy to newspapers and agencies. We are heading south at a rate of twenty knots, but still we are not sure of our final destination. It could be the Maldives or it could be Sri Lanka. That decision is out of our hands. People on the spot will decide where we will be best deployed, and already a tri-service recce unit (Observation, Liaison and Reconnaissance Team or OLRT) is on the ground, assessing the situation.

Location: Arabian Sea
Date: 31 December 2004
Time: 19.00.

Ship's Daily Orders. Our Mission: 'Prepare for disaster relief operations'
Notes: Well done to everyone for the enormous efforts in storing ship and for ensuring that we sailed on time yesterday.

We continue to make good speed south, but everybody is impatient to know where we are heading. Just before supper, Steve Chick addresses the ship's company on the main broadcast system.

'This is the Captain speaking. It has been confirmed that we are to head for Colombo in Sri Lanka, although the area is in such a state of flux that even now we could be rerouted . . .'

Throughout the ship, in cabins, passages, messes, galleys and dining rooms, the entire ship's company listens in silence, but with excited anticipation.

'We find ourselves in extraordinary circumstances, but be assured we are preparing to get fully involved in the humanitarian effort now unfolding in the aftermath of this unheard-of tragedy.'

Steve Chick pauses and reins in the urgency of his tone.

'This is certainly the most sober I will have been on a New Year's Eve and I am sorry you are at sea yet again, but I have been most impressed by your attitude and demeanour at this critical time. Thanks for that and Happy New Year. That's all.'

An hour later, Rab Butler starts a session on the punch bag in the hangar.

'Yeah, well, it's a bit of a bugger missing out on New Year as well as Crimbo, but the job's there to do. Frankly, most of us just want to get stuck in – and I'll tell you something else: it'll beat the hell out of the patrolling malarkey we've been doin'.'

He pushes his great fists into his 16 oz gloves and starts some light shadow boxing to warm up.

'. . . by the way, I got a text from…er indoors", telling me NOT to eat any more from the big tin of bleedin' Quality Street she gave me. Says I've got to keep the sweeties for the little kids where we're going. Quite right. Proper saint my missus . . .'

Whereupon he unleashes a massive right hook to the battered punch bag which was peacefully swinging with the motion of the ocean.

New Year's Eve night is a muted affair. A lot of people have gone to bed early, although some stay up to toast in the New Year. Ginge Grieveson sips absent-mindedly on a can of Carling.

'I'm pleased we're going down there. Makes me feel useful. Just hope we make a difference. It'll do my head in if we just arrive and float around for days, doing nothing.'

He takes a long swig of lager.

'I can't imagine what we might see. No idea what it must be like – all those bodies everywhere. Poor bastards . . . I think the thing that will get me is seeing dead kids or even just injured ones. Being a dad of four, I think it will cut me quite deep – but we're there to help aren't we? No point in blubbering. Got to get on with it.'

He crushes the empty Carling tin and throws it in the gash bag.

'Right, I'm off to my pit. Happy New Year, you lot.'

Location: Arabian Sea
Date: 1 January 2005

Ship's Daily Orders. Our Mission: 'Prepare for disaster relief operations'
Notes:

a) <u>Energy Economy Measures</u>. Due to uncertainty regarding the availability of fuel, the following measures are to be taken by ALL Ship's Company in order to maximise our endurance. Every little helps!

Lighting in compartments that are not frequently visited is to be switched off.
50% lighting routine is to be exercised in flats and passageways.

b) <u>Malaria Tablets</u>. Tablets have now been issued to the Whole Ship's Company.

c) <u>Wills/Personal Accident Insurance</u>. You might wish to consider making a will or taking out insurance. See the Ship's Office for details.

d) <u>Release of Information to families</u>. Be careful about what you say or write to families – despite our high profile, the details of where we are going have not been officially confirmed.

e) <u>Skills questionnaire</u>. If you have any specialist skills, fill in the questionnaire that has been distributed – any expertise welcome.

It is another day of hard sailing and the ship is buzzing with activity and preparation. In the junior rates mess, Lieutenant Surgeon Alison Dewynter speaks to her team of medics – made up mostly of stewards and cooks.

'Right, we still don't really know what's going on,' says the young doctor, 'but my guess is that most of the initial casualties will have been sorted by now, and the secondary stage of the disaster will be setting in. The four biggest killers are likely to be measles, diarrhoea, acute respiratory infections and malaria. There may be some infected wounds – in that case always refers to a doctor. If the wound is not infected – clean it and dress it.'

She pauses and surveys her largely inexperienced team.

'You may also have to deal with dead bodies. If you are part of a burial party, remember the cultural beliefs of the people there. Be sensitive to their religion, and of course their bereavement . . .'

Out on the flight deck the preparations are of a completely different nature and reflect the fact that nobody knows quite what to expect when we arrive in the disaster zone. Standing at the stern are several officers, practising pistol shooting into the ship's wake. This is in case law and order should fail, leading to anarchy and civil unrest, something that can easily occur in a fractured society that is suddenly deprived of basic resources. For the same reason, 'Zippy' Howard, the Royal Marine Colour Sergeant, is also on the flight deck, teaching baton handling techniques and riot control.

'If we go in with stores or water, there might be a reaction,' he says matter of factly to about twenty sailors. 'The people might be desperate and just want to grab it. We have to protect ourselves – but use the minimum of force. Right, so here's what to do if there's a crowd coming at you . . .'

He lifts his baton in a way that suggests he knows a hundred ways to use it to great, good and probably painful effect.

In the aviation office, Toby Clay and John Turner are briefing some of the aircraft handlers.

'We have a second crew arriving later today, so we will have two operational Lynxes on board,' says Toby Clay. 'It seems to me that our main job is going to be ferrying supplies into forward positions, but we will probably have to take the doc around too – so we need to keep nimble.'

Tommy Goodwin is spending even more time than usual touring the ship. He wants to make sure everybody is of good heart and ready for the challenge in front of them.

'There is a sense, for me anyway, of being overwhelmed by the sheer size of this catastrophe,' he confides in me. 'I still can't quite get my head around it, even now, but I do know there is a deep and driven desire in the ship's company to get down there and help – to make a difference. We are likely to see horrific scenes and it will be harrowing for all of us, but one thing about sailors is that they will always be there for each other – that is the great thing about the Navy – and if one person needs a bit of support from his or her shipmates, they will get it. No question.'

Lieutenant Commander John Gardner, the first lieutenant or executive officer, is second in command. Among other things he has to keep

HMS CHATHAM ON HER
WAY TO SRI LANKA

a finger on the pulse of the ship's morale. Every night at around 19.00 hours he pipes the ship.

'Good evening. XO speaking. A lot of you have approached me, saying how you want to get ashore and do something useful. I appreciate your sentiments and your intentions, but frankly it will not be possible to let you all off the ship. We still need to man the ship and make her safe. Rest assured, whatever you will be tasked to do, you will be contributing to this very important operation. Finally, we need to conserve water, so from now on – one shower a day for everyone. And that is a brief shower please – not a Hollywood shower. I do not want to have to turn the water off, but rest assured I will if I have to. I will let you have more information as I get it. That's all.'

A firm officer but with a friendly touch, John Gardner is good at reading situations, and tonight he feels the need to lighten the mood a little in the wardroom – it has been a heavy day of training and preparation. At dinner he makes an announcement.

'Film tonight everyone – I recommend *Shrek 2*. Also, I suggest we start a beard-growing competition. I've cleared it with the captain. Who's in?'

Everyone raises their hands eagerly, except for the four female officers – one of whom suggests that perhaps they should stop shaving their legs – and a couple of the more fresh-faced young lieutenants who think they might get a drubbing in the facial hair stakes.

We continue to make good speed, have passed the Andaman Islands, and are well on our way to Sri Lanka, but we need to take on fuel. In the middle of the night, in the middle of the ocean, we do just that by making a rendezvous with the Royal Fleet Auxiliary supply ship *Diligence* – a floating petrol station and food store that restocks Royal Navy ships all over the world.

RFA *Diligence* is a large ship, but tonight, when we first spy her a mile off our port beam, she is but a tiny glow in the overwhelming darkness of this gigantic ocean. Gradually, the glow gets bigger. Soon it becomes several glows, and before long the outline of a ship illuminated by red deck lights becomes visible. There is something incredibly comforting about this meeting of ships on the high seas, for she is, as they say, 'one of ours' – a little bit of Britain bringing us succour and a huge boost to morale. Because of our untimely diversion from Dubai before we were able to fill up with diesel, and the subsequent need to travel at top speed to the disaster zone, we are now down to only thirteen per cent of our fuel capacity – much lower than the permitted official minimum. If we had not been able to take on fuel at this point, we would have had to drop our average speed from twenty-five knots to about fifteen knots, which would mean it would take at least another two days to reach Sri Lanka.

Diligence edges towards us. Before long we are side by side, only metres apart, but the rough swell of the sea means that neither ship is ever on the same level or height. When we are up on a wave she is down in a trough, then within moments the positions are reversed. This makes it seemingly impossible to winch over the gigantic rubber hose that must inject us with the fuel we so badly need, but sailors are, if nothing else, supremely practical people. They are also some of the most stubborn SOBs under the sun. This is a killer combination and, whilst not always a match for a raging sea, tonight it finally gives the upper-deck teams the initiative they need to coax the fuel hose into place in the side of HMS *Chatham*.

It takes two hours to fill the fuel ship's tanks, after which we resume our course southwards.

Location: Southern Arabian Sea
Date: 4 January 2005
Time: 10.00

Ship's Daily Orders. Our Mission: 'Prepare for disaster relief operations'
Notes: <u>Water Rationing</u>. Until we can ascertain our role, and how close we will be to land (which affects our water-making ability), water rationing will be in force until further notice. This means everyone is now limited to one brief shower a day.

At last we are approaching Colombo, the capital of Sri Lanka. Toby Clay and JT took off earlier in the Lynx to collect the British High Commissioner and members of a forward British military reconnaissance team, who have been trying to assess the situation on the ground. They are now on board and ready to address assembled officers in the wardroom.

Colonel Gordon Messenger of the Royal Marines comes straight to the point.

'I know you all want to get stuck in and do something, but I am afraid you will have to be patient. We need to co-ordinate our efforts with everyone else – and remember, we are here under the direction of the Department for International Development and of course the Sri Lankan Government. What we do not want to do, under any circumstances, is give the impression that we, as the military, are here to take over the show. It might mean a bit of lip biting but that's the way it is.'

Captain Chick and the officers of HMS *Chatham* exchange glances. They know very well that there is as much politics in disaster relief as there is in anything else.

'We need to assess our role and our usefulness very carefully indeed, or our effectiveness could be compromised. We also need to understand the realities of what faces us – we don't want theory, we need 'ground-truth'. In one area, for example, aid was delivered days ago, but it still has not been distributed because the village headman is not around and he insists he has to be there for its distribution so he can get the kudos.'

Stephen Evans, the British High Commissioner, breaks in.

'The situation is still in flux. It is an unusual disaster in that it's in a strip – 1,450 kilometres of destruction, but only along an approximately 400-metre-wide margin. Inland of this margin things are virtually normal, but the immediate coast and its people and economies are devastated, particularly the local fishing communities. They need help quickly to get on their feet again, otherwise they will fragment and wander off to the cities like Trinkomalee and Colombo. They will become displaced urban migrants and probably therefore dispossessed as well.'

Colonel Messenger reclaims the floor.

'I think it will be at least forty-eight hours before you can make a real start. What I can tell you is that I think you will be directed to the eastern coastline – possibly up in the north, but we have to consider politics here because that is Tamil Tigers territory, but more probably you will be in the south because that was by far the hardest hit.'

'By the way,' interrupts the diplomat, 'you will need a policy on bodies – there are still bodies in the water and also being washed up. You need to decide whether you pick them up or not. Do you bring them on board or what? Your choice . . .'

Everybody on the ship is straining to get ashore and do something useful, so this is not the start everybody wanted.

'Would you credit it, eh?' says Rab Butler, after he hears that we are to remain on the ship until further orders. 'Bomb down here like a bat out of bleedin' hell to help out. Then it's the old "hurry up and wait" routine. Thought this was a friggin' emergency, and all we're doin' is bobbin' in the oggin!'*

He sniffs dismissively before adding, 'I'm goin' boxing . . .'

Rab is interrupted by the main broadcast system: 'Hands to flying stations! Hands to flying stations.'

'Oh bugger it!' says Rab despairingly. 'The friggin' hangar will be out of bounds now! That's fuckin' boxing binned then!'

Sure enough, the hangar is closed up and flight-deck handlers take their positions as a Lynx helicopter comes in to land. It is not Toby Clay and JT coming in – they are already on board and so is their helicopter. It is a second Lynx and a second crew that have been sent out to join *Chatham* for the duration of her visit to Sri Lanka. This will increase our effectiveness enormously, because an aerial capability is bound to be of primary importance in any disaster relief scenario, even if it is just a case of transporting personnel or lifting aid supplies.

I have told 'Peter' Sellers that I would like to send some of my film material back to London. I reckon the fact that HMS *Chatham* has actually arrived in Sri Lanka is newsworthy in itself and that most networks would carry it. My aim is to track down Reuters News Agency and 'pool' my material, so that it will be available to any broadcaster who wants to run it. Although I am working for the BBC, in situations like this it is normal for otherwise competing news organisations to share material. Peter agrees and arranges to have me flown ashore that afternoon.

'Toby will take you in to the military airport,' he says as we stand on the flight deck. 'Then you are on your own – so do what you have to do, but then make your way to the Sri Lankan Naval Base. Any taxi will take you there, so I am told by the High Commission, but you MUST be there by 22.00 – no later – and be at the water's edge on the main jetty. We are going to send in a RIB† to pick you up and whisk you back on board, because we are sailing at 22.30 to the south of the island.'

*Sea.

† RIB – Rigid Inflatable Boat.

'Right,' I reply. 'I will be waiting.'

'You'd better be, Chris, because we can't wait. If you are not there, we will have to go without you.'

It is a short flight to the military airport where I pick up a cab that takes me to the Colombo Hilton. Reuters, I have found out, is in the building next door. Once there, I start to download my selected material, so that it can be digitised and sent by satellite to the BBC, Sky and ITV, all of which have said they are keen to run with the story as soon as possible. I look at my watch. I still have plenty of time before I have to be at my rendezvous with HMS *Chatham*'s fast seaboat at the Sri Lankan Naval Base.

Mission completed, I head out to the street in front of the Colombo Hilton, hail a three-wheeler 'chuk chuk' and ask the driver to take me to the Naval Base. I sit back in the glorified motor scooter, delighted that I have managed to place my first news story for HMS *Chatham*, and then watch Colombo at night as it flashes past me – busy, bustling, colourful and noisy. How strange it is that just on the other side of the island there is, by all accounts, indescribable devastation – yet here life carries on as normal, almost as if nothing had happened.

I arrive at the Naval Base with plenty of time to spare, but I decide to go straight down to the jetty anyway and wait – I do not want to take any chances of missing my pick-up. I walk up to the sentry post at the main gate, show my press pass and ask the way to the main jetty.

'You may not come past this barrier!' says the guard.

'Sorry?' I say, startled. 'This is an arrangement with the Royal Navy.'

'Ah, Royal Navy! You are Royal Navy?'

'No. Not exactly. I am a journalist, but I am working on HMS *Chatham*. They are picking me up, you see, from the main –'

'Sorry, if you are not Navy, you can't come in. No journalists.'

'But they are sending in a RIB to pick –'

'You can't come in here!' says the sentry, now gripping his rifle with rather more intent than I feel comfortable with.

'Excuse me,' I say, trying hard not to allow my voice to rise with the tension of the moment. 'If I am not there, they will leave me and I will miss the ship – and I will not be able to catch her up. All my clothes and my cameras are on board, as well as my passport!'

This time the sentry simply glares. He is steadfast so I try another tack.

'Can I see your commanding officer please?' I say as politely and as calmly as I can. It is now ten minutes to ten.

Five minutes later a lieutenant commander strides up to see what is going on. I explain once again.

'No, no, no, sir. I am very sorry, but your ID is not good. We need Navy ID. Sri Lankan Navy, US Navy, Royal Navy – all good. Press ID no good.'

'If I do not get down to that jetty,' I remonstrate, 'I will miss HMS *Chatham*. Don't you understand, I work on her. I live on her!'

'Then you should have Royal Navy ID,' comes the reply.

I know he is right and only doing his job, but I am now beginning to panic. If I miss the RIB I will be stuck in Colombo with no chance at all of finding the ship again, let alone reboarding her. I am stuck at the barrier searching frantically through my wallet for any other sort of ID that could win the day. A Blockbusters membership card leaves the officer and the sentry singularly unimpressed. A Royal Geographical Society membership card causes a flutter of interest, but no access to the base.

'Sir, we can't take chances. There are bad people around. We just need some military ID, sir, or you can't come in.'

'But you could ask the guys bringing in the RIB,' I say pleadingly. 'They are Royal Navy and they will vouch for me – but if you don't do it now they will leave. They said they are not going to wait – the ship has to set sail. Look, it has gone ten – they are probably leaving already!'

'Sir, sir, do you have no military papers at all?' says the lieutenant commander, who seems genuine in his desire to help me. 'You have nothing from the Navy, sir?'

'No, nothing,' I say, cursing myself for not getting a letter of introduction from the captain or the XO. 'Except this,' I say somewhat facetiously, holding up a pen with a Royal Navy logo on it. 'Look, that says Royal Navy!'

The Sri Lankan officer looks at the pen. He holds it up. Then nods his head.

'Ah, that is good, sir. Yes, that is Royal Navy. Please come. We will escort you to the jetty.'

I virtually hurdle the barrier and rush with my armed escort to the jetty where I find the RIB just about to cast off. I have made it with seconds to spare.

'Bloody hell, Chris!' says the bosun. 'You're cutting it a bit fine, aren't you?' What kept you?'

'Don't ask,' I exclaim, leaping into the furiously revving craft.

I settle back for a fast ride over the moonlit sea to HMS *Chatham*, which has already raised her anchor. That was a close call. In the end it seems, I accessed a major military establishment with a biro!

CHAPTER EIGHT

After the Wave

Location: South coast of Sri Lanka
Date: 5 January 2005
Time 10.00

Ship's Daily Orders. Our Mission: 'Reconnoitre the disaster-hit coastal areas of southern Sri Lanka'
Notes: We are running low on cling film*, which is being saved for operations ashore. Also, try not to spill your drinks – if you do, mop it up.

*Cling film is important for wrapping food taken by teams going ashore.

Clearly, the situation on the ground is chaotic. Captain Chick knows that to move in too quickly, without having a proper plan of action, could easily exacerbate an already dire situation. He decides, in consultation with the OLRT and the British High Commission, to sail in an anti-clockwise direction around the island from Colombo. The wave would have hit hardest in the south and in the east, so this is where we need to do proper and detailed reconnaissance.

HMS *Chatham*'s two Lynx aircraft take off on an initial sortie to get an idea of the damage, but also to start assessing the needs and identifying tasks – what Colonel Messenger called 'ground truth'. I have joined Toby and JT in their Lynx, and it is not long before we can see, far below us, the first signs of devastation. We swoop low over countless smashed fishing boats – some have been lifted hundreds of metres inland and rammed into buildings, two or three storeys up. Cars are scattered, overturned, crushed. Huge sections of railway have been ripped up, twisted and contorted. Houses have been shattered – reduced to kindling wood. Trees have been felled by the immense swell of water that seemingly came from nowhere. Some of the larger trees left standing are still laden with bodies that have been swept up into their branches.

OVERLEAF:
FLIGHT OBSERVER JOHN 'JT' TURNER AND FLIGHT COMMANDER TOBY CLAY FLY OVER DEVASTATED SRI LANKA

Looking down on this desolation, I am reminded of the OLRT briefing yesterday and the description of the wave's impact as a 'strip' disaster. Indeed, seeing it for myself gives me the overriding impression that the place has been blitzed – systematically destroyed by massive and deadly accurate precision bombing that had only targeted a three- or four-hundred-metre strip along the entire coastline. Inland of this strip is unscathed, but within the band of destruction, annihilation is, in some places, total. Thousands perished without warning and now, just over a week since the tsunami struck, the heavily silted sea washes gently on to the once golden beaches which are littered with the detritus of countless wrecked homes. It is as if the lapping water is licking the very wounds it had inflicted when suddenly possessed of a strength and power that it could not control.

Back on the ship, everybody is getting impatient to get ashore and do something.

'Everybody's itching to get stuck in. We can see the coast just a few hundred metres on our port side, but we're stuck on the ship. I reckon if people don't get off soon, they are gonna bust,' says Rab Butler, finally managing to get rid of his frustrations on his battered punch bag.

Frustrations apart, however, most people on the ship, including Rab Butler, do realise now that disaster relief is not just a simple case of pitching up and getting involved. This is still a military operation and it has to be approached as such. There is a saying in the Navy that is frequently bandied around and which, it seems to me, is of great relevance to HMS *Chatham* right now – 'Prior planning prevents piss poor performance'.

Location: Just off the east coast of Sri Lanka
Date: 5 January 2005
Time: 11.00

We have carried on around the island and arrived at a place called Baticoloa, about halfway up the east coast. This place evidently took the full force of the tsunami and looks from the ship as if it is in a very sorry state indeed. Initial helicopter reconnaissance confirms this, reporting widespread destruction of both houses, roads and infrastructure.

The ship's command soon decide that this place looks like somewhere that we could make a difference – but again it is not a straight-

forward matter of just pitching up with a spade and looking helpful, like
so many scouts on bob-a-job week. First of all the ship's navigators,
hydrographer and boat's coxwains will have to find safe landing places
for the ship's boats – otherwise nobody is going ashore. At the same
time, small recce parties will have to be flown in by helicopter, to talk to
the local people and military, and any non-governmental organisations
in the area, to decide how best the ship and her company can contribute
to disaster relief. And then there has to be some sort of assessment of
priorities. Just where do you start when a place has been hit by a tidal
wave?

At midday Captain Chick flies ashore with a selection of his senior
officers, warrant officers and chief petty officers.

The military are welcoming and friendly, as are the local politicians,
but the NGOs, including UNICEF and UNHCR, greet the naval officers
with initial suspicion. Being a warship, HMS *Chatham* is instantly
associated, I think, with death and destruction rather than peace and
rehabilitation. The British naval officers, however, are persuasive – none
more so than Steve Chick.

'We have two helicopters,' he explains. 'We could transport emergency supplies in minutes that would take hours by road. And we have
willing hands – 250 crew members who want to get stuck in. We are
simply putting ourselves at the disposal of the people. We will help in
whatever way they want us to, if we possibly can.'

The NGO workers begin to change their opinion. They are very
impressed with the offer of two helicopters, and soon start to suggest
other tasks that might be suitable for the *Chatham* crew to undertake.
These include cleaning out houses full of mud, sand and raw sewage;
pumping out fresh-water wells that are now full of sea water, and also
mending and refloating holed fishing boats, many of which are now
scattered throughout the town – including one, seen from the helicopter, which has been lifted and smashed straight into the fourth floor of
an apartment block.

The wave smashed into this coastal town with such force that many
of the estimated 2,000 dead have not been found. They were simply
washed out to sea. Entire neighbourhoods have disappeared. Whole
sections of the population are homeless. Wells have become polluted
and brackish, the water undrinkable. Thousands of people are displaced

– most refusing to return to anywhere near the coast. They no longer trust the sea. Families who for generations had lived by the sea and from the sea are deserting the sea. They are refugees. They have no possessions. They have no livelihood.

Chief Petty Officer Rick Bennett, who has accompanied the Captain's party, but is tasked to reconnoitre some of the most severely damaged parts of the town, strolls down a street near the coast. He surveys the houses on either side of him – that is to say the piles of rubble that were once houses – and he nods with a smile at huddles of shocked-looking people who simply stare at the blue-uniformed stranger.

'You can't even imagine what these people have been through, can you?' he says, shaking his head. But we can help them, of course we can.'

'What in particular do you think you can do?' I ask. 'This is near-total devastation.'

'Yes, but there are some houses that got away with it – just need a bit of attention. There are others that need demolishing because they are dangerous. So shelters need to be built, latrines dug, you name it.'

We go on down what must have been a bustling street just a couple of weeks ago – a gaggle of children following us, egged on by their natural curiosity.

'We have a lot of skills on board, you know,' says the stocky but tough-looking chief. 'Not just Navy skills, but skills people have brought with them from Civvy Street. We have carpenters, electricians, engineers, tailors, brickies. All sorts. It's amazing, when you ask round, what you find you've got at your disposal. Add to that a bit of military discipline and organisation, then Bob's your uncle!'

He turns around and holds out his hand to one of the children.

'Shake, partner?' he says gently.

The child looks nervous, but then, as Rick's smile grows wider, he ventures closer, takes the proffered hand and returns a delighted grin.

Once they are back on the ship, Captain Chick and his heads of department quickly draw up plans. There will be a four-pronged attack, as it were, on the needs of the people of Baticoloa: repairing, cleaning and rebuilding homes; cleaning wells; mending and repairing fishing boats; transporting stores, medicine and food to places still isolated where roads and bridges have been washed away.

Location: Baticoloa
Date: 7 January 2005
Time: 08.00

Ship's Daily Orders. Our Mission: 'Conduct disaster relief operations'
Notes: Bingo. The sale of bingo tickets has recommenced! Your last chance to buy a ticket will be at Standeasy, Sun 9 Jan. Remember! Don't be a dingo, play bingo!

Early this morning a forward party of Royal Marines went in to check the beach area for land mines. This is a Tamil area and, following years of war between the government and the separatist Tamil Tigers, the Sri Lankan army laid down mine fields. Even though there has been a ceasefire that has held for the last two years, the minefields have remained intact – until the tsunami that is. Many live mines had been washed away from their fields and scattered by the giant wave and, of course, posed a real threat to naval landing parties. Once the marines were happy that the mine threat was minimal, fifty-six sailors and more marines were landed, some by helicopter but mostly by seaboats at beachheads established by a number of forward recce parties. The waters were treacherous with many shallows inhabited by salt-water crocodiles.

'I hear one of the recce boats flipped earlier on,' says a sailor as we enter the inner lagoon. 'I bet those buggers moved fucking fast with these snappers around.'

'You know what?' responds a Marine commando with a wry smile. 'Them crocs won't touch us – they'll be too well fed right now, with all them people that got washed away.' Marine humour – but we all know he is probably right.

Once we land, without mishap, about thirty sailors make their way to the northern district, called Kalady, where they will simply start to clean out houses left standing, just to make them more habitable.

In the southern district the plan is to start work on damaged fishing vessels but, whilst they lie along the banks in their hundreds, nobody can immediately find their owners, so we go in search of them. Nearby, we are told, is a Franciscan convent and orphanage called Saint

Theresa's. They might know there who the boats belonged to. We head straight for the convent, a large stuccoed building, and enter it through its non-existent gates – they were washed away by the wave, along with the convent's entire perimeter wall. The head sister, Sister Sulosana, greets us with a friendly smile and an effusive handshake.

She says most of the boat owners have fled inland, or to some of the refugee camps that have been established on the fringes of the town, but

ON THE BEACH AT
BATICOLOA

SISTER SULOSANA

that some are beginning to return and she will get word to them for us. She then asks if we could possibly help put up a fence or barrier around the convent because, she explains, they need security for the orphans who stay there.

Everybody agrees vigorously, and starts the work even more vigorously. Here at last is a chance to get the hands dirty, and all in a good cause. Working gangs are organised which then set about clearing the rubble of the old walls. All morning huge slabs of concrete and brick are manhandled on to the other side of the road. Then concrete pillars are erected into holes dug at intervals and barbed wire is strung across. The work takes all day, but nobody flags – backbreaking and sweltering though it is. The sailors are so pleased to be doing something useful, in a tangible, observable way. The nuns are, I think, a little nonplussed by the sudden appearance of these men in blue, but are grateful none the less. Throughout the day they provide us with fresh fruit and tea. Extraordinarily, the crockery they bring out – about a dozen cups and saucers – has on them the portrait of a fully bearded British sailor, the one you see on the front of a packet of Senior Service cigarettes. They were probably donated to the convent by someone, and I do not think the nuns even know that the head on the cups is a British sailor, and so do not realise the irony. The sailors do.

'Look, they knew we were coming,' says one of them with a laugh. 'It's in your honour, Nobby. Spitting image of you, mate!'

'Bog off,' retorts Nobby. 'I ain't got a full set.'

'You should grow a beard, mate,' comes the reply, '. . . on the principle that it would hide your ugly mug!'

Nobby is about to say something, but thinks better of it as he notices Sister Sulosana approaching with another plate of pineapple.

CHATHAM SAILORS START CLEARING THE DEBRIS IN BATICOLOA

It is 16.00, and I have joined Chief Petty Officer Jim Wharton and Warrant Officer 'Simmo' Simpson, who are going across the lagoon in a seaboat to check out a mini-bus that needs pulling out of the water. It belongs to a farming co-operative and we are accompanied by the co-op secretary who insists it is only slightly damaged. Eventually we find the bus lying on a sandbank, in about four feet of water. It is a hopeless case. The vehicle is upside-down, the chassis bent, the roof crushed, and the engine by now full of sea water.

'Needs a bit more than a paint-job, mate,' says Simmo Simpson, a big bear of a man.

'Maybe you could fix it?' says the optimistic co-op man.

'Sorry, mate. I couldn't, and I don't even know a man who could. It's a gonner.'

The co-op man looks crestfallen. 'But I am responsible for this van.'

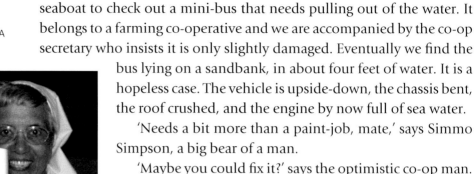

SISTER IRENE WITH A NAVY MUG

WAS IT AN OMEN THAT BRITISH SAILORS WERE COMING?

'Well, it's been totalled by a tsunami. I don't reckon there's anyone could pin that one on you, mate,' says Jim Wharton sympathetically.

The co-op man nods.

We walk along the beach to survey some of the damage. Most buildings are flattened. One had been the Kalady Nautical Engineering College – now all that is left standing are a couple of battered metal dolphins that had formed part of a fountain at the front of the building. As we walk back to the seaboat, we find the beach littered with possessions. It is totally random – surreal, like a Salvador Dali painting – the arm of a child's doll here; a green and gold sari there; then a black shoe; then, a few yards further on, a photograph album lying open, showing a young couple

CLEANING WELLS IN
BATICOLOA

smiling, holding hands; and then a kettle, another shoe, a lipstick . . .
Who did these things belong to? Are they alive or dead?

To our surprise the co-op man suddenly confides that he has lost his
own mother to the tsunami. Literally. She was washed out to sea and
has not been found. There is a pause as we digest this information and
decide the best way to respond. Jim Wharton gently puts his hand on
the man's shoulder and simply says, 'Sorry.'

Half an hour later we have returned to the convent. Sister Irene is
beaming. All the rubble of the old walls has been shifted and a brand
new barbed-wire fence is in its place.

'Bloody hell,' says Simmo Simpson. 'We can't get them to turn to on
the ship, but give them a wall to clear and a fence to build – and they're
off! First class job.'

Over the next few days work continues apace. More and more sailors
are brought ashore, not only from HMS *Chatham* but now also from
Diligence which has arrived to join the effort. Helicopters and seaboats
continually ferry working parties to and from the ships. On the mainland, work continues on house clearance, but also on erecting tents for
displaced people, well cleaning and boat repair. One party cleans out a
church, ready for it to celebrate Mass for the first time since the disaster,
and another party continues with building work at Saint Theresa's
Convent.

Location: Baticoloa
Date: 8 January 2005
Time: 14.00

Ship's Daily Orders. Our Mission: 'Conduct disaster relief
operations (OP GARRON)'
Notes: <u>Bottled water</u>. Do not take any bottled water – it is for use
ashore.

I have joined a naval patrol. Our task is to walk the length of a long sandy peninsula which must have taken the full brunt of the wave. It is about five miles long and apparently there is an orphanage at the end of it, but nobody seems very sure whether it is still standing, or if the orphans and staff are safe. This is not a stroll. The ground is soft, water-logged in places and littered with rubble and wreckage. For hours we trudge through the sand in sweltering heat and suffocating humidity, clambering over the remains of countless buildings and temples. I notice that the only things left standing are palm trees complete with coconuts – flexible enough, I surmise, to have bent with the enormous force of the water and then spring back to the upright position. I notice at the bottom of each and every tree something that initially looks like some sort of highly colourful conceptual art. On closer scrutiny I see what it is. The wave, when it came, simply picked up anything and everything in front of it and carried it in temporary suspension – swirling, bending, twisting, crushing and contorting. Some of this load was then wrapped around the trees in a random, colourful tapestry of horror that is now a bizarre testament to the awesome strength of nature. Red, yellow, green and silver saris – some patterned, some not – other clothing, rope, fishing nets and curtains are rather beautifully entangled and wrapped around the base of the palm trees. In amongst these multi-coloured arrangements of people's possessions are twisted forms which again need careful inspection to identify them – they are bicycles, car doors, number plates and iron gates themselves twisted and bent around the trees as if they had been made of soft putty or Plasticine.

At the base of one tree I see a human skull. And then I see another. And another. Skeletal remains are everywhere around us, but they are clearly not of the recent dead. These are the bones of the long dead, cruelly raised from their resting places and scattered by the giant wave.

Eventually, we reach the end of the peninsula. There are no buildings left standing. No orphanage. No orphans. The wave seems to have blasted everything from the face of the earth. We pause for a brief rest and drink some water, depressed at our discovery of absolutely nothing save desolation and emptiness.

On our way back, we chance on two old men struggling with a body wrapped up in a blanket. They want to bury it, but are having problems digging the grave, so we stop to help them. It is a difficult task because the friable sand keeps falling as the hole gets deeper, but eventually it reaches the desired depth.

The body is then gently lifted and lowered into its resting place – but now it emerges that the two old men do not know the identity of the body. They found it washed ashore and just want to give whoever it was a decent burial.

One of our patrol makes a wooden cross and writes on it with black biro:

Killed by the Tsunami, 26th December 2004
Unknown
Rest in Peace

That night we do not return to the ship, but stay in Baticoloa, because it has been decided that we are spending too much time travelling in from the ship every day. The Sri Lankan Army has given us the use of an empty barracks, and it is there that we gratefully put down our bed rolls and, exhausted, prepare for a good night's rest.

My place is next to Rab Butler.

'I better warn you, shipmate,' he says to me as we settle down. 'I'm a bit of a snorer. Apparently I could do it for England, so you might like to bung in some ear plugs.'

'Thanks for the warning,' I reply, 'but I don't reckon anything will stop me sleeping tonight.'

'OK, bud. Sleep well.'

'Right! Lights off you lot!' shouts Steve Bennett. 'Up at 05.00!'

The lights go out. There is an initial round of sniffs and coughs and a short-lived wind-breaking competition.

'Shut up!' shouts Steve Bennett. Silence descends on the barracks and the breathing gets generally heavier as people start to slumber . . .

'Oh, bollocks!' shouts Rab suddenly. 'Fuckin' bastard. Take that!' He then sets about slapping his own head vigorously and repeatedly.

'Bleedin' blood-sucking mosquitoes!' shouts another voice in the dark. 'They're everywhere!'

Soon, everyone in the dormitory is writhing and slapping their bodies as the entire building becomes infested with the night-loving insects that find they have a veritable feast on their hands.

I do not think any of us slept properly last night. I certainly never heard a single snore from Rab – just a fairly constant torrent of swear words directed at yet another buzzing tormentor. When we rise at 05.00, all of our bodies testify to the night's onslaught – countless spots, angry red welts and scratch marks decorate our torsos, legs, arms and faces.

'Somebody should have thought of insect repellent,' says one sailor, who looks as if he has a bad case of the measles and leprosy all at the same time.

'Bleedin' 'ell,' says Rab. 'Them flamin' mozzis were the size of Lancaster bombers. We didn't need repellent, we needed a fuckin' anti-aircraft battery!'

'Quit dripping,' shouts Steve Bennett, 'and get some scran down you.'

The Sri Lankan Army have brought over some breakfast for us – dry bread and sweet tea. Excessively sweet tea.

'Eeeeeeerrgh! Sugar or bleedin' what!' says Rab with a scowl. 'I'm drinkin' flamin' treacle!'

Most people find the tea too sweet and the bread too dry, so resort to some of our own supplies.

'Not exactly a full English breakfast is it?' says Rab, opening a tin with relish. 'But I could never say no to a nice rice puddin'. Lovely!'

Mosquitoes apart, most people prefer the idea of staying ashore because they can get more done. Countless wells still need to be pumped out, countless buildings need to be cleaned out, and countless fishing boats need to be mended and refloated, but one thing is becoming increasingly clear: the people are getting used to having the British sailors around and are treating them increasingly as friends. I have seen more than a few Sri Lankans wearing RN blue shirts, and most evenings there is a game of cricket between HMS *Chatham* and Sri Lanka.

'Great in'it?' says Rab. 'The people around here are really beginning to respond to us, and I know our girls and boys are made up with what we are doing here – bloody marvellous.' He looks around at the remaining devastation and a group of small children looking at him expectantly.

'Only thing is, I'll have to get the missus to send out some more Quality Street.'

Location: Baticoloa
Date: 12 January 2005
Time: 08.00

Ship's Daily Orders. Our Mission: 'Conduct disaster relief operations (OP GARRON)'
Notes: <u>Pen Pal Letter</u>. A Pen Pal file is located in the Ship's Office, containing lots of letters from people who are interested in writing to personnel on board. If you are interested, please sign for the file and read through the letters. Should you wish to contact anyone, then please submit your letters via the Ship's Office. Many of the people are from Medway in Chatham, who you may get the opportunity to meet with in September when we sail there for a visit!

We have heard reports of an entire community cut off from the mainland somewhere south of Baticoloa. Apparently, the causeway that linked it to the outside world has been smashed by the tsunami, so we have been asked to locate this place, called Kallar, and assess its needs.

After about half an hour's flying from the ship, Toby Clay guides our Lynx low over a wide coastal lagoon and, as we pass over a cluster of tall trees, we see what we are looking for – the broken causeway. Toby slows to a hover right above the break in the road, whilst JT has a closer look through his open window. 'It's washed away,' he says, 'a whole section has simply disappeared. This is Kallar all right.'

I am sitting in the back of the aircraft and at my side are Alison Dewynter and Zippy Howard, the Royal Marine Colour Sergeant. As Toby turns the aircraft, we see the broken road for ourselves and also a long snake of bedraggled people, wading through the thick mud where the bridge once was. Some are carrying loads on their shoulders; some pushing bikes; some leading cattle. They pause briefly to look up to the grey helicopter circling above them.

Expertly, Toby lands the Lynx on what remains of the causeway while Alison, Zippy and I get out. Toby immediately takes off again to return to the ship, where he is going to pick up another six people who will join us for a reconnaissance of the area. Alison needs to find out exactly how the Royal Navy can help in Kallar. What are the main needs? What are the priorities?

CHILDREN FROM KALLAR
GREET THE BRITISH SAILORS

Whilst we wait for the helicopter to return we are surrounded by dozens of giggling and inquisitive children. Zippy decides to amuse them by taking pictures of them with his digital camera and then showing them the image. Big mistake! Zippy, a tough Royal Marine Commando, a fearless killing machine, is helpless as he is enveloped by small boys and girls, all screaming for him to take their photos.

Alison and I are looking on with amusement when an elderly man approaches us.

'Are you American or British?' he enquires politely.

'British, sir,' says Alison. 'Royal Navy.'

'Have you come to invade us?' he asks, looking up to the sky as we hear the sound of the returning Lynx.

'We are not invading, sir,' replies Alison gently. 'We have come to help.'

'Thank you,' says the man, 'but couldn't you invade us as well? My father used to say it was much better under the British.'

'No, sir,' laughs Alison. 'It's not what we do these days, I'm afraid.'

The old man turns and walks away disconsolately.

The Lynx approaches the causeway for the second time and prepares to land, but now so many people have been attracted by the arrival of strangers that there is nowhere on the causeway left for it. Toby immediately aborts his landing and flies off to do a circuit of the lagoon, whilst we do our best to clear a space for the aircraft. Eventually, after much

GINGE GRIEVESON AT
KALLAR

shouting and gesticulation, we manage to create room for Toby to put down the Lynx. As it roars in low over the water, its downdraught throws up a fine spray that drenches us all and delights the children, but soon it lands again. The rest of our party join us and I am delighted to see that one of them is Ginge Grieveson, the clock-watching chef who is normally imprisoned in his galley or store room.

'They let you off the ship, then, Ginge?' I say.

'Yes, they couldn't stand any more of my moaning, I shouldn't wonder,' he replies with a smile. 'Actually, I am first-aid trained, and they reckoned the doc might need some back-up.'

Once congregated, we share out the water and rations we have to carry and set off to investigate, but it is so relentlessly hot and humid that we sweat through our clothes within minutes. We trudge away from the causeway and into the sprawling settlement to the south – or at least what was once a settlement. Kallar has been virtually destroyed by the tsunami – only the sturdiest of buildings still stand, but even they are badly damaged. Most homes have simply been razed. There is just

OVERLEAF:
DR KATIE BRAY WAITS FOR
TOBY CLAY TO LAND THE
LYNX AT THE BROKEN
CAUSEWAY

rubble where an entire community once lived – rubble and despair. Much-needed aid simply cannot get through by road and the isolated people are clearly desperate: food, water, shelter, bedding, medicines – you name it, they need it. We find that some of the main needs are specifically for asthma inhalers, insulin for diabetics and drugs for heart disease, because many people whose lives depend on these items have lost them to the wave. Chronic diseases are not being managed, and Kallar's main hospital has been so swamped that it has closed down.

At first Alison feels dwarfed by the situation.

'What can one frigate and one RFA support ship do amidst this chaos?' she says angrily. 'What could a thousand frigates do?' She looks around and shakes her head. 'We are too little, too late!'

It is impossible to know where to start and we all share Alison's frustration, but she does not let it get the better of her. Almost immediately her training kicks in, as does her natural determination. Grasping the nettle, she starts talking to the people. She searches out community leaders and quizzes the local doctor. She visits refugee sites, she goes to a local school, now a shelter for displaced families, and finally she goes to talk with some NGO representatives staying at the local YMCA. There she meets Cathy Bellaert. a young South African volunteer medical worker who eagerly embraces the possibility of help from the Royal Navy. She spends a good hour briefing Alison on Kallar and its people.

By the end of the afternoon the young surgeon lieutenant is well on the way to formulating a plan of action. She now has some solid recommendations to take back to the captain.

Back on board, Alison attends the evening command briefing, where she reports to Captain Chick and his operations team. She explains the immense problem of medications lost to the tsunami, and explains that patients are dying and will continue to die if their diseases are not treated. She stresses that the psychological trauma is taking its toll. She tells of faces that no longer smile, of people deeply depressed by their losses, of families broken by bereavement. She emphasises the need to treat simple infections, which have got out of control because people are now living in crowded conditions in refugee camps and makeshift squatter sites. She describes in graphic detail the rashes, bacterial infections and fungal infestations that are rife.

Captain Chick and his team listen carefully to what their doctor has to say and then ask for her recommendations and plans. She replies that she thinks the best thing the ship can do is to help re-open the flooded hospital. Once that is functioning again, she explains, the whole community will benefit physically and spiritually. It is, she thinks, the best way to kick start Kallar.

Steve Chick and his heads of department wholly endorse her recommendations, and tell her to prepare to start work tomorrow morning at dawn.

Location: Off the Coast of Kallar
Date: 13 January 2005
Time: 06.30

Daily Orders. Our Mission: 'Conduct disaster relief operations (OP GARRON)'
Notes: A working party of 50 will be transported to the mainland to commence work on the hospital at Kallar.

Fifty sailors and marines have been flown in groups of six to a central landing site in the middle of Kallar. From there, everybody has made their way on foot to the YMCA hall where we are to be billeted. It is only a walk of about a mile, but again the heat and humidity are unforgiving, so we are grateful for the cool shade of the YMCA compound with its overhanging trees. The hall itself is basic but spacious, dry and well ventilated.

'Open windows!' says Alison Dewynter with alarm. 'That's fine by day, but by night the mosquitoes will be everywhere. We need nets for everyone, because I don't want another flood of bitten bodies to look after. We have enough on here as it is.'

'Excuse me, ma'am,' says Ratz Rackliff. 'I will go on a search for nets if you like. I saw some small shops on the way here, and they may have what we want. Or else they will know where we can get them.'

'OK. Sounds good. Take a hundred dollars and see what you can find.'

'Yes, ma'am!' replies Ratz.

'You'll never find fifty-six mozzie nets, mate. Not around here – they've been washed out.'

'Yes I will. Just you watch!' retorts Ratz who, regarding himself as a bit of a Del Boy, rises to a challenge like this.

Ratz disappears on his quest – now one of honour. The rest of the party gather and make their way to the central hospital about 400 metres away. Miraculously it is still standing and seems structurally sound, even though the wave washed right through it, depositing a thick layer of mud, rubbish and raw sewage. It is deserted – a ghost hospital. The men and women of HMS *Chatham* prepare to reclaim the building, resurrect it and re-establish it, as well as trying to salvage whatever they can of the beds, screens, cabinets and tables that lie scattered and twisted around the hospital grounds. For a moment everybody just stares at the task in front of them, assessing its magnitude, but then, literally and metaphorically, simply roll up their sleeves and wade into it. They are armed with spades, hoses, axes and, above all, resolve – buckets of it. Nobody who saw this could fail to be moved by the fortitude of these sailors, who are as resolute as the surgeon lieutenant who leads them to make a difference to this ravaged community.

The back-breaking work continues all day. The local people, so traumatised by recent events, look on as the strangers in blue slowly, almost imperceptibly at first, wrestle the hospital back from the dirt and stinking mud in which it has been encased. By the late afternoon the progress can be seen. Encouraged, a few locals join in. The ball is rolling . . .

Exhausted, hungry, sweaty but above all thirsty, the naval party returns to the YMCA, and after we have taken off our boots and enter the hall we see something that stops us in our tracks.

'Bloody hell!', exclaims one sailor. 'Is it real?'

'It can't be,' answers another, 'unless we've bleedin' died and gone to heaven.'

'It's a mirage,' suggests another. 'The work and the heat have gone to our heads.'

'No, shipmates,' says Ratz Rackliff, walking over from the other side of the room. 'It's real, it's cold and it's beer! Might not be John Smith's, but it's the right colour and it's got a kick.'

'How much you got, Ratz?'

'Crates of it, mate, but go easy – it's gotta last.'

'I could kiss you, Ratz – bloody tongues an' all!'

'Don't worry. A simple thank you will suffice!'

'What about the mozzie nets?' interrupts Alison.

'Fifty-six of them, ma'am. Wrapped up over there – one for every-body. Got the beer as part of the deal.'

'Excellent. Well done,' says Alison, grateful that she will not be treat-ing mosquito bites in the morning. 'Grab yourselves a net everyone and we will hang them on ropes we can stretch across the room.'

We all take one of the packages and proceed to unwrap them.

'Ratz! What the fuck are these?' shouts one sailor.

'Whaddya mean?' replied Ratz defensively.

'It's flaming pink! And it's got bloody frills!'

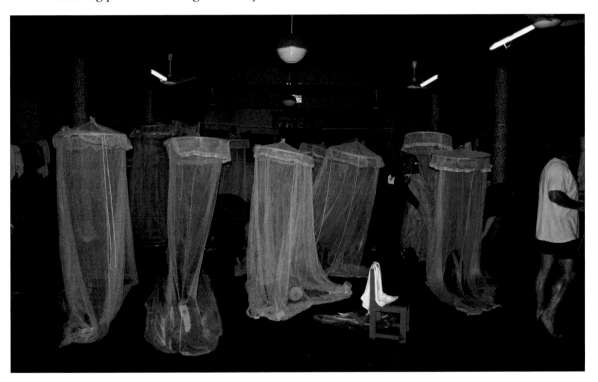

THE JELLYFISH MOZZIE NETS – COURTESY OF RATZ RACKLIFF

'Quit complaining! It's a mozzy net ain't it? Anyway, some of them are blue.'

'Yes, mine's blue,' retorts someone else, 'pale blue with more frills – and sparkly bits!'

'Well, it's all I could find and I did a good deal, so like 'em or lump 'em.'

All the mosquito nets are either baby blue or pale pink and they all sport frills. One by one we tie them to ropes stretched across the hall. Soon there are ten lines of these delicately coloured bell-shaped nets hanging seemingly from mid air – looking for all the world like so many jellyfish bobbing in the sea.

'Looks like something out of *Finding Nemo*,' says someone from inside one of the pink jellyfish.

'Just be grateful the Bootnecks ain't here to see this, shippers!' says another. 'We'd never hear the end of it.'

'Frankly, I would wear one of them as a dress if I had to – just so long as I can have one of them beers.'

'Right, listen up!' says Warrant Officer Steve Price. 'No beers, no scran till everybody's washed and all shoes are cleaned. Don't let that mud dry on. There's a couple of showers, so don't all rush.'

Everyone lines up for a wash, but then someone comes in from outside with an alternative plan for ablutions.

'Oi, there's a well outside and a bucket on a rope. Nobody around, so I just stripped off and poured it all over me. Bloody lovely it was.'

About a dozen of us go straight outside. The bucket on a rope option seems much more attractive than queuing for a couple of dilapidated showers. We strip off in the darkness and take it in turns to haul up the bucket and pour its contents over our heads. The cool water is as refreshing as it is cleansing, and at last we are beginning to feel more alive.

'Hang around!' says a voice. 'My eyes are getting used to the dark now. Oh Christ!'

'Bleedin' 'ell!' says another.

'Oh cobblers!' exclaims yet another.

Gradually we all see the same thing. We have inadvertently wandered into someone's garden. Not only that, but the well is situated right by their veranda, and to cap it all the owner, a little old lady, is sitting in her comfy chair no more than five yards from a dozen naked, male bodies. We all grab our towels, conceal our modesty, and scamper inside. The lady does not budge nor say a word, but she is smiling from ear to ear.

This evening we are dining like kings on Pot Noodles, Ambrosia creamed rice and a bottle each of the local beer. Spirits are high and everyone is looking forward to getting to grips with the hospital again tomorrow – the bit is between our collective teeth. We chat amongst ourselves for a couple of hours. A couple of sailors separately try, but fail dismally, to trap Cathy the South African volunteer worker, who is charming, urbane and more than a match for a couple of tiddly Jack Tars.

As a finale to the evening, however, Steve Price finds Alison Dewynter's personal camera, which she has left lying around unattended – a big mistake if there are sailors about. Click, click, click – one after another buttocks are bared to add to the doctor's photo collection.

Finally, Steve Price thrusts the small digital camera down the front of his shorts and takes a 'flash' photo.

'Bloody hell!' he says, looking at the image on the camera. 'It looks gigantic!'

Some time in the future Alison will discover these rogue photos, but it strikes me that, being a doctor, she will have seen it all before.

Location: Kallar. YMCA
Date: 14 January 2005
Time: 06.30.

The next day, more sailors arrive from the ship. Now, in addition to the cleaning, a work party starts pumping out the main well that serves the hospital. It is full of sea water. The ship's two Lynxes make continuous flights, delivering aid from Baticoloa in a huge net slung underneath it. This includes food, medicines and bedding from UNICEF and UNHCR, and other NGOs.

Meanwhile, Tommy Goodwin, the ship's chaplain arrives for a bit of morale boosting with the local kids. A veritable pied piper, Tommy soon has a crowd of delighted youngsters howling with laughter as he teaches them everything from Scottish dancing to an exhausting game of chase called 'Port and Starboard'. This involves him standing in the

TOMMY GOODWIN MEETS THE CHILDREN

TOMMY GOODWIN PLAYING
'PORT AND STARBOARD'

middle of a large area and shouting randomly 'Port', 'Starboard', 'Bow' or 'Stern', at which point the kids have to rush to the appropriate position already marked out. Last one there is 'out'. If Tommy shouts 'Man overboard', everybody has to dive to the ground, and if he shouts 'Captain on the bridge', they all have to salute and cry out 'Aye aye, sir!' 'Port and Starboard' is a great hit with the children of Kallar.

Ginge, meanwhile, tries to appeal to other local children by trying to distribute small cartons of orange juice out of a large rucksack. Trying to make the task simpler, he opens the zip of the bag to reveal his full cargo of drinks to the small crowd of innocents before him. He is about to hand them out when WHOOSH! In a flash, they descend. Crazed like psychotic piranhas, they strip the bag of every drink in it and then run away.

'Just like bloody sailors!' says Ginge, dumbfounded. 'No "thank yous", no gratitude – just get it down yer neck and run!'

This afternoon, as work continues in the hospital, a lorry full of pots and pans arrives nearby. It has come up from the broken causeway, where it was loaded by local volunteers after an airdrop. Volunteers have organised the delivery, knowing that people urgently need not only food to cook but something to cook it with, but as soon as word gets around, people seem to appear from nowhere to demand the utensils.

The crowd, mostly women, starts to get angry, but distribution under these circumstances is impossible. The young man in charge of the valuable cargo is in a visible state of panic, but someone has already mentioned to him that the Royal Navy is in town. Relieved, he sends a runner to the hospital a quarter of a mile away. Within minutes Chief Petty Officer Steve Bennett is on site. Faced with the angry mob of baying women he acts quickly. 'Go back to the hospital,' he shouts to an accompanying sailor, 'and get twelve blokes. Big blokes. And run!'

Within an hour the situation is under control. A small army of slightly perplexed sailors have won the day by lining up and separating the crowd from the lorry until some local armed police arrive to distribute the assorted saucepans and frying pans to the now tamed women.

ME IN FRONT OF THE HOSPITAL AT KALLAR

'That's what you call the thin blue line,' says one exhausted matelot as he trudges back to the hospital.

'Don't know if "thin" is the right word, mate,' says one of his oppos. 'Seen yourself in a mirror recently?'

Meanwhile, Alison Dewynter, the bit between her teeth, has formulated an ambitious plan. Encouraged by the progress in the hospital, she has decided that tomorrow she will actually try to open a clinic.

*laundryman – traditionally, since the Second World War laundrymen on HM ships have been Hong Kong Chinese civilians.

'I think we can do it,' she says hopefully. 'We won't be able to do much at first, but at least we can bring in some drugs and bandages from the ship and start treating people. We can show them that things are getting back to some sort of normality. It will give them some hope.'

That evening, as I wander back to the YMCA, I bump into Lieutenant Kenny Dalgleish who is in charge of a team cleaning out the hospital's Hindu temple, so that worship there may resume without much more delay. I notice him deep in thought and looking at something in his hand – what from a distance seems like a small furry animal. As I look closer, I see he is holding a teddy bear – muddy, stained and wet.

'I found it in the mud,' he says quietly. 'I just keep wondering whose it is. Whether they survived or whether they . . .'

He pauses to let the thought pass, and with it the terrible sense of tragedy that pervades the place.

'I'm going to take this little fellow back to the ship and give it to the dhobeyman* to clean up. Then he can come and live in my cabin. A sort of souvenir – or, rather, a reminder . . .'

Location: Kallar. YMCA
Date: 15 January 2005
Time: 06.30

The next morning a small party continues to clean and disinfect the hospital whilst others sort through the twisted wreckage of beds, screens, wheelchairs and tables to see what can still be used. By midday a ward in the hospital is virtually transformed. There is a consultation area, a treatment room and a drug dispensary. Alison has been joined by her colleague from RFA *Diligence*, Surgeon Lieutenant Katie Bray, and by two o'clock the doors are opened.

A large crowd has waited patiently, and slowly, one by one, they troop in to see one or other of the Royal Navy doctors. There are cuts and bruises, headaches, eye infections, tummy aches, and lots of crying babies with worried mothers. Alison and Kathy work patiently through them all, diagnosing and treating each case as it comes. However, this is not about the aspirins they give out or the bandages they apply – this is about showing the traumatised survivors of one of the biggest natural disasters the world has ever seen that life carries on; that people care; that whilst it will take years for normality to return, there *is* hope.

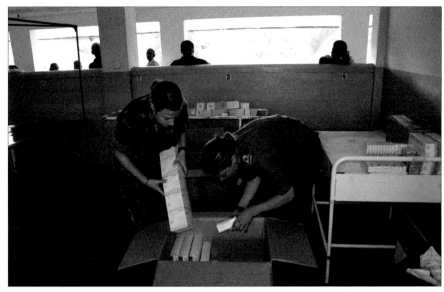

ALISON AND KATIE PREPARE
TO OPEN THE CLINIC

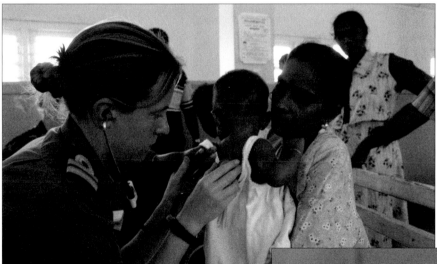

DR ALISON DEWYNTER
AFTER THE CLINIC HAS
OPENED

DR ALISON DEWYNTER AT
WORK

This is a vital message to give the people of Kallar. This is what Surgeon Lieutenant Alison Dewynter has eventually realised a lone Royal Navy frigate can provide – in its own way the most important and most valuable thing it could bring.

That evening, in the warm light of a dying sun, the men and women of HMS *Chatham* play a game of cricket with the locals, whilst in the background can be heard the laughter of children still playing the game Tommy Goodwin taught them. Shouts of 'Howzat' mingle with the distant echoes of young voices crying 'Port', 'Starboard' and 'Aye Aye Captain!'

One way or another, the Royal Navy has left its mark on the people of Kallar.

Postscript: Extract from my diary on the day I left Sri Lanka to return to the UK

I have to return to Plymouth to catch up with other people and other stories, so I am cadging a lift from Baticoloa to Colombo on an American Black Hawk helicopter. As I leave, HMS *Chatham* and RFA *Diligence* are starting some bridge-building work to the south of Baticoloa. There is still so much to do. It will take years for these areas to return to anywhere like normal, but work has started. Baticoloa and Kallar have become important to the men and women of the Royal Navy and the Royal Fleet Auxiliary and many of them hope they can stay long enough to make a lasting difference. However, operational requirements will eventually force them to leave. Maybe other Royal Navy ships will take over – who knows? Our Navy is stretched as it is, but when you lob in a couple of natural disasters to add to the workload – a hurricane there, an earthquake here – there simply are not enough ships in the fleet to cope. That, however, is for the politicians and Sea Lords to work out . . .

Two days later I am back in Plymouth, and here I find just how proud of HMS *Chatham* everybody is – and nowhere more than at HMS *Raleigh*.

Location: HMS *Raleigh*. Plymouth
Date: 14 January 2005
Time: 10.00

It is the day after I returned from Sri Lanka. I have come along to HMS *Raleigh* to attend the 'Passing-In' Parade of the Forty-Sixers – the recruits who arrived in Plymouth last November to start their Phase One training. Jenny, Sharon, Paul, and Amy have passed all their courses, and today will officially become sailors in Her Majesty's Senior Service. They will now go on to their Phase Two training and begin their specialisations: Jenny still wants to be a hydrographer; Sharon wants to become an aircraft mechanic; Paul, of course, wants to be a chef; and Amy wants to be a stores accountant.

THE ROYAL MARINES BAND AT THE FORTY-SIXERS PASSING-IN CEREMONY

They are lined up in their ranks – resplendent in their Number Ones and shouldering SA 80 rifles with bayonets fixed. The Royal Marine band is playing stirring marching music, and everyone's families are here to witness the occasion. There are many cheeks wet with tears of pride and emotion.

At the end of the ceremony, Commodore David Pond, the commanding officer of HMS *Raleigh*, makes a speech that welcomes the recruits into the Navy proper.

'You should all be very proud of yourselves. It is a great achievement to have got through Phase One training. You are now part of the finest Navy in the world, and of course our core business is fighting war where it is necessary to protect the interests of the nation, as well as helping to maintain global security. But the Navy is more than this as well – we have to be an adaptable service and our purpose is sometimes not to confront enemies with weapons of destruction, but to help our fellow man in times of despair and tragedy. I know we have all been watching with great concern the terrible events unfolding in the regions struck by the Boxing Day tsunami, but I know also we have been watching with pride the sterling work of the Royal Navy in Sri Lanka, through the work of the men and women of HMS *Chatham*. They are the Royal Navy at its best, and they are making a difference – that's the sort of thing that you're going to be trained to do, and that's the sort of difference you're going to be able to make in the world. You are now part of the naval family. Good luck, have fun, stay safe and committed. God Bless.'

CHAPTER NINE

The Thursday War

Location: Royal Navy Hawk Jet
Date: 21 January 2005
Time: 13.30

I am flying in the back of a Royal Navy Hawk jet which is skimming the sea at an altitude of just 100 feet at 500 miles an hour. The water seems close enough to touch, and the sense of speed at this height is extraordinary and exhilarating. Suddenly the nose of the Hawk rises and the plane soars into the sky. five hundred feet, 1,000 feet, 2,000 feet in seconds. The aircraft keeps going up, but then starts a long backward loop before suddenly twisting out of it to go into a steep dive . . .

'OK, Chris. Breathe hard. We are about to pull about five Gs. Breathe, breathe and watch the horizon . . . here we go!'

Lieutenant Commander Russ Eatwell is flying the plane – exactly the same sort of plane flown by the Red Arrows, except ours is black – and is taking me on what the Navy euphemistically calls a 'benign sortie'. Simply put, this is to test my stomach in extreme flying situations, to make sure it stays where God intended it to be – inside my body. I am due to do some filming from this same plane during war exercises next week, when it will 'attack' warships in a simulated war scenario. The Navy will not let me fly on such a sortie unless they are confident that I can keep my breakfast to myself.

'Breathe, Chris . . . suck it in . . . watch the horizon . . .'

The Hawk is in the middle of a tight turn and exerting terrific pressure on our bodies – pulling us powerfully down into our seats. Gravity is now increased by a factor of five. Under my overalls I am wearing air-controlled G pants, which automatically tighten around my lower body as the G forces increase, but still it is important to force the lungs to breathe deeply and regularly. It is also a useful trick to keep your eyes on the horizon, as it helps the inner ears to adjust. I can't say my stomach is ecstatic about the sensation, but it decides to stay put.

MY BREAKFAST STAYED PUT!

Russ goes through a series of manoeuvres, pushing both the plane and my inner anatomy to their limits. After about half an hour of continually 'pulling Gs', we head for home – Royal Navy Air Station Yeovilton in Somerset.

It is starting to rain so Russ climbs above the cloud base, putting us into bright sunshine.

'That's good, Chris,' says Russ through the microphone on his helmet. 'I reckon we can let you come with us next week. It'll be good to have you along for the ride.'

'This has been amazing – real adrenaline-pumping stuff. I suppose it's just another day for you, Russ?'

'Not at all. It's always a thrill and it's better than crack cocaine. Not that I know what crack cocaine feels like, of course, but flying jets is addictive. I used to feel as if I wasn't complete unless I was in a plane travelling at MACH 1* or above, but then I got married and had a daughter – so I discovered something even better.'

'How long have you been flying?'

'I have been twenty-one years in the Navy, and flying jets for fifteen of those.'

'What were you flying before jets?'

'Helicopters, but I seldom admit to that – it's a bit like having VD in your medical records – not something to shout about!'

I am well aware that there has long been a healthy sense of competition between helicopter aircrew and fast jet pilots within the Fleet Air Arm, and it continually expresses itself in typically raunchy naval humour.

'What's wrong with helicopters?' I ask, probing his prejudice.

'I could never trust an aircraft in which the wings go faster than the fuselage.'

Russ begins the descent to Yeovilton.

'What about this plane – the Hawk. Do you like flying it?' I ask, as we descend back into the grey weather below the clouds.

'Yes, it's a very agile little plane with a very good rate of roll. As a trainer plane for fighter pilots, it is designed to be unstable so we can throw it around the sky. You'll see what it can do next Thursday, when we go to war!'

One week later I am back in the Hawk. We are flying alongside two others, and are about to attack a convoy of ships in the English Channel – two Royal Navy frigates, a Greek destroyer and a German minesweeper. Russ Eatwell peels off from the other Hawks and prepares for his first bombing run – a low approach, again at about 100 feet above the water, directed at the Greek ship.

'Basically, we are the baddies today,' he tells me from his forward cockpit. 'We are not carrying missiles but iron bombs – imaginary ones of course. We want to plant them on the ships, but first I have to try and get through their air defence systems.'

He adjusts the trim as we approach the first of the ships to be attacked.

'I need to stay as undetected as I can, so I stay low and try not to sky-line myself. Seen against the sky, I am a much easier target – and the

*MACH 1 – speed of sound.

OVERLEAF:
THE HAWKS ARE
SCRAMBLED

higher I am, the further away they can see me. In a training situation, 100 feet is as low as we're allowed to go, but in a real situation we go as low as we need.'

OFF TO ATTACK THE ENEMY – ME AND LT CDR RUSS EATWELL

The Greek destroyer in front of us is manoeuvring violently to throw us off our aim. As we scream over the top of the ship, Russ calls out, 'Bombs gone!' and immediately starts to climb.

'You have to be very careful, dropping bombs at low level,' he says as we reach an altitude of one thousand feet.

'If you don't get it right, you get caught up in the fragmentation envelope – that is, the bomb blast itself, because some of the fragments will be travelling at supersonic speeds, much faster than we are. The speed of approach and altitude of bomb release is critical.'

He now prepares to dive-bomb the German minesweeper, so he gains some more height and then levels off, ready to attack.

'There are two kinds of bombing approach,' he explains casually as he prepares to dive. 'The one we just did at low level – that is a 'lay down' attack – and the one we are about to do. The dive-bomb attack is much more accurate, and the steeper the dive the better. That is why the Stuka dive-bombers in the Second World War were so effective – they were coming down almost vertically.'

We begin our own steep dive from about two thousand feet. The German ship looks like a toy beneath us. Again she starts to manoeuvre violently as the Hawk bears down from right above her.

'This is a ten-degree dive,' Russ says, as we hurtle seawards. 'I am pretending to drop a 1,000 lb bomb, so I will release it at about 555 feet at a speed of 450 knots.'

The toy ship gets larger and larger as we get nearer and nearer. 'Bombs gone!' says Russ again, as he pulls the plane out of the dive, pulling a good six Gs. The small handheld camera I am using becomes so heavy I can hardly hold it up.

BOMB'S GONE!

'People probably think we just fly along as fast as we can, drop a few bombs and hope for the best – but it is a very complex process. The logistics of dropping bombs involves all manner of trigonometry and algorithms. A lot of arithmetic!'

'And a lot of experience?' I suggest.

'Yes. There is a lot to think about when you are attacking something like a ship. You are having to fly the plane, and launch your own attack as well as defend yourself from counter-attack. A lot can go wrong, and the slightest deviation from your bombing run will throw the bomb wide – and then some other poor bugger has to go in and do it again.'

WITH RUSS EATWELL AFTER THE 'BENIGN SORTIE'

Russ joins another aircraft at 1,000 feet. It is a Falcon – slightly bigger than the Hawk. 'OK,' he says cheerfully. 'Last run, and this time we are going to emulate the flight profile of a missile. We will fly under the wing of the Falcon which will "release" us at some distance from the target. We will then do what a missile does, keeping low and fast. This gives the ship an opportunity to test out their anti-missile defence systems.'

We continue to fly next to the Falcon, immediately under its right wing, and then suddenly we drop away. We have become a missile. We skim the sea once again, and stay level for several minutes before a Royal Navy frigate comes into view. We keep going, pointing directly at her midships, and do not pull away till the last moment. We then climb again steeply and join the other two Hawks in formation. Russ gives them the thumbs-up.

'All done!' he says. 'Mission accomplished. That's it till next Thursday, when we'll be attacking HMS *Ocean* – the biggest ship in the fleet and a lovely large target!'

Location: HMS *Ocean*
Date: 4 February 2005
Time: 09.30

I am on the bridge with Captain Tony Johnstone-Burt.

'It's Thursday and so it must be war!' he says with a bright smile. 'In Plymouth, we go to war every Thursday without fail.'

He points down to a chart in front of him.

'This might look a bit familiar,' he says, 'in that it appears to be the outline of Great Britain and Ireland, but you will see that, because it's Thursday, the political geography has changed a bit. Devon becomes part of the Republic of Brownia, essentially the good guys, and is surrounded by the Republic of Ginger – the bad guys. They are always having problems, and every week there is another scenario and the Royal Navy has to come in and sort it out.'

'And do you know beforehand what is going to happen?'

'No. We have a general idea that we are going to be attacked in some way, but we just have to stand by and see what they are going to throw at us – it could be anything.'

'They' refers not directly to the Republics of Brownia and Ginger, but to a central organisation within the Royal Navy called Flag Officer Sea Training, or FOST. The rationale of FOST is best illustrated by its own maxim – 'The most important single factor in a naval service is the quality of its personnel and their training.' Every ship in the Royal Navy will go through a period of FOST before it is considered ready for duty on the high seas. The five- or six-week course will test the ship and her company to the extremes of their abilities, in all manner of situations and scenarios that the ship might confront in the real world, with a particular stress on expeditionary warfare. These scenarios range from battle damage exercises to naval gunfire support, as well as disaster relief operations, ship protection, counter-terrorism exercises and even the VIP visits which are an important part of the diplomatic responsibility naval warships carry. So successful is FOST that ships from many other navies now put themselves through the extremely testing, and often very stressful, training involved. A friend of mine who served in the Navy during the Falklands War once told me, 'The war was hell, but at least it wasn't as bad as FOST!'

One of the key evolutions in the FOST package is the Thursday War. This is regarded as the most realistic and exacting multi-threat training it is possible to mount, short of a real war. The basic scenario is that a multi-national taskforce is operating in the

THE GEOGRAPHY OF THE THURSDAY WAR

shallow waters off the friendly, fictitious state of Brownia. Their mission is to escort a 'High Value Unit' (HVU), normally a Royal Fleet Auxiliary

HMS *OCEAN* PREPARES FOR THE THURSDAY WAR

tanker, along a pre-set navigational path. To accomplish this it must counter the air, surface and sub-surface threats deployed by Ginger, a fictitious rogue state that is subjecting Brownia to continued aggression in defiance of international law.

'These Gingians are unstable chaps, always up to no good,' says Tony Johnstone-Burt as he walks into the ship's darkened operations room. This is the nerve centre of the ship where he would always be in the event of attack, and it is crammed with radar screens and electronic monitoring equipment. 'We are in an area where we might well expect an air attack, so we have closed up for action.'

Upper-deck gunners are watching out for aircraft. Radar operators in the ops room are also scanning for hostile aircraft movements.

ME WITH TONY JOHNSTONE-BURT

BANDITS IDENTIFIED (HMS *OCEAN*'S OPS ROOM)

It is not long before the Gingian Air Force comes hunting for us.

'Unknown aircraft approaching from the north!' comes a voice from the ops room over the central broadcast system. Gunners on the bridge wings point to a couple of specks in the sky just above the horizon and prepare to fire their GPMGs. The specks get closer and grow into the unmistakable outlines of Hawk jets. I wonder which one of them is being piloted by Russ Eatwell, that well-known Gingian topgun!

'Flash, flash, flash! All positions APS*. Bruisers inbound bearing 221, now strength two!'

*APS – Air Picture Supervision

The Hawks approach low, scream overhead and then climb rapidly. One of them flies away, probably to prepare itself for another low-level 'laydown' attack, whilst the other climbs, ready to dive-bomb. HMS *Ocean* is defending herself against sustained aerial attack. The Captain and his principal warfare officers mastermind the ship's defence and anti-aircraft posture.

'Bruisers inbound, 225, range 12!'

'All positions APS, missile carrier inbound bearing 223, 4 miles – green four zero!'

ATTACK!

'Second aircraft – one mile! Bombs released!'

'Brace! Brace! Brace!'

The ship is defended by a wide range of weaponry including both gunnery and missiles, but today cannot prevent both damage and casualties. The FOST staff on board, or Fosties as they are called, stand outside the attack simulations and announce what damage the ship has sustained, according to their own pre-arranged plan. Without warning they suddenly announce that the ship has been hit and say where the damage has been sustained. They will have set off smoke canisters in the 'damaged' areas and volunteers from the ship's company will already have been opted out of the actual exercise to become casualties. This is a very popular job for any frustrated thespians, as they are encouraged to act out their injuries, shock and panic as realistically as they can. They are all 'made-up' with blood, horrific wounds, burns and even bones projecting from their limbs.

MIKE BROTHERTON AT THE
THURSDAY WAR

Right now the ship has sustained a major hit on its port side at the stern. Some have been killed and there are many wounded. This is where Mike Brotherton, the ship's chaplain, gets involved.

'If there are dead and dying, I have to give the last rites,' he says as he rushes to the sickbay where the wounded are being taken. 'I also need to be around to help with the injured and console them, and even the fit-bodied need support at a time like this. It is amazing how quickly people turn to God in real-life war situations!'

Dozens of walking wounded are coming into the sickbay. Others, more seriously wounded, are being carried in. Medics tend to them as quickly as they can, trying to identify the ones that need more immediate attention. One sailor with a bandaged and bloodied head is screaming.

'I can't see! I can't see! Help me!'

A woman sailor, pallid and drained of colour, is lying flat and staring with wide unblinking eyes.

'We are all going to die,' she whimpers.

'No we're not,' says Mike Brotherton, gently taking her hand. 'Everything will be all right.'

'We are! We are! The ship is going to sink.'

'No it's not. The Captain has control of the situation. Everything will be fine . . . look, here's the doctor. He will make you feel more comfortable.'

The doctor is just about to tend to the patient when a Fostie walks over.

'Sorry, doc. You're dead! Smoke inhalation.'

Mike Brotherton looks up at the Fostie, startled.

'It's all right, Bish. You're still alive!'

'Oh, thank you!' says Mike gratefully.

The bandits seem to have flown off, but whilst any danger of attack remains, the ship stays at action stations. Even in the heat of war, however, people have to eat, so the galleys continue to cook, and of course food provides a huge boost to morale in extreme and dangerous circumstances. I go down to the junior rates' mess with Mike Brotherton.

'Obviously, we don't sit down and eat a three-course meal,' says Mike. 'We do what's called action messing – in other words, very fast eating!'

The entire ship has to be fed in an hour and a half including cooking and washing up. The ship's company has to eat by quarters – that is, twenty-five per cent at a time – to ensure weapons and sensors remain manned. They eat in four minutes flat and return nourished back to their action stations. The cooks have to provide hot, tasty food at a precise rate to feed the queues, then eat themselves before returning to their own action stations. Cooks are often also medics or fire-fighters.

'Chicken stew, beef stew or vegetarian stew,' says Mike. 'Help yourself, Chris. We have less than four minutes now.'

I take a helping of chicken stew and start to eat fast.

'Action messing food will always be "sloppies",' says Mike. 'There is no point in having something you have to cut up and chew. You just need to be able to pour it down your throat!'

This morning's air defence exercise (ADEX) is over and Tony Johnstone-Burt now has a quite different situation to handle.

We are stationed in potentially hostile waters near the Republic of Ginger, on our way to the Republic of Brownia. The British government has sent HMS *Ocean* a signal that an opportunity has arisen for peace talks to be convened between the Brownian and Ginger governments, to resolve the recent crisis in which Ginger took a highly aggressive stance in its will to unite the two countries. Although both governments are willing to attend peace talks, the Brownian officials refuse to leave their country in the current climate and the Ginger delegation refuse to meet on Brownian soil. For talks to take place it is therefore imperative that a suitably high-profile venue can be found in international territory close to Brownia, and both sides have agreed that HMS *Ocean*, a major Royal Navy asset, meets their need.

Tony Johnstone-Burt is back on the bridge and preparing to take *Ocean* into the Brownian Port of Freeport (Plymouth) where he is to host the peace talks.

'We have been told to expect trouble on our way in,' he says, showing me a recent signal from the commander of the Joint TaskForce (CJTF).

You are to proceed into Freeport in a suitable posture to defend yourself against probable terrorist attack and the delegates against interference from protestors until arrival of local police forces. Terrorist threat level now high. The Pro Ginger Front (PGF) have stated they are against the peace initiative as it jeopardises their aim to unite Brownia and Ginger, and they are likely to attempt to sabotage the talks. The PGF are well organised, trained and equipped, and have a wide range of attack capabilities including small water craft, mortars, RPGs* and small arms.

* RPGs are Rocket Propelled Grenades

† Zulu Time is Greenwich Mean Time

You are to report to CJTF if you believe the mission is not achievable by 2000Z (Zulu† Time) and the talks need to be delayed. It is imperative the talks commence at the latest by 2359Z. They must not be cancelled outright.

HMS *Ocean* proceeds to Freeport, but then all hell lets loose at the outer breakwater (the entrance to Plymouth Sound). A terrorist attack is launched from fast speedboats carrying masked men firing machine guns. Tony Johnstone-Burt has already deployed a number of the ship's landing craft full of Royal Marines to escort the ship. They quickly repel the attempted attack.

Another signal is received.

The People's Popular Front for Ginger (PPFG), a fanatical group that split from the PGF 3 years ago as they regarded the PGF as weak, were successfully infiltrated by the Brownian police and are now largely considered a spent force. However, a small suicide bomber cell was not neutralised and remains unlocated. It is believed that they could mount a suicide attack using individuals, vehicles or boats.

As soon as the ship is tied up alongside, a Royal Marine guard is posted on the jetty whilst the Brownian and Gingian delegates are awaited. FOST now exert further pressure on HMS *Ocean*. Several aggressive and pushy 'journalists' arrive at the ship to ask awkward questions of any of the ship's personnel they come across.

'Why are you here?'

'What is the British interest in this conflict?'

'Is the Royal Navy siding with one side over another?'

All the ship's company have been well briefed to ensure that the media gain a positive impression of UK involvement in the talks without affecting their neutrality as host. The Royal Marines, keeping a sharp look-out for any possible suicide bombers, deal with the press questions politely but briefly.

'We are here to facilitate the talks.'

'Britain is interested in helping both sides reach a peaceful settlement.'

'The Royal Navy, like the UK, is neutral in this matter.'

Or, there is the catch-all 'You will have to ask my superior officer.'

After two hours, the guards spot a figure walking up the road to the jetty. At the same time another attack is launched from one of the terrorist speedboats that fires its machine guns at the upper deck of the ship, but the upper-deck gunners are quick to return fire.

'Halt! Identify yourself!' shouts a Royal Marine corporal to the approaching figure who, ignoring the warning, keeps advancing.

'Halt or we shoot!'

The figure breaks into a run and throws open his coat to reveal sticks of 'dynamite' tied to his body.

'Fire!' shouts the corporal. The bomber falls dead.

On the upper deck of the ship a gunner has been hit and is dying. Mike Brotherton is at his side.

The Thursday War is over and everyone is ready to drop. HMS *Ocean* has endured six hours of continuous high-pressure activity, and now the FOST staff will debrief the ship's heads of departments and award a mark for each aspect of the ship's reaction to the different scenarios. The marks range from 'unsatisfactory', 'below satisfactory',* 'satisfactory', 'very satisfactory' to 'very good' (B.Sat, Sat, V.Sat, V.Good). 'Very Good', however, is virtually an impossible mark to achieve, certainly as an over-all mark, as it would represent a virtually perfect score. In matters of war and conflict there is seldom, if ever, a perfect action, so it follows there must always be room for improvement. Today HMS *Ocean*'s overall score is a shining 'V.Sat'.

*If this is too far below satisfactory, the ship may be required to redo the exercise from scratch. Colloquially this is called a 'Rescrub'.

'It might all seem like a big game,' says Tony Johnstone-Burt, sitting exhausted in his cabin, 'But it does give everybody the most amazing insight into some of the actions they might be called upon to take part in. I am very proud of my ship today. I think we all did extremely well, in all departments from warfare to logistics. It is very high-pressure stuff with the scenarios continually changing, but then, that is what happens in the real world. There is no script to war. And the action messing was terrific. I wish we could have that beef stew a bit more often, actually!'

'Can you relax now?'

'Yes, until tomorrow morning. Then the Fosties are back on board with more tricks up their sleeves. And next Thursday it will be war again!'

Mike Brotherton, back in his cabin, collapses on to his bed. 'Goodness! Air attacks, terrorists, suicide bombers. What a day!'

'Obviously it's all pretend . . .' I say to the drained cleric, 'but any of it could happen.'

'Of course it could. A lot of stuff they give us is based on real situations that have occurred.'

'How do you reconcile your spiritual beliefs with the fact you are serving on a ship of war whose business is or can be fighting?'

'Good question – and it is a question, if I'm honest, I do have to struggle with sometimes. Then I remind myself that the Royal Navy is not a belligerent navy. We don't go looking for trouble – far from it. We are there first and foremost to preserve peace.'

He points to a photograph on his wall of himself and a group of Marines sitting in a Land Rover.

'That was in Sierra Leone. I was sent in with the first wave of marines because the place was in such a state, with people hacked to death, dying, wounded – it was terrible. There were orphans everywhere, the bereaved relatives, and the simply shocked and frightened as well. We went in to help, not to fight, but, if we are attacked in those situations, we would have to defend ourselves. I think God understands that.'

'So who cares for the carer, Mike?'

'Hah! Another good question. Well, I have a very close relationship with the captain. He's a friend really, and we support each other much of the time. If I need a bit of companionship or just a chat with some-one, I usually drop in on him. Very good company is our captain.'

Mike yawns widely.

'In fact, that is exactly where I'm going now. His steward makes a very good cup of tea . . .'

CHAPTER TEN

Rab's Run Ashore

Location: Arabian Sea
Date: 7 February 2005
Time: 13.00

Ship's Daily Orders. Our Mission: 'To detect, disrupt and destroy terrorist elements operating in the region'
Notes: Today's Bingo numbers were drawn by LWEM Agutter.
They are 60, 22, 66, 26, 82, 10, 20, 45, 80, 21.

HMS *Chatham* is back on patrol in the Arabian Gulf. After her dramatic diversion to Sri Lanka, following the devastating tsunami on Boxing Day, the ship has resumed her normal duties on Operation Calash – the policing of the ocean approaches to Iraq and its neighbours. Once again *Chatham* is hunting down any suspect shipping which may be carrying illegal cargoes such as arms, drugs or al-Qaeda operatives. All day and all night the ship looks out for ships and small fishing dhows which need to be checked by armed boarding parties. The oceans are wide and the search can be frustrating.

'Fuckin' borin' is what it is, mate,' says Rab Butler as he searches the distant horizon with his binoculars. '*Groundhog Day* – bleedin' monotonous. It's difficult to find the bad guys at the best of times, but I s'pose we have to be seen to be here. Deterrence like.'

'Do most people find this patrolling boring?' I ask.

'Well, the Bootnecks probably find it all right 'cos they are the ones doin' the boardin', but for the rest of us – well it's like watching paint dry. This is the most difficult part of the deployment now – halfway through, but still can't really think of goin' home yet. Just gotta get on wiv the job – staring at the soddin' horizon all day. Oh look, there's a seagull – that's made me fuckin' day that has!'

Down in the wardroom galley, Ginge Grieveson is on duty. Up to now he has been in charge of stores, but he has swapped duties and will be cooking for the officers for the rest of the deployment.

'It's good to have a change, just to stop me going slowly out of my mind,' he laughs, but only half jokingly. 'Being back on patrol does most people's heads in. Search and board, search and board. Same old same old – no variation. It was good down in Sri Lanka. It made us all feel like we were doing something useful. Getting our hands dirty and contributing. But this patrolling leaves most of us cold. Don't get me wrong, I know it's important, but most of us are too remote from the action.'

'You still clock-watching, Ginge?' I ask. 'Still counting the days?'

'Nah. What gives you that idea?' he says, looking up at the calendar on the bulkhead. 'Two months, three weeks, four days and ten hours. Haven't worked out the minutes and seconds yet – just give us a moment . . .'

The ship is working hard in a difficult region and at a difficult time. The policing work, as monotonous as it may be, is essential to help maintain stability in the Middle East as Iraq slowly attempts to achieve a toehold on its future as a democratic country. HMS *Chatham*, along with other ships in Operation Calash, provides a military platform from which policing of the seas is possible. The boarding parties led by Royal Marine Commandos and the warfare department locked away in the darkened operations room, with all its radar and secret squirrel gadgetry, are at the sharp end of the surveillance work, but most of the ship's company are there to make sure the ship, as a seaborne community, continues to function – that is eat, drink, wash, float, navigate and, of course, protect itself should the need arise. Caterers, stewards, store accountants, writers, stokers, weapons mechanics, radar operators, gunners and navigators all do their bit to ensure the ship operates at peak performance in the pursuit of its duty.

'Gotta look on the bright side though,' says Rab, still peering through his binoculars. 'In just one week we will be back in Doobers! Then it will be another sort of *Groundhog Day* – the good sort. Beer, beer and more beer! Bring it on . . . !'

Location: Approaching Dubai
Date: 13 February 2005
Time: 10.30

Ship's Daily Orders. Our Mission: 'To have a good time!'
Notes: FLAGO 1616 – Drunkenness. The definition of drunkenness
is in section 28 of the NDA and is set out as follows:

'A person is drunk if owing to the influence of alcohol or any drug,
whether alone or in combination with any other circumstances, he
is unfit to be entrusted with his duty or with any duty which he
might reasonably expect to be called upon to perform or behaves
in a disorderly manner or in a manner likely to bring discredit on
Her Majesty's Service'

We approach Dubai for the second time on this deployment. The first time we had just spent Christmas at sea and the entire ship's company had been looking forward to a tempestuous New Year run ashore. That, of course, never happened, thanks to the tsunami.

Today, however, it looks as if the ship's company will get ashore and at last be able to sample the many and varied delights that make modern Dubai, that oasis of hedonism set like a sparkling jewel in the arid deserts of the Arab Emirates, one of the most popular destinations for a sailor wanting to let his or her hair down.

THE ILLUSTRATED MAN

'Look at that!' says Rab, focusing his binoculars on Dubai's dramatic skyline. 'A sailor's paradise and no bleedin' mistake. Fingers crossed we don't get no more tsunamis, earthquakes, tornadoes, floods or plagues of fuckin' frogs.'

'What are your plans for Dubai, Rab?'

'Well, apart from drink a great deal of beer, I'm gonna get a new tattoo.'

'Anything in mind?'

'Oh yeah. I know exactly what it will be, and I know just the man to do it – a Russian called Anton. He's a bleedin' genius with the old electric needle!'

HMS *Chatham* has tied up alongside at Port Rashid, as before, at Jetty 74. Many of the ship's company, not on watch, have headed straight into town. At midday Rab and I go to the main gates of the dockyard, where Anton is there to meet us.

'Rab! How are you, my friend? Welcome back to Dubai.'

'Anton, thanks for comin' to pick us up, mate – I wasn't sure you'd get my text.'

'No problem, my friend. So what is it you want tattooed this time?'

'Something very special this time, mate! Let's get to the parlour and I'll show you a picture of it.'

Anton drives us to a tall office block on the outskirts of town, where we take the lift to the fourteenth floor and enter a spacious and well-lit room, full of what, at first sight, look like medieval instruments of torture – his needles. On the walls are pictures of arms, legs, torsos, hands, feet, buttocks and breasts that have been adorned by Anton and his multi-coloured inks. He has etched just about any animal you could think of, from mythical dragons and unicorns to roaring lions, soaring eagles and charging horses. Then there are the obscure Celtic designs, Maori patterns or North American Indian motifs and symbols. Anton has tattooed just about anything, on to just about any part of the human body.

'Have you got room left, Rab?' says Anton. 'I thought you were all full up.'

'Nah, got a space I've been keepin' for this one on my back. Anyway, I got a picture here . . .'

'OK . Show, please.'

Rab takes an envelope from his bag and carefully takes out a sheet of paper. It is a faded black and white photograph of a sailor.

'That's my granddad,' he says proudly. 'He was in the Mob during the Second World War and, though he's passed away, I've always reckoned he is there for me – my guardian angel. I want 'im on me back. Reckon you can do that, Anton?'

Anton holds the photograph up to the light at the window and studies it hard.

'Show me space on back, please.'

Rab pulls off his T-shirt to reveal a well-tattooed torso, but turns to show his back. The left side is covered with two crossed flags – the cross of St George and the White Ensign – a pair of lions, an imperial crown and an English rose. The right-hand side is vacant.

'I can do,' says Anton. 'Please sit.'

Rab sits with his back to the window. The strong Dubai sun burns down on his white English skin, illuminating a broad, fleshy canvas for the Russian tattooist to work on. Anton carefully prepares a series of needles and inks . . .

'Me granddad was a leading sick-berth attendant. He died when I was about fourteen of a heart attack.'

'Keep still, please,' says Anton, as he carefully starts to trace the outlines of the photograph on to Rab.

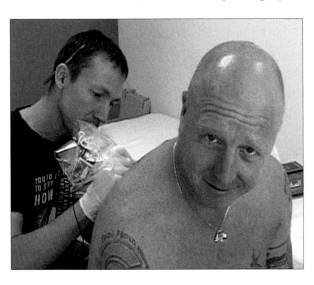

ANTON THE RUSSIAN STARTS WORK ON RAB

'OK, mate. No worries.' Rab straightens his back. 'Anyway, later in life, when I was goin' through some personal problems, a friend took me along to this spiritualist church for some solace. The spiritualist bloke had a look at me and said there was a man in naval uniform lookin' over me, and that he 'ad died of a heart attack . . . Hello, he's about to start drilling.'

Anton has turned on the needle.

'Steady, please.'

Rab braces himself and then winces as the needle starts to inject ink into his skin. 'Bugger me, that don't half smart . . . anyway, me granddad served on HMS *King George V*, in Gibraltar and in Alexandria. The old fella didn't talk too much about the war because he had nightmares about it. I do know that once he was told to bury three Italians when he was in Alexandria, but they were in bits and came in buckets – he had to sort of pour them into the graves . . . full military honours though!'

At half-past two, Rab walks into the Seaman's Mission in central Dubai, where dozens of sailors from HMS *Chatham* are gathered around the swimming pool.

'Let's have a look, Rab! Let's see yer tat!' they shout out as soon as they see him.

'Nah, can't yet. Still got the bandage on. Not allowed to . . .'

'Ah go on, Rab. Quick look won't harm!'

'Oh, go on then,' says Rab, dying to show it off.

A dozen sailors crowd round whilst Rab carefully peels the Vaseline-saturated lint bandage from his back to reveal the perfect portrait of his grandfather as a young sailor.

'Fuckin' quality, mate!' says one of Rab's messmates.

'Bloody superb!' says another.

'How much did that cost, mate?'

'Hundred and fifty Dib Dobs.'*

'Bargain, mate! It's real lifelike that . . .'

'Right,' says Rab, delighted with the reviews of his latest body art. 'Time to start drinking beer … mine's a Guinness!'

Sitting by the pool is Tommy Goodwin. Along with everyone else, he is relaxing in the sunshine, although he is writing intently in a notebook.

'You're looking very thoughtful, Tommy,' I say.

'Ah, yes. Well . . . you see I leave the ship tomorrow.'

'I know. You're going back to Scotland, aren't you?'

'That's right. I'm taking up my new job as chaplain at the submarine base in Faslane. I am looking forward to that and I can't wait to see my family, but in another way I am sad to leave *Chatham*. It has been home for me for a while, and we – all of us on board – have been through a lot together. I will miss the ship and I will miss the ship's company.'

'And I am sure they will miss you too, Tommy,' I say.

'Well, I'm just writing down a few thoughts about my time on *Chatham*, about the people I've met and the things we have done. . . .'

* Dib Dobs – foreign currency of any kind. Another term often used is Ickies. Either can be subdivided into Klebbies.

THE TATTOO RAB ALWAYS DREAMED OF

By six o'clock we are arriving back at the ship to get ready for a night on the town. Rab walks up the gangway and is immediately stopped by the armed guards – not because he has done anything wrong but because they have already heard about his tattoo and want to have a look.

Once again he pulls his T-shirt off and turns his back towards the glowing red sun just sinking below the horizon.

'Nice tat, Rab!' says one of the guards.

'Yeah, it's a good'un,' says his companion. 'Pity about some of the others though, mate. What's that one on your arm?'

'James Brown. Look, it bloody says so underneath!'

'Really? Looks more like the elephant man. Did you do it yourself?'

'No!' laughs Rab, 'but I can't remember who did, to be honest. In fact, I don't think I was quite compos mentis when I had it done!'

'Lathered, eh?'

'Of course! And in a couple of hours I intend to be just that again. I will think about you poor sods on duty all night – not!'

Five of us cram into a taxi at eight o'clock and head back to the Seaman's Mission.

'Right, we'll start at the mission. Have a few there and then move on,' says 'Reg' Gutteridge, an operator mechanic in above water warfare.

'Apparently the Yanks are in town,' says Rab. 'One of their big flat tops. Hope they behave themselves.'

'Do you have trouble with the Americans?' I ask.

'Sometimes, yeah!' says Rab. 'It's usually "handbags", though it can get rougher occasionally. You know, it's all about who has the best navy, and that can get a bit heated.'

'And the Yanks can never take their drink, either,' says Reg. 'Their ships are dry, no alcohol allowed, so once they come ashore it only takes half a pint and they're all over the place.'

'You know what they are told by their commanding officers when the Royal Navy is in town, don't you?' says Rab.

'Yeah, not to go anywhere near us!'

'That's right. They are told don't drink wiv us, play cards wiv us or fight wiv us, because they will get a drubbing on all counts.'

'Says you, shipmate!' exclaims Reg. 'Have you seen some of them Yank sailors? Muscles on muscles they've got!'

'Nah, they're all poofters, mate!'

The Seaman's Mission is full of sailors from HMS *Chatham*. Rab, Reg and I order a steak and chips and a round of Guinness.

'We'll just have some scran and then head out to the main strip,' says Rab. 'I reckon we should go to Waxy O'Connor's, and then end up at Rock Bottom to dance the night away.'

At last the ship's company is getting its long promised run ashore in Dubai. It has been a long time coming, but now it is here everybody is going to take full advantage of it.

'Come on, Chris!' says Rab. 'Your round, mate. Mine's another Guinness!'

And so it starts. The British sailor, generally speaking, can drink for Britain – and in a sense he does. I remember my time with Scouse Ashton, the regulator back in Plymouth, when he told me that the British sailor seeks out alcohol wherever he is. That is largely true. It seems to be part of British naval culture, but that is not to say that all sailors are drunkards. In some ways it is quite ritualised behaviour; it's what sailors do en masse to underscore and emphasise their comrade-ship. It is what shipmates do – and if you are invited to drink with sailors, you *do* become their shipmate, even if it is only for that night. It is an inclusive thing and in some ways, I suppose, a very important part of being in the Navy. It is a bonding thing and was explained to me once by an old Navy friend called Bob Hawkins, a lieutenant commander in the diving branch, and a legendary party goer. He said that to drink with your oppos is as important a part of Navy life as any other because it heightens morale as well as a sense of brotherhood/sisterhood, but he added that 'If you are going to hoot with the owls you have to make sure that you can soar with the eagles the next day.'

Right now, as I order another round of drinks at the crowded bar, everybody is quite clearly and quite rightly only interested in the hooting part of the equation.

It's now ten. We have arrived at Waxy O'Connor's – and walk into a little bit of Dublin transplanted to the Arab Emirates: draught Guinness, Irish accents behind the bar and a shoulder to shoulder clientele, all laughing and many singing. As my eyes adjust to the low light I begin to pick out some familiar faces from the ship. It is strange seeing everybody in civilian clothes, and particularly seeing some of the girls now dressed to kill in all their finery and make-up.

Rab, Reg and I set up camp by the pool tables where we are soon drawn into a game by a crowd already playing. Rab is now quite well oiled and still sinking Guinness, but his cue control is impressive and we are soon ahead on games. With each win comes another round, and so the evening progresses.

'Actually, I'm fuckin' useless at pool when I'm sober, but when I've 'ad a few I get me eye in somehow. Strange old thing!'

A few Guinesses later Rab is leaning against the wall and beginning to look a little glazed when an Irish jig blasts out of the loudspeakers. Reacting immediately, he launches into an extraordinary display of Irish dancing that Michael Flatley of *Riverdance* fame would be proud of. His head and body are virtually motionless with his gaze fixed, but his legs are pumping out the steps with staggering speed. Everybody around the pool tables looks on, impressed, and when the music finally finishes they applaud loudly.

'Awesome mate,' says Reg. 'I didn't know you could do Irish dancing.'

'I can't, mate,' slurs Rab. 'Don't know what came over me.'

One o'clock – and we are now at Rock Bottom, a famous Dubai venue. If Waxy O'Connor's was busy and loud, this is frenetic and ear shattering. Again, it seems to have been taken over by HMS *Chatham*, and I immediately spot half the Royal Marine boarding party on the dance floor, as well as several stewards, stokers and weapons engineers. A lot of the sailors seem to be concentrating their dancing efforts in the vicinity of a tall and amply endowed blonde who, well aware of the attention she is receiving, is taunting everyone with sultry glances and flashing smiles.

RAB AT THE ROCK BOTTOM

'Classic!' shouts Rab into my ear. 'That's Jack on the pull. Bet nobody traps that busty blonde though – she's way out of their league!'

He takes to the dance floor himself and puts on a remarkable display of what can only be described as flamenco crossed with Russian cossack dancing and boxing.

Suddenly, he lurches across the floor to a man pouring tequila down people's throats.

'In here, matey!' Rab shouts, pointing to his open mouth. The man pours a stream of the liquor into the gunner's capacious mouth.

'Aaaaargh!' Rab steps back, spluttering and choking, his eyes bulging out of his head, looking as if he is about to have a seizure. Then a broad grin spreads across his face.

'Bloody great place this, ain't it! Come on, I'm gonna dance again!'

Three o'clock – and Rab, Reg and I wander down the street, sucking in the cool night air. We are holding each other up.

'Gotta eat!' says Rab. 'Need food!'

Reg and I grunt agreement and head for the nearest burger bar. Somehow we manage to order and pay for three chicken burgers and chips.

'Good run ashore, shipmates!' mutters Rab with his mouth full.

'Still standing!' says Reg.

'Only just!' I say.

'That was a mild night out, Chris!' says Rab with a crooked smile. 'Just to get you started.'

Rab has at last got me drunk in Dubai. I have now been formally initiated. I know I will suffer a sore head tomorrow but, even in my intoxicated state, I am pleased, once again, to have been able to consolidate my relationship with these sailors in the time-honoured way.

We stagger towards the ship. It is 3.30 in the morning.

'OK. The rule is if you can walk up the gangway unaided, you won't get pinged. So concentrate, guys, or we'll be on report.'

One by one sailors are making their way on to the ship, up a gangway angled at about thirty degrees. Most seem to be making it to the top, but some look very wobbly indeed. Soon it is our turn and, whilst I am not subject to the terms of naval discipline, I consider it to be a matter of honour that I make it up under my own steam. I do. So does Rab and so does Reg. Like everyone else they then 'peg themselves in' – that is, move the coloured peg by their name on a display board from 'Ashore' to 'On board'.

We are just about to head into the ship and make our way to our bunks when a figure rushes out, practically knocking Rab over. Seconds later a girl rushes out too, shouting after the figure, 'Come back Trev! Trev!'

'What's up, Suzy?' asks Rab. 'What's up with Trev?'

'It's Debbie. She's chucked him. There was a blazing row and he said he's going to leave the ship. I was trying to stop him.'

At that point we hear the voice of a duty chief petty officer on the flight deck.

'Do not leave the ship! If you go down that gangway, you will be for the high jump.'

'Don't go, Trev!' shouts Suzy.

'Trevor!' shouts Rab. 'Don't be a mug, mate!'

Trevor does not even look back. He runs down the gangway and disappears into the darkness of the dockyard.

'Bugger it!' says Rab. 'I could see that coming. They've been having trouble for a while; Trev can be a bit hot-headed sometimes – too much for his own good.'

'Should we go after him?' says Reg.

'No,' says Suzy. 'Someone's gone to get Tommy. Tommy should deal with this.'

Minutes later the chaplain emerges from the ship.

'Where is Trevor?' he asks.

'Somewhere over there, Bish,' says Reg. 'I think he might be by those containers.'

'OK,' says Tommy. 'Suzy, why don't you come with me? Is Debbie all right?'

'Yes, she's with the girls in the mess.'

'Come on, then. Let's go and get Trev.'

Nearly everyone witnessing this scene is inebriated, apart from the duty watch of course, but that does not stop people being concerned for one of their own in trouble. I watch the drama unfold with fascination. It is another dramatic example of how close a ship's company gets. Obviously, relationships *do* develop, despite the rigorously enforced No Touch rule, but they can seldom exist in a vacuum on board. Because most people know each other, particularly on a frigate, the complexities of an emotional attachment will ramify through a mess deck and beyond. This is just part of the reality of life on board ship – especially since women started coming to sea. Of course, relationship complications occur all the time in other walks of life, so why shouldn't they on warships? This is not an argument against having women at sea, but it does emphasise the increased importance of people management on board a ship, as well as the need for pastoral care. Much of this pastoral responsibility will naturally fall at the feet of divisional officers, each of whom will have a specific number of junior or senior rates placed under their wing, and it is their duty to safeguard the emotional health of these wards.

Not all ships have chaplains on board all the time, but when they do it follows that much of the pastoral as well as the spiritual welfare of the ship's company will become that person's main responsibility. That is the case tonight.

We wait on deck to see what happens. Eventually, we see three figures emerge from the shadows and head back to the ship. Trevor is flanked by Suzy on one side and Tommy on the other. Both have their arms around his shoulders.

'Sorted!' says Reg.

'*Coronation Street* has nothing on us,' says Rab. 'Right, I'm off to my pit. Goodnight!'

Location: Dubai. Port Rashid, Jetty 74
Date: 20 February 2005
Time: 09.00

Many of the ship's company have congregated on the flight deck. Tommy Goodwin is leaving this morning and he is being given a proper ship's send off. John Gardner, the XO, steps forward to address all those assembled.

'We are saying goodbye today to Tommy Goodwin – our chaplain who has been with us since before Christmas. Tommy has been vital to our welfare on HMS *Chatham* during this deployment – there for everybody all the time . . .'

As he extols the considerable virtues of Tommy Goodwin, I look around at all those who wanted to come and say goodbye to their chaplain. It is not compulsory to be here, but every rank and every branch is represented. Tommy stands in front of them meekly, but wearing his trademark smile.

'Of course, Tommy has had a particularly hectic time on board,' continues the XO. 'We spent Christmas at sea, as well as the New Year, always busy times for a man of the cloth, but Tommy also had to provide all the moral and spiritual support for the ship's company as we confronted the huge challenge of providing humanitarian aid and relief to Sri Lanka immediately after the tsunami. Tommy, we will miss you, but we wish you lots of luck in your new post in Scotland – and we would like to give you this as a small token to remember us by.'

John Gardner hands the chaplain a framed picture – it is a collection of photographs taken of Tommy throughout his time on board. It shows him taking services on the flight deck, in the senior officers' mess (the ship's makeshift chapel) and of course in the thick of it in Sri Lanka.

Tommy accepts the picture gratefully and then steps forward to say a few words.

'Brothers and Sisters,' he starts in his characteristic way. 'I would like to thank you for this magnificent memento of my time here. It has been a very special time, and I will never forget HMS *Chatham* and all of you who make her the ship that she is. Yesterday, at the Seaman's Mission, I was relaxing with a lot of you around the pool. I took the opportunity then of making a few notes about what to say to you today, and I ended up writing a short poem. It is quickly written, but it is from the heart. I would like to read it to you now if I may. I have called it simply "Shipmates".'

Tommy unfolds two sheets of lined writing paper that he takes from his back pocket and begins to read a poem about his time on board HMS Chatham. Everyone listens attentively, drawn in by his soft Scottish brogue and warmly remembering all the times shared.

Minutes later Tommy is walking down the gangway and leaving for the next adventure in his career.

HMS *Chatham* prepares to depart as well. She is heading back to the Arabian Sea for a final period of patrolling the Gulf. In three weeks she will be heading home – but on the way she has already been tasked with two very special and unique duties: one in Egypt and another in Turkey.

CHAPTER ELEVEN

Raising the Dead

We are born, we live, we die. We are remembered by the loved ones we leave behind and anybody else whose lives we touched or influenced through our own existence. As it is with people, so it is with ships. In my time with the Navy many of my experiences touched on the metaphysical. the spiritual and, sometimes, the downright spooky.

Location: Devonport dockyard. Weston Mill Lake, Wharf 15
Date: 15 April 2005
Time: 09.30

The last time I saw Tommy the Bish was in the United Arab Emirates. He was on the quayside at Dubai, waving us all goodbye as *Chatham* returned to her duties in the Gulf. He was returning home for a spot of well-deserved leave before taking up a new appointment at the Faslane submarine base in his beloved Scotland. Today, however, he is back in Plymouth for a funeral – well sort of. He is presiding at the decommissioning ceremony of HMS *Norfolk* – a Type 23 Frigate and a hapless victim of the recent defence cuts. Be that as it may, when a ship comes to the end of her working life in the Royal Navy she is not simply discarded like some decrepit 'old banger', but celebrated by her present ship's company as well as many of those who may have served on her in the past. This is testimony to the fact that, in a very unworldly sense, a ship is deemed to have a soul – and her passing is imbued with religious symbolism and ritual.

HMS *Norfolk* is tied up alongside at Berth 14 in Frigate Alley. She is spotless and gleaming, with the Union Jack fluttering at her bow and the

White Ensign waving proudly at her stern. Visitors are arriving by car
and coach and beginning to fill up the temporary stand erected on the
quayside in front of the ship. Tommy saunters up the jetty with his customary smile and an outstretched hand.

'Glad to see you got back from Dubai OK,' I say to him.

'Ach, it's good to be back in Scotland, but I miss everybody on
Chatham. Have you heard from them?'

'No,' I reply, 'but I am actually rejoining her tomorrow – out in
Alexandria.'

'Great!' says Tommy enthusiastically. 'Please send the ship my
regards. She is having quite a time isn't she? Extraordinary deployment.'

'Absolutely,' I nod, as I follow his gaze over to HMS *Norfolk*.

'Oh, she's looking great, isn't she?' he says. 'Shame we have to say
goodbye to her today, but it has to be done. She is one of the other ships
in my parish, along with *Chatham* and *Newcastle*, so it is down to me to
officiate today. Always a bit sad these events. Anyway, I'd better go and
get ready. See you later for a drink, Chris.'

As I wait for the ceremony to start, I wander over to the edge of the
quay and have a closer look at HMS *Norfolk*. She has the classic sleek
lines of all Type 23s, as well as a steely, stealthy poise that is all her own.
Over the past fifteen years she has become like all ships, more than just
a ship of war. She has also been an important instrument in the government's overall foreign and domestic policy, keeping the peace and
flying the flag in such diverse areas of the world as the Falkland Islands,
Brunei, Sierra Leone; at home during the fire-fighters' strike as well as in
the northern Arabian gulf. She certainly seems to have lived up to her
motto: 'Serviens Servo' ('Serving, I Preserve').

The decision to decommission her was a political one and part of
the defence cuts that have reduced the Royal Navy to just thirty-one
major warships – three short of the French Navy. Defence cuts are
always controversial, but I know from the time I am spending with
sailors that they are finding it difficult to come to terms with some of the
strangling reductions in budgets that are so constraining a navy that has
ever-increasing global duties to perform.

As I look at HMS *Norfolk* I remind myself of HMS *Chatham* having to
redeploy to Sri Lanka, leaving her post in the Gulf that could not be
filled by another Royal Navy ship. I also think of *Chatham* not handing
over to HMS *Portland* as planned when she left the Gulf, because *Portland* had to be redeployed to the Falklands. Then I think right back to

the Inter Command Boxing Championships, when half the boxers had to leave for West Africa on the *Albion* before the final bouts could be fought. The Royal Navy is nothing but overstretched, and yet here is a warship, only fifteen years old, that will either be scrapped or sold on to another navy.

The ship's company has mustered on the jetty by 10.25, and all the guests have arrived and taken their places in the stand: family members of the ship's company, former ship's company representatives, and VIPs. The Royal Marine Band strikes up with 'Life on the Ocean Wave' and marches smartly past the ship to take its place by the side of the public stand. An honour guard follows, carrying rifles with bayonets

THE ROYAL MARINE BAND
MARCHES PAST HMS
NORFOLK

fixed and with chin straps down. It comes to a halt in front of the public stand, forming into two ranks, ready for inspection. Now, the entire ship's company, immaculate in their brushed and pressed Number One uniforms, complete with medals, form up smartly in front of their ship. They are led by officers, all of whom carry ceremonial swords.

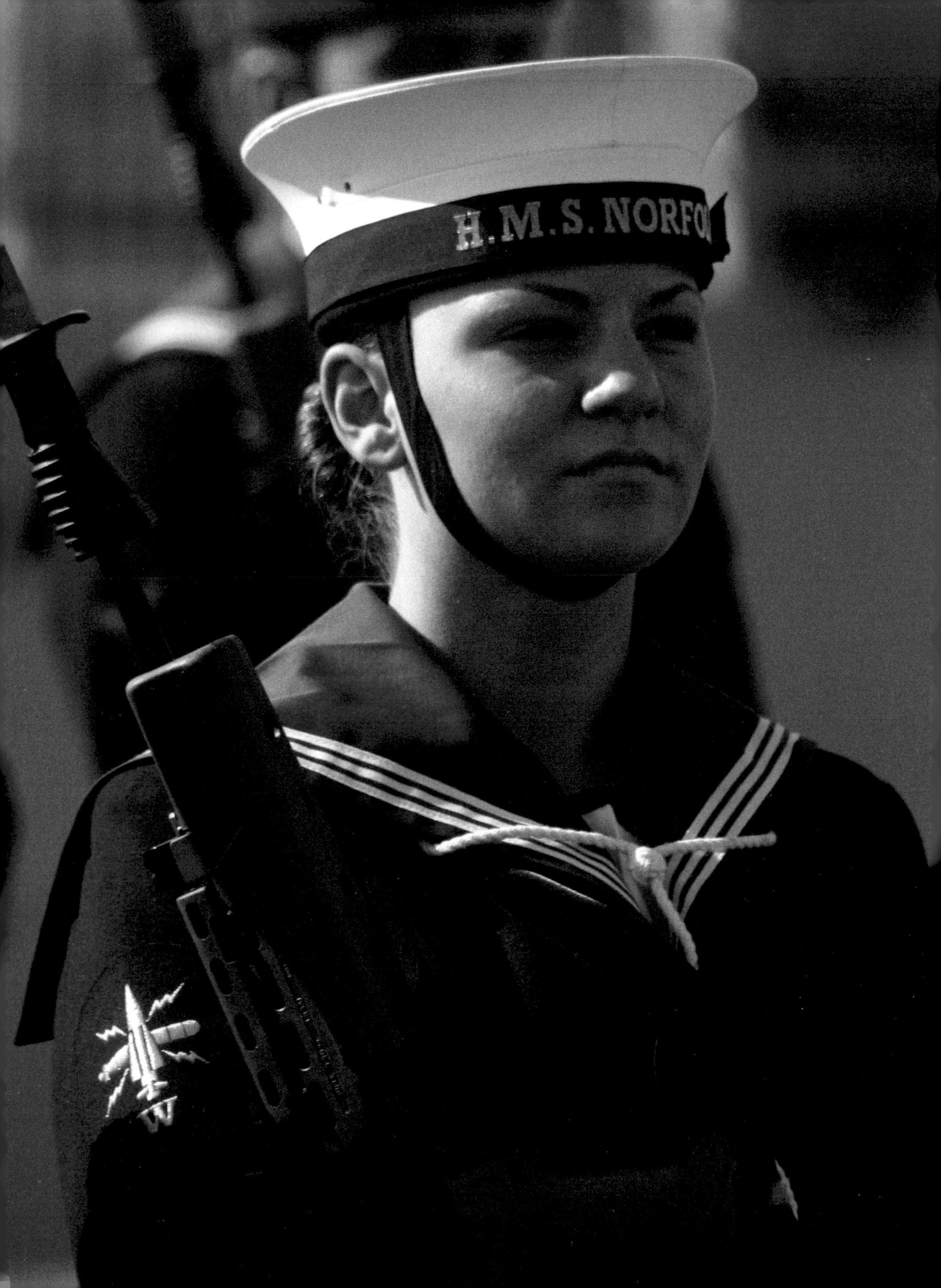
H.M.S. NORFO

At 10.30 the guest of honour arrives. He is Admiral Sir Jonathan Band, KBE, Commander in Chief of the Fleet and the first Commanding Officer of HMS *Norfolk* when she was newly launched. This tall and charismatic admiral, who, it has recently been announced, will be the next First Sea Lord, inspects the guard. Resplendent in his admiral's dress uniform, he stops to talk to most of the young men and women, some of whom he probably recognises because he makes it his business to get to know the sailors that serve him. Jonathan Band is typical of many of today's high-ranking officers: despite that phenomenally high rank, he is not remote or aloof. He does not hide behind his seniority, but commands through force of personality and a completely genuine interest in, and respect for, the people under him. He is highly respected himself, and admired by sailors and officers alike because he is always willing to talk to them on their terms. He does not talk down. I have met him many times in many different situations within the Navy, and I am always fascinated by his natural ability to put his subordinates at ease – and let's face it, that is nearly everyone else in the Navy and, when he becomes First Sea Lord, it will be everyone. As I watch the commander in chief move from the guard to the ranks of the ship's company, where he continues to chat with stokers, gunners, stewards, store accountants and weapons engineers, I am struck by the symbolism of the scene playing out in front of me. Here is a warship that has served her country and is about to be consigned to the history books, but her final tasking is to provide the dramatic backdrop to a ceremony that not only marks her own demise but is one in which the man whose duty it will be to lead the Royal Navy into the future is talking personally to the very young sailors who will make that future happen. The past, the present and the future are here before us strangely entwined.

Admiral Band takes his seat in the stand and the current commanding officer of HMS *Norfolk*, Lieutenant Commander Martin Simpson, walks up the steps of the dais to make his address. He does not face the assembled guests, but speaks in the direction of the ship's company and the ship herself.

In a strong and steadfast voice he welcomes everybody to the decommissioning ceremony and service of thanksgiving in honour, as he says of 'HMS *Norfolk* and all her people past and present'. He contin-

FACING PAGE:
A SAILOR OF HMS *NORFOLK*
SAYS GOODBYE TO HER SHIP

ues by thanking everybody for taking the time to pay special tribute to a ship that has been their workplace and home over many years.

He thanks Admiral Band for attending, and then gives special thanks to Tommy Goodwin, saying that he had become an integral part of the ship over the last eighteen months. He describes him as a 'man of great passion, cheerfulness and fortitude', adding that 'he has my undying admiration as a man who ministered in the city of Glasgow and still believes in God!'

Martin Simpson waits for the wave of laughter to die down before continuing in more serious vein.

'As we decommission *Norfolk*, we should be careful not to consider this necessarily a sad day, but there is always a sense of wistful inevitability about saying goodbye to a ship at the end of her service life . . .'

His voice is already reverberating with emotion, but his delivery is stage-perfect. All eyes and ears are on him as he continues his speech. He projects with passion – this is his moment and he clearly has a message to impart.

'I'm very aware of the feeling of many gathered here today that, whilst ultimately predictable, *Norfolk*'s decommissioning may be somewhat premature . . .'

The commanding officer pauses to look up at the assembled ship's company before him and seems to catch their collective eye, as if to say, 'This is for you guys.'

'From the day she was launched *Norfolk* has taken on the life and spirit of those who have served her, becoming variously a home, an office, a workshop, schoolroom, restaurant, conference centre, diplomatic mission, party venue and even, at times, a sunbed . . .'

The joke relieves the growing emotional tension that is rising in everyone.

'. . . It is this versatility and constant metamorphosis that embodies the character that is inherent in every Royal Naval warship, and *Norfolk* is no exception.'

A flock of raucous seagulls interrupts the proceedings, but once they have passed the speech is continued.

'A ship is an expression of the personality of the ship's company, and one that goes beyond the mere shape and lines of her hull. I am extremely proud of the ship's company here before me who, despite the knowledge that *Norfolk*'s days were numbered, have maintained the standards of professionalism and pride in our ship right up to the last.

Even though shortly she will no longer be part of the Royal Navy, she has been looked after with such obvious pride and dignity that, fifteen years on, she is still looking good – and, if necessary, still ready to do her duty . . .'

I look back to the stand and see more than one naval wife, girlfriend or mother dabbing at their eyes with a tissue.

The CO steps down and Tommy Goodwin steps forward. For a small man Tommy always packs a punch, and he is immediately into his stride, unleashing his vibrant, rich Scottish brogue.

'Brothers and Sisters, we come together to worship God, our heavenly father, and to give him thanks for all those, past and present, who have served our Sovereign and country faithfully on HMS *Norfolk*. As one ship's company we celebrate the fellowship of the Royal Navy, and we rejoice in our ship's achievements . . .'

REVEREND TOMMY GOODWIN AT THE DECOMMISSIONING OF HMS *NORFOLK*

I have seen Tommy in action so many times now, but I still find his style completely compelling. So do all who hear him. It does not matter whether you are a Christian, a Muslim, a Hindu or an atheist, Tommy manages to appeal to something deep within you.

'Brothers and Sisters, I guess farewells bring strange emotions. I think it was a songwriter who penned the words "Breaking up is hard to do", and this morning there is a sense in which this act of decommissioning is hard to do, because all of us gathered here invested something in the ship we have come to say goodbye to. We were all sent to serve in different ways, at different times, in different places and given different tasks, yet it was HMS *Norfolk* that brought us all together. Her commission gave us a sense of purpose. Her commission gave us a sense of being involved in a shared assignment. She gave us a place to belong to, a place to experience life and community as men and women. And in a strange way, as she was sent to protect the weak and defeat those who would disrupt world peace through her steely presence, she gave us some stability, security and safety as she sailed the high seas.

'And so for us this act of decommissioning is hard to do. And yet it's also an act in which we're happy to share, because HMS *Norfolk* has brought us all together again, and as we gather together this morning, we acknowledge together as a ship's company that she has fulfilled her mission. She has completed her part in the ongoing task facing the Royal Navy. She has done what was asked of her. She has fought the good fight. She has finished the race. She has finished her deployment. She has finished her commission. She has kept the faith. It's hard to do. Yet we must be happy to share in this passing, because the reality is, though we are saying farewell to a shell made of steel, we are not actually saying goodbye to HMS *Norfolk* because in your heart and my heart, in *our* hearts, her spirit lives on. Because you are HMS *Norfolk*, I am HMS *Norfolk*, we are HMS *Norfolk* together. As we accept new assignments, go on new missions, we take the spirit of *Norfolk* with us. And as we do what we do, we will help the Royal Navy to continue to be the best navy in the world. Let us pray . . .'

Finally, Admiral Band steps forward. His deep voice promises gravitas but instead delivers emotion. He is clearly moved by the occasion.

'Ladies and Gentlemen. I . . . I have to admit, even though I was the first commanding officer of this ship, the guard is better today than the one we had fifteen years ago . . .'

I am interested to see if the admiral will refer to the defence cuts that have cost the Navy not only HMS *Norfolk* but at least two other frigates as well. He has to be careful because right now, in mid-April, we are in the lead-up to a general election, and he has to avoid anything remotely political in his public speeches. In the Navy this period is referred to as 'purdah', and that is why no press, other than myself, are present at this ceremony. The admiral knows I will be writing about today's decommissioning, but not till long after purdah is ended, so I am wondering whether he will let his guard down, just for a moment.

'We all knew that ships would be decommissioned when we heard the defence budget announcements last year . . . and I feared then that *Norfolk* would be one to go.'

The admiral pauses to look up at the ship and then at the ship's company before continuing.

'Right, it's not just because of the election that I think I will *not* say something I might want to . . .' he says enigmatically, '. . . but the decision has been made and that's that. All I will say is that I accept it, if the price for paying off *Norfolk*, *Marlborough* and *Grafton* is the safety of the future equipment and capability programme in the Royal Navy, because we must continue to modernise and there is a premium on quality in the world we face . . .'

Again, he pauses and looks around at his audience.

With a rising voice he launches into an impassioned defence of the Type 23 Frigate, pointing out that not only is it ideal for patrolling duties, force protection, boarding and interdiction operations, but also that it is able to step up to the exacting demands of 'a high-intensity operation' – in other words, war, – at a moment's notice. It is this flexibility that Admiral Band clearly values in his strategic overview of the modern Navy, and he is making it clear that it is something that must be appreciated by the politicians as well.

ADMIRAL JONATHAN BAND GIVES AN EMOTIONAL SPEECH AT THE DECOMMISSIONING OF HMS *NORFOLK*

'Most of the remaining ships in this class, like *Norfolk*'s sister ship *Westminster*, are the guardians of surface-based anti-submarine warfare well into the future and, by God . . .' he says with pointed emphasis, '. . . we had better keep that core skill. I know if I was an enemy submarine commanding officer coming across a Type 23, with new low-frequency sonar, with surface ship defence and torpedo defence, I would be pretty sure I would not be picking up my pension . . .'

There is no doubt that the admiral is struggling with his emotions. As the first commanding officer of a ship that is minutes away from her demise, he must be feeling the sense of finality very acutely.

'The great thing is . . . and this . . . is my final message to you . . .'

The admiral's voice begins to waver.

'Excuse me . . .' he says, as he composes himself.

'My final message to you is…take the *Norfolk* spirit with you, wherever you go. Thank you.'

It is 11.25, and the ceremonial officer shouts a simple order: 'Ship's company will about turn. About turn!'

The entire ship's company turns through a hundred and eighty degrees. All now face HMS *Norfolk*. A Royal Marine bugler steps forward, comes smartly to attention and raises his bugle. The people in the stand get to their feet. There is a moment of silence before the guard of honour presents arms – the signal for the bugler to play the haunting strains of the Last Post. As he does so, dutymen at either end of the ship start to lower the ship's flags. At the bow the Union Jack descends slowly, as does the White Ensign at the stern. When they are fully lowered it will signify that HMS *Norfolk*'s decommission has been completed.

It is 11.28. *Norfolk* is no longer a Royal Navy warship.

Location: Egypt. Alexandria
Date: 17 April 2005

I have flown into the sprawling city of Alexandria, Egypt's second city and famous naval port into which HMS *Chatham* is due to sail tomorrow morning. She has finished her patrol duties in the Gulf and is on her way home, in a roundabout sort of way. She still has a heavy schedule of duties to fulfil, including one here in Alexandria – an unusual one to say the least.

The press release from the British Embassy in Cairo describes it thus: 'The primary aim of the visit of Her Majesty's Ship *Chatham* is to undertake a suitable ceremony by the Commanding Officer and the Ship's Company to rebury the remains of 30 British sailors and soldiers dating from the Napoleonic Wars.' Royal Navy ships are often required to perform ceremonial duties but, by any standards, this one is extraordinary.

It all started 207 years ago at the Battle of the Nile – long considered the Royal Navy's most daring operation. In 1798, Napoleon Bonaparte sailed with a French invading force to occupy Egypt, from where he planned to challenge British domination in India. Nelson, sent to hunt for Napoleon's fleet across the Mediterranean, finally sighted the seventeen French vessels in the late evening of 1 August, at a place called Abu Qir, off the coast of Egypt. The French admiral, Admiral Brueys, had set his gunships in a line close to the shallow coastal waters, fully assuming that no vessel would or could sneak behind. Such was his certainty that he did not even bother to prepare the land-facing guns. He also believed the British would wait until the next morning to join battle. Nelson, who was to suffer serious head wounds in the ensuing fight, had other ideas. Five British vessels sailed into the shallows behind the French fleet, while the British admiral led an assault from the front. Combining surprise with far superior seamanship, the Royal Navy ships swarmed around each French vessel in turn, destroying or capturing all but four of the enemy ships. The French lost 1,400 men. Nelson lost just 218 men and no vessels, establishing him as the pre-eminent admiral of his time. Notwithstanding Trafalgar, this is widely seen as his finest hour. Overnight, the British had annihilated their French foes and left Napoleon's army stranded in Egypt. Napoleon fled to France, his ambition, to use Egypt to challenge British domination of India, in tatters. Three years later the Royal Navy returned, this time to deliver General Abercrombie's 12,000-strong army to Abu Qir bay, in order to rout the remaining French troops in Egypt and take the country for the British crown. It was another successful military operation for the British forces, even though casualties were lost both to the battle and to disease. It is some of these casualties, killed over 200 years ago at both the Battle of the Nile and the Battle of Abu Qir Bay, that HMS *Chatham* is coming in to re-inter tomorrow.

Location: Green Plaza Hilton. Breakfast bar
Time: 08.30

Whilst I am in Alexandria, I am staying at the Green Plaza Hilton towards the north of the city, where I am told I will be able to meet with several key people responsible for the burial ceremony – notably I need

NICK SLOPE AT NELSON'S
ISLAND

A NELSONIAN SAILOR
REVEALED

to look out for Nick Slope, the British archaeologist who recovered the remains.

I have taken my buffet breakfast to a small table next to a massive potted palm in the middle of the expansive dining hall. My plan is to leaf through the itinerary for the day, given to me by a British consulate official who met me at the airport, and then, after breakfast, check at reception for the room numbers of the various people I need to track down – in particular Nick Slope. As the waiter pours my coffee I notice the man at the table next to mine. He is middle-aged, with cropped reddish hair, and hirsute, but that is not what catches my attention. It is that he is frantically fielding telephone calls on his mobile which keep coming one after the other.

Ring, ring. 'Hello, who is that? . . . CNN?. . . . Yes, I am Nick Slope. I could give you an interview later, around 11.00 . . . OK. Goodbye' . . . *Ring, ring* . . . 'Hello, Nick Slope . . . BBC radio? . . . an interview . . . yes . . . about 11.30. Call me on this number . . . Bye.' . . . *Ring, ring* . . . 'Hello, Nick Slope here . . . Who? . . . the *Egyptian Chronicle* . . . ?'

In a lull between calls I lean over to his table and catch his attention.

'Nick Slope?' I enquire needlessly.

'Yes,' replies the bearded and bewildered archaeologist.

I introduce myself.

'Oh, you are with the *Chatham*?' he says effusively. 'Great. Come and join me. Would you like some more coffee?' . . . *Ring, ring* . . . 'Good God, it never stops . . . do excuse me . . .'

After the request for yet another interview, Nick calls over the waiter to ask for more coffee, and then explains what is happening.

'It's gone completely mad. The press are going crazy over this story, and yet I have had such trouble getting funding for the excavations – you just wouldn't believe it . . .'

'It's an amazing story,' I say. 'So how did it all start? When did you make the discovery?'

'Well, I didn't make the initial discovery – that was an Italian archaeologist called Paulo Gallo. Since 2001 he has been excavating on a small island just off Alex called Nelson Island, in Abu Qir Bay. He was looking for Greek-Roman artefacts but then started discovering human bones – lots of them. Also, whole bodies in coffins.'

'That's when you got involved?' .

'Yes. It soon became apparent that these were British bodies, because of the uniforms, and I specialise in military, especially naval, archaeology.'

'And the bodies are from Nelson's Navy?'

'Oh, yes. Some are from the Battle of the Nile in 1798 when Nelson beat up the French Fleet, but most are probably from the British Expeditionary landings in 1801 at Abu Qir Bay, when the British returned to kick the French out of Egypt. British casualties from both the Navy and the Army were buried on this small island which they named after Nelson himself.'

'How many bodies have you found?'

'Thirty-two – but I reckon there could be at least another hundred on the island. The thing is, Nelson Island is being eroded by the sea and is slowly disappearing. That's why we are here now, to bury the ones we have found. We will be putting the remains of many bodies into the same coffins, although complete remains will have a coffin of their own. Tomorrow the burials will be done with full military honours. As you know, HMS *Chatham* will be doing the honours, literally. It's very exciting. Great to have the Navy with us – so appropriate – especially

Chatham, because the *Chatham* at the time was the ship that was eventually to carry Nelson's body down the Thames from Greenwich to Whitehall.'

'Do you know the identity of any of the bodies?'

'We know one of them is a woman known only as G, and another is an infant who was almost certainly her newborn child – possibly the wife and child of a sailor. Because they were away at sea for such long periods, they were often allowed to bring their wives and children on board. The women would be given duties, like helping the surgeon with the wounded, or providing gunpowder to the gunners during battle. So, having women at sea is not as recent a development as people think.'

'What about sailors?' I enquire. 'Have you identified any?'

'Just one. Master and Commander James Russell of HMS *Cerise*, who died of fever, aged thirty-four, in 1801. We have two of his relatives over from the UK to attend the burial – Gordon and Joan Watson. I arranged to see them in the lobby about now. Come on, I'll introduce you.'

Gordon and Joan Watson are two of the most extraordinary people I have ever met. He is eighty-seven and she is eighty-three and they are throwbacks to a bygone era – charming, witty and wonderfully eccentric in that 'terribly British' sort of way.

'Hello!' says Gordon when he meets me. 'BBC, eh? Do you know Sally – the girl on the Southern news? I like her tremendously. Very gutsy – always going off to somewhere or other.'

GORDON AND JOAN WATSON ATTRACTING A LOT OF ATTENTION

'Sorry,' I say, 'I'm afraid I don't know Sally.'

'Oh, no matter. Joan dear, this is Chris from the BBC.'

'Hello, Chris,' says Joan brightly. 'We like the BBC – you can stay.'

'Thank you,' I say rather coyly.

'Isn't this marvellous?' says Gordon. 'Absolutely thrilling. Didn't know I had an ancestor in the Navy, so what a turn-up for the books eh? Flew in yesterday. Haven't flown since the Second World War, you know. I was RAF actually, not Navy. So was Joan.'

'Yes,' says Joan with a broad smile. 'I was a WAAF. A mechanic on Lancaster bombers.'

POST CAPTAIN JAMES RUSSELL – ANCESTOR OF GORDON AND JOAN WATSON

JAMES RUSSELL EXTRACTED FROM THE SANDS OF NELSON ISLAND

'Loved the WAAFS,' pipes in Gordon. 'Looked terrific in uniforms, don't you know,' he laughs, before adding, 'I still have an eye for the ladies, even now.'

'It's true!' says Joan. 'I think that's what keeps him young!'

The constant repartee betrays an energy and a youthfulness beyond their considerable years. Gordon is small, a little shrunken with age, but sprightly. He has snowy white hair and wears a permanent, beaming smile. Joan is about the same height, with short-cropped white hair and a sparkle in her eyes. When they are not holding hands, Gordon has his arm slung over his wife's shoulder.

'I say, dear,' says Gordon, peering out of the window. 'Look at that view. Isn't it marvellous? Absolutely terrific.'

There is something inspiring about this elderly gentleman who is not only completely unconcerned by his advancing years, but also continues to be amazed by life and all its riches. He is also, totally unselfconsciously, desperately proud of being English. Somehow it seems entirely appropriate that one of his ancestors was a Master and Commander in Nelson's navy.

Location: Alexandria. British Consulate
Time: 12.00

We have come to the British Consulate to see the coffins before they are moved to the Chatby Cemetery (the British and Commonwealth War Graves Cemetery in Alexandria), where the ceremony will be held tomorrow afternoon. Nick Slope leads us through the gates of the consulate and towards the back of the building. As we walk into a small courtyard, Gordon Watson takes a deep breath as he sees the first of five coffins being brought from the building and laid on the ground.

'Oh my goodness gracious! Heavens above. Joan, my dear, will you look at that.'

Nick Slope gently guides the couple to the first coffin in the line.

'That's James Russell, your ancestor.'

For the first time today, Gordon and Joan are silent. They look at the wooden coffin for long minutes. I think maybe Gordon is even saying a prayer. Eventually, he stoops down and gently touches the lid of the coffin.

'I say, I do think these coffins are darned smart. I like the brass adornments. Joan, aren't they marvellous?'

The Egyptian workers who have been lifting the coffins are resting in the shade, and have been watching the elderly English couple with interest. Gordon walks over to them.

'Thank you so much for doing all that hard work and treating the coffins so gently. I do thank you tremendously,' he beams. He then goes round to each man to shake his hand. 'Thank you very much,' he says to each bemused Egyptian in turn. Despite not speaking any English, they all return a genuine smile to the old Englishman with his heart so clearly pinned to his sleeve for all to see.

'This is bloody amazing,' says Nick Slope. 'Three years ago, when I started this work, I never thought it would get to this: a military burial for these men, found under the sands of Nelson Island. It's like a dream – and you only meet people like Gordon and Joan in dreams, don't you?'

We leave the consulate as the coffins are loaded on to a lorry and transported across town to the Chatby Cemetery, where they will wait overnight.

The Following Morning
Location: Alexandria. Naval Base
Time: 08.58

I am standing on the quayside with the naval attaché to Egypt, waiting for HMS *Chatham* to arrive. She is due at 09.00 and, once she is tied up alongside, sixty sailors are being bussed to the Chatby Cemetery for a full rehearsal of the ceremony to be performed this afternoon. It will be a tight schedule.

We peer out to sea, but the visibility is poor due to a combination of heat and the after-effects of a sandstorm. I look down at my watch and at that very instant the naval attaché shouts out briskly, 'I have visual of HMS *Chatham*.' On the dot of 09.00, HMS *Chatham*'s bow appears round the headland. She turns to starboard and heads past a line of Egyptian warships, towards Jetty 16 where she will berth. She is dead on time.

It is good to see the familiar outline of the frigate emerge out of the Egyptian haze and, as I watch this little piece of Britain glide towards us, I am reminded of the words of HMS *Norfolk*'s commanding officer just three days ago at his ship's emotional decommissioning: 'A ship is an expression of the personality of the ship's company, and one that goes beyond the mere shape and lines of her hull.'

Since she left Plymouth in December, HMS *Chatham* has assumed many identities – a ship of war in the Gulf, a ship of peace and hope in Sri Lanka, a ship of fun in Dubai and now, in Egypt, she is about to become a ship of ceremony and national pride. She will have ticked all the boxes: operational, recreational, and soon decorational. Yet, all the time, in whatever guise, she has remained a home and sanctuary for a community of men and women who have been welded into a family of kindred spirits. They might have their ups and downs, as in any family, and some days might be better than others, but when all is said and done, these people 'are' the ship; HMS *Chatham* 'is' her ship's company. Her steely identity as a cold instrument of war is belied by the collective identity she is given by the people on board, from Captain Chick down to the most junior rating.

HMS *Chatham* nudges herself, with a little help from a single Egyptian tug, into her position alongside. The mooring lines are thrown ashore and are secured around several bollards. Then there is the final flourish of any berthing by a British warship – the raising of the Union

Flag at the bow of the ship. The flag, hauled up the jackstay, immediately catches the warm Egyptian breeze and patriotically signals the ship's presence for all to see. The Navy is here. HMS *Chatham*, 'Up and At'Em', has arrived.

'Hello, mate!' shouts a familiar voice from the flight deck.

'Hello, Rab,' I shout back. 'How are you doing?'

'Mustn't grumble, but then again I'm a sailor, so perhaps I should!' he laughs.

'Have you recovered from Dubai?' I ask, recalling that the last time I saw Rab was the night when we had helped each other to get up the gangway after that particularly alcohol-driven run ashore at the Rock Bottom night club.

'Oh, yeah. Well over that one, mate. Looking forward to the next, but it won't be for a while 'cos of all this ceremonial we gotta do. Stopped doin' the "operational", now we gotta do a bit of "decorational" before we can get on with the "recreational"!'

Ratz Rackliff is on the quarterdeck, dressed in civvies. 'I'm off home!' he shouts. 'Got to get home for the last few weeks leading up to the birth. Can't let Theresa do it all on her own!'

'Good luck Ratz!' I shout. 'See you back in Plymouth.'

'You bet! I will be on the quayside when the ship comes home, with the baby Rackliff in my arms!'

Location: Alexandria. Chatby Cemetery
Time: 10.30

Three coaches of sailors from Chatham have arrived at the cemetery. Sixty men and women in blue working rig walk into the tranquil grounds to rehearse for this afternoon's ceremony. Twenty are to form the guard of honour, who will fire three rifle volleys over the graves. Another thirty will be the coffin bearers, and the rest, mostly officers, will lead the procession to the graves into which the coffins will be gently lowered. The *Chatham* sailors have tried to practise their ceremonial duties on the ship as they came up through the Red Sea and the Suez Canal, but it is difficult to march on a moving ship and graves could only be imagined. They have just two hours to rehearse, and want to get it right because there is going to be a lot of press present. Then I notice that Rab Butler is one of the honour guard.

'Rab,' I say. 'Were you told to do this, or are you on punishment or something?'

'Nah! Volunteered for this one, didn't I?' he replies with a broad smile. 'Learned a long time ago to never volunteer for nothin' if you want to keep your life sweet, but this is different, I reckon. Really wanted to do this – but Jesus, we 'ave to get crackin' 'cos we were all over the bleedin' place on the ship. It's always dangerous to ask a sailor to march, and we can't afford to get this one wrong.'

All over the cemetery, sailors are practising marching, coming to attention and shouldering arms, or else they are rehearsing how to pick up coffins and slow march to the strict funereal beat of sixty-four paces to the minute to music which is provided by an Egyptian Army band.

Gordon and Joan Watson have arrived to take a look at the proceedings, and are immediately impressed by the efforts being put into the day.

'I think it is wonderful that the Navy is here,' says Gordon. 'It makes me proud to be British. It's fantastic . . .' He breaks off from what he was going to say, and his voice falters. 'I . . . I . . . find it all very emotional here,' he says, looking at the rows upon rows of graves in the cemetery. Many of the inscriptions on the headstones simply say: 'An Unknown Sailor. Died 1939' or 'An Unknown Soldier. Died 1940'. The ones that are specific with names and ages betray the youthfulness of those who fell, many as young as nineteen or twenty years old.

'They were . . . just so . . . young,' Gordon stammers, his eyes filling with tears. 'We lost so many of our friends, and they were all so very young. If they had survived, our country would still be great today, I can tell you that.'

'You don't think our country is great now, Gordon?' I ask.

'Oh, it has great things about it, terrific things. Absolutely! But you see, we lost the cream of our young men back then. I don't think they have ever quite been replaced. These young sailors here today are splendid of course, quite splendid. And I love to see the girls there now – at first we weren't in favour of women at sea, but now we have come round, haven't we, dear?'

'Yes,' says Joan. 'We were a bit worried about it when they first announced it, but look at them now – just as good as the boys.'

'I just hope these young people never have to go through what we went through. All these graves are full of young men who died when they were the same age as these sailors in front of us now. Can you . . . can you . . . imagine that . . . so . . . so young.' Gordon falters again.

I try to imagine Gordon and Joan as young people. In 1939, at the outbreak of war, Gordon would have been twenty-one and Joan would have been seventeen.

'Of course, your friends who died will always be young,' I ventured.

'Absolutely,' says Gordon. 'What's that wonderful thing they say at Remembrance? "They shall grow not old, as we that are left grow old" … how does it go . . . um?'

A chief petty officer standing nearby overhears.

'Excuse me, sir,' he says softly, 'it continues like this: "Age shall not weary them nor the years condemn. At the going down of the sun and in the morning we will remember them." '

As the chief finishes, Gordon repeats the words under his breath, 'We will remember them.'

'Thank you, young man,' says Joan.

'Oh dear,' gasps Gordon, 'I am a very emotional man – I fear I will be overcome this afternoon.'

'No you won't,' insists Joan standing at his side. 'You might have a little cry later, but this afternoon you will be fine.'

Gordon nods in agreement and takes his wife's hand. This was team-work. Gordon and Joan are a well-practised team.

At midday the rehearsal is complete and the sailors return to HMS *Chatham* for lunch, and to change into their dress uniforms. Gordon and Joan Watson return to the hotel, also to get refreshed and to change – for this is to be their afternoon.

Location: Alexandria. Chatby Cemetery
Time 14.30

Everybody and everything is transformed. The coffins, laid out in a neat row near the entrance to the cemetery, are all draped in Union Jacks. The sailors are in their white tropical Number Ones, with many wearing medals gained from places like the Falklands, Afghanistan and the Gulf. The officers, also wearing whites and medals, carry swords. Gordon Watson is wearing a dark suit and Joan a floral dress. Both of them, like the sailors, wear their own medals, but theirs, of course, are from the Second World War.

FACING PAGE:
HMS *CHATHAM*'S BURIAL
PARTY AT ALEXANDRIA

'Did nothing particularly brave to get these – just served my country,' says Gordon. 'Very proud to have them, though. Do you think they are in the right place?'

'I think they might be a little higher, sir,' suggests a naval officer standing nearby.

'Really? Well, you chaps know the drill. Will you do it for me? Pin them a bit higher. Just above the pocket, you think?'

Once the medals have been adjusted, Gordon and Joan take their places in two of the front seats reserved for them as VIPs.

The couple sit flanked by the British Ambassador to Egypt, Sir Derek Plumbly, and the British Consul-General in Alexandria, Alan Cobden. Next to him is Nick Slope, looking excited, emotional and absolutely exhausted.

A seated group of about two hundred, including Egyptian ministers and even representatives of the French Navy, wait for proceedings to commence. To the left of them, a massive press corps is poised with every type of lens and microphone you could imagine. Immediately in front of them are six freshly dug graves. A silence descends over the crowd as an officer delivers a clear crisp order to the guard of honour at the front of the cemetery.

'Guard, slope arms! Guard, by the left slow march!'

Two Royal Marine buglers lead out the guard of honour and firing party in two marching ranks of twenty sailors. Every man and woman is immaculate – tropical whites, gaiters, SA 80 rifles and chin straps down. The marching is perfect and proud. 'Rab' Butler is at the head of the right-hand rank, looking as serious and as intent as I have ever seen him. He might act the clown and nurture an image as a bit of a hard man, but he has a soft centre and I know he will be feeling the emotion of this event very deeply. I am sure he will be thinking of his grandfather, tattooed on his back for posterity.

The guard of honour reaches its place next to the graves. 'Guard, Halt!' shouts the young officer leading them. 'Guard, lower on your arms reverse!'

The two ranks of sailors slowly bow their heads in one graceful, collective movement lasting exactly three seconds. Their heads will now remain bowed for the entire ceremony until they receive orders to fire a salute.

One of the Royal Marine buglers sounds an alert. This is the signal for the pall bearers on the other side of the cemetery to stand by the coffins – six sailors to every coffin, three on each side. 'Coffin party, lift!' comes the order. The coffins are slowly and steadily raised, and then lowered on to the shoulders of the bearers. 'Coffin party, by the left slow march!' The Egyptian Navy band strikes up a slow dirge – sixty-four beats per minute.

With measured steps the bearers take the remains of the British sailors, soldiers and marines towards their final resting place. It is a journey that has taken over two hundred years, and it will now be completed in a matter of minutes.

The procession winds sedately towards the graves, but the press pack are anything but sedate. Hemmed in by the VIPs, the guard of honour and a huge palm tree, some cameramen break ranks to get a better view. British Embassy officials and senior naval officers run to cut off the recalcitrant journalists and herd them back to their pen. Some photographers, meanwhile, are running between the ranks of the guard of

HMS *CHATHAM'S* BURIAL PARTY CARRY A COFFIN

honour. I notice Rab flinch as someone brushes next to him, trying to get a shot of the approaching coffins. Another photographer has decided to kneel right in front of the officer in charge of the guard, who is standing holding his sword upright. The officer whispers beneath his breath, 'Sir, in a little while I have to bring my sword down in front of me in a flourish. If you stay there, you are likely to lose an ear at the very least.' The photographer moves without hesitation and gladly seeks the safety of the pack from whence he came.

The pall bearers finally reach the burial place where they lower the coffins on to slats over the graves.

There follow addresses and prayers, before the Reverend Godfrey Hilliard, the Royal Navy Chaplain of the Fleet performs the Committal, during which the coffins are slowly lowered:

> Forasmuch as it hath pleased Almighty God of his great
> Mercy to take unto himself the soul of our brothers here
> departed, we therefore commit their remains to the ground;
> earth to earth, ashes to ashes, dust to dust . . .

I look over to Gordon Watson who has his eyes firmly on the coffin of his ancestor, Master and Commander James Russell. He watches it all the way into the grave. He then closes his eyes tightly and retreats into private thoughts and prayers.

Moments later the guard of honour is brought to attention and given a short sharp set of orders:

'Firing party, shoulder arms!

'Firing party, volleys with blank cartridge – load!

'Firing party, pre . . . sent!

'Volley one – Fire!

'Volley two – Fire!

'Volley three – Fire!'

The buglers sound the Last Post, then all becomes still for the observation of one minute's silence.

Gordon reaches for his wife's hand.

What goes through people's minds at such times? I can only tell you my own thoughts. They are a jumble of surreal images: white, weathered bones in shallow, sandy graves washed by lapping waves; nineteenth-century sailors and marines firing muskets from wave-tossed longboats; twentieth-century sailors manning anti-aircraft guns against swarms of attacking enemy aircraft; my Uncle Billy, whom I never knew – an RAF pilot, who was killed when his aircraft blew up in 1926 . . .

After the minute has run its course, the buglers sound Reveille and our thoughts are returned to the here and now.

Wreaths are now laid at the graves, and the Union Flag that draped the coffin of James Russell is carefully folded and then presented to Gordon Watson.

The guard of honour and coffin bearers march off and are dismissed. At this point, the press pack descend on Gordon and Joan and pepper them with questions: 'What did you think of the burial? How much do you know about James Russell? What did you do in the war? How long have you been married?'

The two of them field the questions admirably and amiably. Quite unabashed by the attention they are receiving, they answer every journalist with great courtesy and disarming honesty. Very soon the hardened hacks become putty in their hands. The quick-fire questions cease and Gordon holds court, speaking on just about anything he wants: England, cricket, the Navy, Nelson, and the monarchy. The journalists, from all over the world, are being charmed and they just sit back and enjoy the experience that is the Watsons.

I walk out of the cemetery to look for Rab and meet him gulping down some water.

'How was that Rab?' I ask.

'Yeah – had to bow me 'ead for twenty minutes during all the speeches and minute's silence. Got quite "emotional".'

'Ah, it got to you a bit, did it?

'Nah, I don't mean emotional in that way. I mean it got bleedin' uncomfortable. That rifle gets 'eavy after a while. "Emotional" as in a pain in the arse . . . well, arm anyway!'

I push him. 'You mean it didn't affect you at all, Rab?'

'Oh yeah. Of course it did. I was proud really. I mean matelots are matelots aren't they, in any time of history. What gets me about these geezers tho' is that they did all their fighting close range – 'and to bleedin' 'and sometimes. In the modern Navy we tend to fight from a distance. Awesome really, when you fink about what they 'ad to go through, eh?' He ponders for a moment and then takes another long swig of water. 'But that rifle did get bleedin' 'eavy after a while, and when one of them journalists nearly trod on me toe when I 'ad me 'ead bowed, I nearly shoved it up 'is jacksie!'

I return to the cemetery gates to say goodbye to Gordon and Joan Watson, and find them talking to a group of sailors.

'Thank you so much for that,' Gordon is saying. 'It made me so proud, and you all did it beautifully. Perfect marching with all the guns and everything. Tremendous!'

'Thank you, sir,' says one young sailor. 'We are very glad to have done it, aren't we, fellas?' Everybody agrees.

'Wonderful,' replies Gordon. 'May I ask how old you are young man?'

'Nineteen, sir.'

'Terrific,' says Gordon. 'Good age. Absolutely tremendous!'

One Year Earlier

An extraordinary counterpart to the Alexandria burials occurred in 2004, when I heard not only that Devonport dockyard was meant to be haunted, but that the Navy was calling in a team of 'ghostbusters' to investigate reports of strange sounds and presences.

Location: Devonport dockyard
Date: 23 October 2004
Time: 11.30

I am walking through the old part of the dockyard, known as South Yard, with Commander Charles Crichton who heads up the Naval Base Visitors Centre. We are going to visit the Ropery, a very long eighteenth-century building that was used for rope-making in the past, but which now houses the dockyard museum. Underneath it is the Hangman's Cell, with a gallows which was allegedly used to execute over a hundred men – all of them French prisoners from the Napoleonic Wars. Many naval ratings have reportedly been unnerved by a 'strange ' atmosphere in this cell. Next to the Ropery is a deserted four-storey house, a listed building, called the Master Ropemaker's House. All manner of ghostly goings-on have been reported here as well. They include sightings of a young girl, aged between five and ten, dressed in Victorian costume and playing with her toys around the house. Naval security staff have seen lights going on and off in the house, even though it has been empty for years. A bearded eighteenth-century naval officer has also been seen on several occasions.

'I try to keep an open mind about all this,' says Charles Crichton in his lilting northern Irish accent, 'but there have been so many reports of paranormal activities over the years, and many of them have been from tough Ministry of Defence policemen who have been patrolling the yard at night. On more than one occasion, I have been told, they have had to "leg it" after sensing something out of the ordinary.'

It is a sunny day and, as we walk around the supposedly haunted locations, they do not strike me as particularly eerie, but the buildings in this part of the dockyard are certainly old and very isolated from the main dockyard.

'We have a big team of paranormal investigators coming later,' says Charles Crichton. 'They are going to spend the next two nights here with night-vision cameras, laser thermometers, dowsing rods and hi-tech sound detection equipment, hoping to gather evidence.'

Commander Crichton has invited the team in to try to prove or disprove scientifically whether the paranormal is at work in the dockyard, and I have permission to be with them for the duration of their experiments. Let me come clean now – I am a sceptic, but, like Commander Crichton, I am going to keep as open a mind as I can.

We return to Commander Crichton's office, set in a beautiful Georgian house not far from the Ropery. The leader of the paranormal team has arrived. Her name is Carole Bromley, although she works under the name of 'Goldie'.

'I have been a paranormal investigator for some years now,' she says brightly. 'I used to be a sceptic myself, but then I started becoming aware of something around me – a different sort of energy – and then I realised these were spirits. There were just a few at first but now – goodness – my home is like Heathrow Airport!'

Soon the rest of the team arrive, about twenty in all, and they are immediately briefed by Goldie.

'We are here to collect evidence,' she says. 'With the history of the place, and particularly the deaths that have occurred here, it's got classic potential!'

After dark, we walk to the Master Ropemaker's House. Without the comforting benefit of daylight, the place feels very different from this afternoon. It does feel spooky. Maybe this is auto-suggestion, or it may be to do with the fact that the wind is blowing up a bit and whistling through the trees, but I am glad none the less to have plenty of other people around.

The paranormal investigators move into the house and spend an hour wandering around it, just feeling for the energies. Some are taking digital photographs, trying to capture the telltale blotches that, they tell me, signify the presence of a spirit. Others, clutching their dousing rods, are feeling for ley lines – energy paths caused by a paranormal energy.

Eventually, the investigators stop taking the spiritual pulse of the house and start to set what they call ghost traps. Children's toys are distributed around the house: a teddy bear, a Winnie the Pooh, a doll. These are placed carefully on pieces of paper and their exact position marked by pen. Elsewhere, brightly coloured marbles are set down and then flour is sprinkled over them. A house of cards is built on the floor of one room.

'We are going to leave the house for a while,' explains Goldie, 'and then, when we come back, we want to see if any of the toys have moved. The teddy or the dolly could be attractive to a child if she is in here, and if she wants to play with the marbles, any movement will be shown in the sprinkled flour.'

Before we go, Goldie sets two more traps. She places a sheet of paper on the floor, and another under an open door, then tapes a pencil to the door, with its sharpened tip touching the paper.

'If an energy moves the door, the pencil will mark the paper,' whispers Goldie. 'The other piece of paper is for the spirit to draw on. I am putting another pencil on it.'

We leave the house to go and have a cup of tea back at Commander Crichton's office.

On our return, one hour later, I am dying to see if we have caught any ghosts, but before we get to the house someone lets out a yell.

'The lights are on!'

'We turned them off before we went,' says Goldie calmly.

'Are you sure?' asks someone else. 'I think we might have left them on.'

'No!' insists Goldie. 'We turned them off. We have spirits!'

As we go back into the house, several of the investigators are monitoring energy levels with sensitive meters, and the digital photographers are clicking way like mad.

'There has been an energy here, I can feel it,' says Babs, a recognised expert on ley lines.

'Look, Winnie the Pooh's leg has shifted, hasn't it?'

'The door hasn't moved, but look at the other paper – there is a drawing on it!'

It is true. On the sheet of paper left for a spirit to draw on, there is a scribble in the middle.

Goldie immediately calls a séance. Everybody sits down in a circle and holds hands. The lights are turned off.

Suddenly there is a scream.

'Get me out of here! Get me out of here!'

Someone turns on the lights and we see Babs writhing around on the floor.

'She's been touched,' says Goldie, as Babs is helped to her feet and taken out of the room.

The investigators are convinced they have happened on a rich seam of 'paranormality'. I am still trying to keep an open mind about things, but I cannot say the Winnie the Pooh and the flour-sprinkled marbles have provided irrefutable evidence of the other world at play – and the one piece of startling empirical evidence that seemed initially exciting – the scribble on the piece of paper – is now discovered, to everyone's disappointment, not to be a scribble at all, but just a piece of old cobweb that has fallen from the rafters.

The first night's work is over. Tomorrow night we are going to investigate the Hangman's Cell.

Location: Devonport dockyard. South Yard, the Hangman's Cell
Date: 24 October 2004
Time: 00.30

Tonight the approach is very different. The investigators have no doubt that there are restless spirits abroad in the Ropery and the Hangman's Cell, so Goldie has invited two psychics along to plumb the depths of this restlessness and its causes. They are 44-year-old identical twins, Gaynor and Joy.

Once again we form a circle, but tonight it is in the Hangman's Cell, just below the trapdoor through which, it is alleged, the French prisoners fell to their neck-snapping end around two hundred years ago.

I sit down outside the circle as I want to observe, but a colleague of mine called Priscilla, who has come along tonight out of interest, elects to go into the circle to take part in the experiment. Goldie calls everybody to silence, and we all look over to the psychic twins sitting together at the head of the circle. Joy raises her arms.

'I will now speak the mantra to draw the power of light towards us. When I have spoken the mantra, Gaynor will start to be drawn into the other world, where she will try and contact her spiritual guide Blue Mountain, who is a Native American killed in the last century.'

Everybody settles back for the mantra.

'May the power of the one light flow into the heart of all true servers. May the love of the one soul characterise the lives of all who seek to aid the wise ones . . .'

This is the signal for Gaynor to leave our world and enter the other. Eyes tightly shut, her head drops forward as she seems to fall into an instant trance. Before long her breathing gets heavier and heavier. After a couple of minutes, a strangled voice emanates from deep in her chest. It is a tortured, indecipherable voice that speaks but makes no sense.

The voice continues for a good six or seven minutes and, as I look round, I am aware of a growing agitation amongst the investigators. I look over to Priscilla and smile. She smiles back and half raises an eyebrow. Suddenly Gaynor stands up, still with her eyes tight shut.

'Hello, Blue Mountain,' says Joy.

'Hello,' says Blue Mountain, through Gaynor who crosses her arms. The spirit guide addresses the circle in a deep and heavily accented voice.

'There has been considerable work done here. We have chosen to join your efforts and allow the light to come forward because we are aware of very many people in the next vibration of existence who are unable to progress further and are disturbing the environment. We have come from the masters of the light to encourage movements of souls to the power of love . . .'

Suddenly a piercing scream breaks the silence of the cell, which is now chilled by the night air. All eyes turn to a figure trembling in the shadows.

'It's Priscilla!' shouts Goldie.

Joy turns to her sister. 'One of us is troubled, Blue Mountain.'

'I know,' replies the spirit guide. 'Let the power of the white light bathe the anxious soul.'

The white light apparently has no effect. Priscilla continues to shake and scream.

'Nina! Nina! Nina!' she is saying repeatedly.

She runs out of the cell, into the dark alley outside the Ropery. Goldie and I follow her and grab her to comfort her. She is in extreme distress.

'Nina! Nina! Nina!' she cries again.

'Who is Nina?' asks Goldie, gently but firmly.

'My wife, my wife!'

It takes five hours to coax Priscilla back from wherever she has gone. She remembers little of what happened, but is exhausted and has a bad stomach ache.

Blue Mountain has reverted to the spirit world, and Joy and Gaynor call the investigators together.

'Priscilla was a vehicle for one of the restless spirits to inhabit,' says Joy. 'We think he was one of the executed French sailors who never saw his wife again, and that his love for her, and his untimely end, prevented him from moving to the next world.'

'When I have my strength back' says Gaynor, 'I am going back to find Blue Mountain – we need to find this restless soul and get him to the next world, or he will inhabit this place for ever . . .'

Postscript

Gaynor summoned Blue Mountain again, but he never managed to track down Nina's husband. Priscilla felt ill and feverish for the next week, and developed a mass of mouth ulcers. When she told Goldie about this, Goldie said, 'Yes, mouth ulcers are very common after direct contact with the afterlife.'

I still cannot explain what happened that night – neither can Priscilla – but, despite my misgivings about the ghost-trapping in the Ropemaster's House, I still would not say with any certainty that we did not, that night, have close contact with the spirit of a dead French sailor . . .

CHAPTER TWELVE

The Royal Potatoes

Location: Eastern Mediterranean – en route to Turkey
Date: 21 April 2005
Time: 09.30

Daily Orders. Our Mission: 'Preps for Gallipoli Commemorations'
Notes: BR81 0221 Policy & Appearance – Sideburns. Sideburns
shall not extend below the ear lobe, shall be of even width, and
shall be taper trimmed and squared off to conform to the overall
hairstyle. Sideburns for Royal Marine personnel shall not extend
below halfway down the ear.

After leaving Alexandria HMS *Chatham* heads north and sets course for Turkey, where she is due to take part in the ninetieth anniversary commemoration of the Gallipoli campaign – that great and tragic battle of the First World War that saw well over 130,000 men perish to bullet, bayonet, military incompetence and ravaging disease. HRH the Prince of Wales, who will be laying a wreath at a memorial service to mark the occasion, will be spending a night on HMS *Chatham*, before flying back to Britain. The heir to the British throne, however, does not just drop in on a British warship for a kip, a sandwich and a cup of cocoa, as Rab is quick to point out.

'What you are now goin' to see is all of us doin' very passable impressions of blue-arsed flamin' flies. Someone like Prince Charles requires special treatment according to established protocol and that means just one thing. Everybody on the ship will be runnin' around chasing their bleedin' tails.'

A visit like this is an honour indeed, but the protocol involved as well as the practicalities of catering for a prince and his entourage are a nightmare to organise. The ship, having already provided the formal burial party for the re-interment of the Nelsonian soldiers and sailors in Alexandria, is now fully attuned to ceremonial duties – a far cry from her patrolling duties in the Gulf and the humanitarian duties carried out in Sri Lanka.

En route to Turkey, however, we stop off at Souda Bay in Crete to refuel. We are only here for half a day, but there is much to be done whilst the ship is alongside. First, of course, there is the fuel itself to be pumped aboard – tons of diesel oil. Second, this is an ideal opportunity to clean the ship – give it a good wash down and a thorough brush up before proceeding to our Royal appointment. Third, it is also an ideal opportunity for 'Sweeney' Todd the clubswinger to carry out some much-needed fitness tests for the ship's company. Everybody in the Navy has to pass such a test every year. It can take various forms, but most people opt for the mile and a half run. The time target varies with age, but however old anybody is they have to attempt it. (Over 50s are allowed to walk if they choose.) A failure to meet the required time does not necessarily mean having to leave the service, but it will entail heavy remedial training to improve matters.

Sweeney Todd marks out the course on the quayside of the military refuelling port just outside Souda Bay. Soon, about twenty sailors are lining up ready to start. One of them is Ginge Grieveson, who badly needs to record a good time.

'I hate running, and it's not as if I am that unfit either – I still play rugby occasionally, but ask me to run any distance and I can't seem to do it. My knees give out.'

'What time have you got to do it in?' I ask.

'For my age group – late thirties – I need to be able to crack eleven and a half minutes. The best I have done is twelve minutes ten seconds. The thing is, I won't get promotion if I don't get the time, and it would be nice to be a petty officer some day. I've been a leading hand long enough.'

'OK, gentlemen!' shouts Sweeney Todd. 'If we are all warmed up – up to your marks please . . . steady. Go!'

The runners move off. Ginge is very near the back.

On the other side of the quay, Chief Petty Officer Dave Wharton, a chief gunnery instructor, is putting a squad through their marching paces.

This is the ceremonial party that will be representing the Royal Navy at Gallipoli for the anniversary commemorations. Dave Wharton is marching them hard because he wants them to perform perfectly on the day. He knows there will be many representatives of navies there, and he wants HMS *Chatham*'s guard to shine.

'Left, left, left right left. Swing those arms higher – up to the level of your shoulders. Left, left, left right left!'

Ginge Grieveson runs past the marching squad, but he is suffering out on the makeshift running track. He is breathing heavily and his legs look wobbly, but he is persevering.

'Come on, Ginge!' shouts Sweeney. 'You could be close. Pick up the pace a bit, shipmate.'

Ginge tries to respond, but he is clearly in pain. With a hundred metres to go he summons up a sprint to the line.

'Bloody hell!' he gasps. 'That was hell!'

'Sorry, Ginge,' says Sweeney. 'Your time is eleven minutes forty-eight. Eighteen seconds short.'

'Well, I'm getting better, aren't I?' says Ginge between breaths. 'If I keep that rate of improvement up, I should be in the Olympic squad by 2008. I could be running in Beijing!'

'Yes mate!' says Sweeney. 'Very probably, but I would just be happy with you passing Pusser's little test first. We'll give it another go next time we have some solid ground to run on. OK?'

'Can't wait, mate!' retorts Ginge, looking redder than the tomatoes he was chopping this morning in his galley.

Rab Butler, who passed his fitness test back in Plymouth, watches the whole thing from the flight deck where he is part of a human chain passing bags of carrots and turnips into the ship. They are being hoisted by a small crane on to the ship from the lorry that has delivered them.

'Poor old Ginge!' he says sympathetically. 'It's bloody hot for running too. Mind you, I wouldn't have minded being in that ceremonial party, but there was too many volunteers.'

'You like marching, Rab?' says one of the others in the chain.

'Well, it's not that exactly, but I'm looking forward to Gallipoli actually. Just before I left on this deployment, my old man told me that my great-grandfather was killed there. I had no idea till then. His name was Charles Andrews and he was in the East Yorkshire Regiment, so I'm gonna try and get up to the memorial and see if I can spot his name. It would be special that. I just thought that I might have had a better chance of getting off the ship if I was doin' some ceremonial.'

'Carrots incoming, Rab!'

'Gotcha!' shouts Rab, grabbing a huge sack and passing it to the next man.

Before the ship heads back to sea, thirty of the ship's company are leaving to be sent home to the UK. This is part of an advance party which, after reaching the UK, will take their leave before the ship arrives in June. The advance party will then man the ship when she first arrives, allowing the rest of the ship's company to take their leave.

'Lucky buggers!' says Ginge, as he watches them get into the coach that will take them to the airport to catch a military Hercules. 'Still, I get to go home early too. I'll be leaving from Barcelona in three weeks – roll on!'

Location: The Aegean Sea
Date: 22 April 2005
Time 06.00

Daily Orders. Our Mission: 'Preps for Gallipoli Commemorations'
Notes: Marching Platoons for Gallipoli. The rig for the ceremony
for the Marching Platoon will be 1b's (blues) and for the armed
personnel 1a's (blues).

We are sailing from the north Aegean Sea into the narrow straits known as the Dardanelles, between the Gallipoli peninsula and the Turkish mainland. Today the weather is fine, the sea is calm and the only sounds are the deep hum of the ship's engines, a light breeze blowing from the south, and the insistent call of seabirds following in our wake.

Ninety years ago, in 1915, a previous incarnation of HMS *Chatham*, a battleship, sailed into the Dardanelles just as we do today. She, however, was accompanied by seventeen other battleships – thirteen Royal Navy and four French – and the predominant sounds would have been those of gunfire, explosions and the screams of dying and wounded men. This was the beginning of the ill-fated Gallipoli campaign – something many of us on the ship are reading up on, for this is what we have come to commemorate.

By early 1915, with deadlock on the Western Front and the Russian Army struggling in the east, First Lord of the Admiralty Winston Churchill became the driving force behind a grand scheme to strike at the Central Powers on a new front in south eastern Europe, knock Turkey out of the war, and open up a much-needed relief route to Russia through the Dardanelles.

The campaign began with an attempt to force the Dardanelles by naval power alone, but the early bombardments on coastal strongholds failed and three Allied battleships were lost to Turkish mines. (HMS *Chatham* was not lost, but was none the less badly damaged.)

In response to this failure, a massive expeditionary force of 489,000 men was dispatched to seize the Gallipoli peninsula and clear the way for the Royal Navy to capture the Turkish capital of Constantinople (Istanbul). Known as the Mediterranean Expeditionary Force, it consisted of the British 29th Division, a Newfoundland battalion, Indian troops, two divisions of the Australian and New Zealand Army Corps (ANZAC), a Royal Naval Division and a French colonial division.

HMS *CHATHAM* IN THE DARDANELLES

The attack was launched on 25 April 1915, but a combination of hostile terrain and an unexpectedly ferocious Turkish defence stopped any advance dead in its tracks. From then on, with the element of surprise lost, the campaign degenerated into the deadlock and carnage of erosive trench warfare. The Turkish force of some 500,000 men, fighting for their motherland, clung grimly to the high ground and succeeded in inflicting heavy losses on the invading forces. The stalemate continued, and soon disease caused by unsanitary conditions and extreme heat claimed almost as many lives as Turkish gunfire.

Of the Allied forces, 205,000 British and Dominion soldiers and 47,000 Frenchmen became casualties – either killed, wounded or evacuated with sickness. British and Dominion forces suffered 43,000 killed – including 7,594 Australians (out of a deployment of 20,000) and 2,431 New Zealanders – and the French 8,000. Only 11,000 Allied dead were identified and buried on the peninsula. Over 30,000 have no known grave.

Turkish troops suffered 300,000 casualties, including at least 86,000 dead.

Eventually, the Allied forces were evacuated, and so ended what has since been described as 'a chronicle of heroism and endurance, incompetence and sheer muddle' that must rank with Passchendaele as one of the most tragically evocative battle honours of the Great War.

At 10 o'clock, HMS *Chatham* sails regally into the calm and sheltered waters off the town of Canakkale – the nearest town to the historic battlefields of the Gallipoli peninsula and the many war memorials that will be the focus of the commemorations over the next two days. We drop anchor and promptly hoist the Union Jack at the bow and the White Ensign at the stern.

Normally, at about this time, Sweeney Todd would be supervising circuit training on the flight deck, but not so today. John Gardner, the XO, has posted an important notice that applies to the whole ship's company:

<u>Circuit Training and Upper Deck Running whilst at anchor at Canakkale</u>. Due to the high-profile nature of our visit, the upper deck will be out of bounds whilst we are at anchor. There will be no circuit training or upper-deck running during our visit.

'It's all a bit of a buggerance if you ask me,' says Rab Butler who is on guard duty on the flight deck. 'I mean, I don't mind so much about circuits 'cos I'll do my own thing on the punch bag anyway, and it's not that we can't come up here for recreation, but we can't go ashore either.'

Rab looks over to Canakkale's enticing waterfront, with all its bustling cafés, bars and restaurants.

'It's 'cos they don't want us to go boozing, you see. They don't want to risk anybody getting into trouble, what with the commemorations coming up and especially with Prince Charles coming on board tomorrow. I understand it, but it's a bit of a bleedin' ball ache!'

'When are you going to look for your great-grandfather's name on the memorial?' I ask.

'Dunno. I ain't in the guard, so I was told I wouldn't be allowed to go ashore, but I've put in a special request. I tell you, I'll be well fucked off if I can't go.'

Location: Canakkale
Date: 23 April 2005
Time: 07.30

Daily Orders. Our Mission: 'Gallipoli Commemorations'
Notes: A yellow power transformer has been misplaced. This is a PLR* item worth over £250. Anyone knowing of its whereabouts return it to the Electrical Workshop.

*Permanent Loan Record i.e. sign for it but lose it and you pay for it!

A Turkish passenger boat is transferring HMS *Chatham*'s marching platoon to the shore. Dressed in Number Ones, with highly polished boots and newly whitened belts and gaiters, the thirty men and women climb from the boat on to the jetty and then straight on to a waiting coach. This promptly takes the party up the coast, crosses to the Gallipoli peninsula and then proceeds to the Abide Memorial to the fallen Turkish soldiers of the Gallipoli campaign. Here they prepare to join the thousands congregating for the commemoration. These include soldiers and sailors representing all the other countries involved in the original conflict – Turkey, Australia, New Zealand, France, Germany, India, Canada and Russia.

LIEUTENANT COMMANDER MICHAEL 'WOODY' WOOD AND HMS *CHATHAM* SAILORS AT THE GALLIPOLI COMMEMORATIONS. HMS *CHATHAM* IS IN THE BACKGROUND

HMS *CHATHAM* GUARD AT GALLIPOLI

FACING PAGE: THE HMS *CHATHAM* GUARD AT THE ABIDE MONUMENT AT GALLIPOLI

First of all Lieutenant Commander Mike 'Woody' Wood, one of the ship's Principal Warfare Officers, and the officer in charge, stands the platoon at ease.

'Today is a very proud but solemn day. You are representing your ship and your country. Hold yourself well, look smart and march as you have been taught. I want to see the Royal Navy at its best out there. Platoon! Platoon – attention!'

Thirty pairs of heels snap together.

'Platoon! By the right – quick march!'

HMS *Chatham*'s marching platoon moves into position between the Royal Australian Navy and the French Navy in the shadow of the enormous stone edifice that is the Turkish memorial. At 10.00, a large Turkish military band strikes up as political representatives of all the attending nations take their position – these include diplomats, foreign ministers and several heads of state. Five hundred men, dressed in traditional Turkish military costume, march slowly from under the memorial, blowing horns and beating drums.

Over the next hour, a splendid and highly colourful ceremony unfolds. Flags are hoisted, speeches are made and music is played. In the waters below us, from where British and Allied battleships bombarded Turkish positions ninety years ago, a dozen warships, including HMS *Chatham*, sail in a line of honour past the imposing memorial. The Turkish Air Force stages a spectacular flypast in close formation, and one by one each country's sailors or soldiers march past the guests of honour and then past the grave of the Unknown Soldier, at which point they salute.

It is a remarkable sight – epic in its scale as well as its concept. All the nations that fought together and against each other are unified in tribute to their fallen.

AIR DISPLAY OVER THE ABIDE MEMORIAL

Rab Butler has managed to get ashore and at five o'clock is in a taxi taking him not to the Abide Memorial but the Helles Memorial, at the top of the peninsula. This is the place of commemoration for missing

Australians who died at Helles, and British and Indian servicemen who died throughout the peninsula and have no known grave. It bears over 21,000 names.

'That was a close-run thing. I thought they were gonna play silly buggers at first and not let me off, but I said I really wanted to see if I could find my great-granddad's name, so they let me go. Bloody hope I find him now!'

The taxi comes over the brow of a small hill, and there in front of us is the Helles Memorial – a massive stone tower surrounded by high-built walls.

'Bloody hell!' exclaims Rab. 'That's great, in'it? Look at that – makes you feel weird, dunnit?'

It is bright but very windy up here on the headland. Today the Helles Memorial is practically deserted, because the main commemoration was at the Abide Memorial, but tomorrow Prince Charles will lead the commemoration here, so it will become very crowded.

THE COMMONWEALTH MEMORIAL AT GALLIPOLI

'There are Aussies and Kiwis everywhere in town,' says Rab. 'They'll all be here tomorrow, won't they? They took a hell of a bashing at the actual battle. Have you seen *Gallipoli* with Mel Gibson? That just shows you what a balls-up it all was.'

We get out of the taxi and begin to walk up the hill towards the memorial.

'My great-granddad's name was not Butler – it was Andrews, because he was my dad's mother's father. Charley they called him, Charley Andrews, and he was a private in the 6th Battalion of the East Yorkshire Regiment. I couldn't believe it when my dad told me about the old chap just before we deployed. I had no idea up to then, but I would love to see his name – it would be like saying hello to him. Showing we ain't forgot him.'

The memorial is large, and 21,000 names written on both faces of all the surrounding walls are a lot to look through. Rab starts to walk round, but can't find the East Yorkshire Regiment.

'I've looked on all the upper walls on the inside. I'm gonna look on the base of the actual monument now. Maybe they ain't put him up. Jesus, I would be gutted – so would my dad.'

I walk behind Rab, letting him draw ahead. Whether he is going to find his great-granddad or not, this is an emotional experience for the normally tough-minded gunner and I think he would like to be alone with his thoughts. He walks around the entire memorial twice and still cannot find what he is looking for. Then the sun, low in the sky and red-

RAB BUTLER FINDS HIS GREAT-GRANDFATHER'S NAME AT THE COMMONWEALTH MEMORIAL

dening into its evening livery, casts a pink hue over the entire west side of the tower where Rab is standing. He looks up once again.

'The East Yorkshire Regiment!' he shouts.

He scans the long list of names in alphabetical order: 'Anders, Andersen, Anderson . . . Andrews . . . Yes! Charles Andrews! He's here! The old boy is here – bless him!'

Rab beams. As the smile spreads across his face, his eyes glisten. He might be a rough diamond, I think to myself, a bit of a geezer with a tough-guy image, but he has depth to him – and the deep centre of Rab Butler, I have concluded, is a lot softer than he would like to admit to his mess deck or his boxing mates.

'I'm gonna ring the old man!' he says, reaching for his mobile phone. 'He'll be well chuffed at this.'

He punches in a number and puts the phone to his ear. 'Hope he's in . . . what time is it at home? Ah, it's ringing! Come on, come on . . . DAD! I found 'im!'

As Rab talks to his father, I step back to take a photo of the memorial. It is now I see an inscription written on the side of the memorial base. It is attributed to Mustafa Kemal, who was the military leader during the defence of Gallipoli – he later became the first president of the new Turkish republic under his new name, Mustafa Kemal Ataturk. He was known simply as Ataturk – the father of the Turks.

> Those heroes that shed
> Their blood
> And lost their lives;
> You are now lying in the
> Soil of a friendly country.
> Therefore rest in peace.
> There is no difference
> Between the Johnnies
> And the Mehmets to us
> Where they lie side by side
> Here in this country of ours.
> You, the mothers,
> Who sent their sons from
> Far away countries,
> Wipe away your tears;
> Your sons are now lying in
> Our bosom
> And are in peace.
> After having lost their lives
> On this land they have
> Become our sons as well.
>   *Mustafa Kemal*

There could be no words more appropriate to the day – whether in the context of the spectacular, mass commemoration at the Abide Memorial or of the personal search by a single British sailor for the name of his great-grandfather on the memorial before me now – in the corner of a foreign field.

'I was right,' says Rab, walking over to me. 'Dad's dead chuffed and so am I. Over the bleedin' moon. This has made my whole deployment, this!'

He reaches up to the memorial and touches his great-grandfather's name for the last time. We turn and walk away – Rab is lost in the silence of his thoughts.

A seaboat ties up alongside HMS *Chatham* at a quarter to eight, and a party of visitors climb the steps up to the flight deck of the warship. One of them is a vice admiral in the Royal Navy who is duly piped aboard and saluted by a welcoming party that includes the captain himself. Steve Chick steps forward to greet his high-ranking guest with a shake of the hand and a deferential bow of the head as befits a future King of England.

HRH the Prince of Wales is on board *Chatham* for the night. Tomorrow morning, at 05.00, he will depart the ship to attend a dawn service of commemoration at the Helles Memorial where he will lay a wreath.

GINGE AND THE ROYAL POTATOES

After that, he will return to the ship to meet some of the ship's company before leaving for the UK. Tonight, however, he will meet no one, but will retire to the captain's cabin, vacated by Steve Chick, where he will have a light supper before retiring.

The Prince's valet is immediately taken to the officers' galley, where Ginge Grieveson is standing by to provide a Royal supper. Tonight, the officers' menu has a choice of chicken Kiev or beef Wellington, with treacle pudding to follow, but none of this will ever touch the future king's lips. Ginge is given a small parcel of food, apparently brought from the Prince's own Duchy Estate, and is asked to prepare it for him.

'Three organic spuds, a bit of salad and some meat!' says Ginge. 'I'm baking the potatoes – only little 'uns – and I've got the rest of it in the fridge. I mean, it's up to him, of course, but I reckon he would have liked my grub tonight – the officers seemed to.'

'But at least you can say you have cooked exclusively for a future monarch,' I say.

'Yeah, that's true,' replies Ginge. 'I thought I might have had to cook for Camilla as well, but he didn't bring her. Shame – they were only married last week, weren't they?'

'Hey, Ginge,' says one of the wardroom stewards at the door. 'Can I have a look at the Royal Spuds?'

'What for?'

'Because they're Royal!'

'Go on then,' says Ginge, opening the oven door.

'They look just like normal potatoes,' says the steward.

'Of course they bloody do!' says Ginge. 'What did you expect – that they all had little crowns on?'

'Ginge!' says another voice at the door. 'Let's have a look, mate!'

Within minutes the galley is full of sailors, not only wanting to look at the Royal Potatoes but take photographs of them as well.

Click, click, click.

'Bloody front line paparazzi, you lot!' says Ginge. 'Oi, don't get too close. That's probably a decapitating offence that is.'

Click, click, click.

'What I'm not telling them,' he whispers to me, 'is that he has also brought with him a piece of Royal Wedding cake. It's in the fridge till he wants it – but if I'm not careful, I can just see that getting half-inched and ending up on bloody ebay!'

Location: Canakkale
Date: 25 April 2005
Time: 13.50

Daily Orders. Our Mission: 'Gallipoli Commemorations'
Notes: Gash bags. The gash compactor is currently being repaired. During this time all gash is to be placed in plastic gash bags only and not paper ones. All tins are to be crushed down to maximise gash bag capacity. The ongoing work on the gash compactor will cease this afternoon as it is on HRH's tour.

HRH the Prince of Wales is back on HMS *Chatham*. He is being given a tour of the ship and the opportunity of meeting some of the ship's company. As his time is short, most people had assumed that his tour would be cursory and his meeting with people perfunctory, so everybody is delighted to find the Prince is keen to take his time and that he is really enjoying chatting with sailors and officers alike. Perhaps this should not

HRH THE PRINCE OF WALES
GREETS *CHATHAM* SAILORS

be too surprising as the Prince was himself a serving officer in the Royal Navy, and well understands the naval mentality.

'Have you had some good runs ashore?' he asks everybody, knowing that any sailor would sooner talk about that than anything else.

'Oh yes, sir. Cracking run in Dubai!'

'Excellent. Good place to go.'

It is impressive the way the Prince puts everyone at ease. Halfway through his tour of the ship he visits the senior rates' dining hall, where he meets a selection of people who worked in key positions during the disaster-relief operation in Sri Lanka. His interest is genuine, and his pride in the ship's achievement comes over clearly in the way he responds to people's personal accounts of what happened in Baticoloa and Kallar.

As the Prince tours the ship Ginge Grieveson remains in the wardroom galley, just in case there is a royal command for a cup of tea . . . and that piece of wedding cake that is still in the fridge.

CHAPTER THIRTEEN

Heads Up, Chests Out, Be Proud

Location: Central Plymouth
Date: 19 May 2005
Time: 07.30

Natasha Pulley picks up her little girl Daisy and sits her on the kitchen table.

'Sit there, Daisy, whilst I put your shoes on.'

'Don't like those shoes!'

'Yes you do. Those are nice shoes. Let me tie them up because we must go to the crèche or Mummy's going to be late for work. You can take one toy – which one would you like?'

'I want dolly.'

'Dolly?'

'No, teddy and dolly.'

'No. Choose one. You can't have both.'

'Dolly.'

'Right, take Dolly and let's go. Alfie, come on – time for school.' She looks around at me. 'Come on, Chris – we gotta go!'

I have come to her home this morning in order to go in to work with her at Her Majesty's Naval Base Devonport, so I obediently obey the order and follow Natasha, Daisy and Alfie as they rush out of the front door. We scramble into her Audi A6 and head off, but not before retrieving Dolly who takes a headlong tumble into the gutter as Daisy tries to close her door.

'Dolly's dirty!' screams Daisy.

'Dolly's fine. We can give her a wash later. Alfie – buckle up!'

'This is the usual morning routine,' she explains as she manoeuvres the car out of its parking space. 'Bob – my husband – works as a manager in the local yoghurt and cream factory and starts early in the morning, so I normally see to the kids on my way to work.'

'What time do you have to be at work?' I ask.

'I like to be in by nine if I can.'

We drop six-year-old Alfie at his school, and then Natasha continues to Devonport dockyard. She queues briefly at Drake Gate (one of four main entrances to the sprawling naval base), shows her ID, and drives down a winding road to drop Daisy off at the dockyard crèche. We then drive around the one-way system to the Wyvern Sports Centre where Natasha works as a chief petty officer physical training instructor. This is where I met her when she was helping to organise the Inter Command Boxing Championships and I was struck then, as I am again now, by her sparky personality and high-octane energy.

Today is a big day for Natasha because she starts serious training. She is attempting to get into the Devonport team for the Royal Navy Field Gun Competition – a tough race that involves pulling a large field gun over a flat course of 170 metres. Many Navy establishments put in a team. It is a hard-fought competition, with little compromise and frequent injury.

'Bob thinks I'm mad doing this,' she says, as we walk into the main gym. 'Normally field gunners are big, hairy and butch, with muscles on their muscles – not five-foot-four mothers of two.'

'You're pretty fit though, aren't you, Tash?' I say.

'Oh yeah – but fit for cross country and netball. Not lugging ruddy great guns all over the park.'

'So why are you doing it?'

'Well, the challenge of it for a start, and to fly the flag for women of course! But also it's an incredible team event that needs different people to do all sorts of different things. We all have to pull the gun and its limber – that's its ammunition carriage – but the big guys are the ones that actually manhandle them and their heavy wheels, which we have to take off at a couple of points in the race. The others need to do more of the nipping in and out sort of stuff, putting the pins and shackles on the wheels double fast – you'll see when we start practising with the gun.'

'So you are a nipper-in-and-out-er?'

'Well, actually, I prefer to call myself a speedy bullet!'

THE BEAST MASTER

Half an hour later, a squad of about thirty very large sailors and the diminutive Natasha Pulley lines up in front of Warrant Officer PTI Ian Binks, a field gun veteran known to some as 'Binksy' but also as the 'Beast Master'. For the next eight weeks of intensive training, he will be referred to officially as Number One.

'Listen up!' he shouts. 'You are all now going to start training for the Field Gun Competition to be held at HMS *Collingwood* in Portsmouth in just over two months. I want complete commitment from you. I want you to put everything you've got into our bid to be champions – and it is champions I intend for us to be. Nothing else. Understood?'

'Yes, Number One!' the squad shouts in close-order unison.

'There will be a lot of sweat, probably some blood and definitely some tears. All right with that?'

'Yes, Number One!'

'The eventual team will be just eighteen of you – so some are going to be disappointed. You need to compete for your places, every one of you. Happy with that?'

'Yes, Number One!'

'If there is anyone who reckons they will not be able to deliver, they are free to leave now – any takers?'

The question is greeted with silence.

'OK. Let's do it. We start now – on the floor. Give me thirty!'

Everyone drops straight down and pumps out the press-ups.

For the next hour Ian Binks puts his newly formed squad through their paces. Pull-ups, push-ups, squat thrusts, sit-ups, shuttle runs and star jumps. Every man and one girl grit their teeth to the bitter end of an intense first session.

That evening Tash and I drive back to her house.

'That was a killer today in the gym – but it was great. I loved it!'

'Big blokes, aren't they?'

'Yes, but they're all great guys – big blokes with big hearts – and Number One is awesome. If anyone can get us to the winner's podium it is Binksy the Beast Master.'

'Do you reckon you can keep up with the training?'

'Physically I reckon I can – but it is going to mean a lot more time training in the evening, so Bob will have to help out with the kids.'

'He'll be OK with that?'

'Yes. He's in Civvy Street now, but he was in the Navy himself and he was five times a field gunner. He understands it – even though he thinks I'm mad to do it. He knows how much you have to put into it.'

Bob Pulley is already at home and looking after the children.

'How was it?' he asks, as he gives Daisy her tea.

'Great! But Number One beasted us just to get started.'

'Plenty more where that came from I should expect.'

Natasha and Bob start to prepare supper – taking it in turns to play with the children, who are now painting at the table.

'You must miss the kids when you go to sea?' I ask.

'I don't go to sea,' she replies.

'What, never?'

'No. Never. I couldn't leave the kids.'

'But don't you have to, if you are told?'

'Not me. You see I joined as a Wren back in 1987, when you could choose whether to go to sea or not. I chose not to at that time. Since then the Wrens have been disbanded, and now we are all the same – men and women are just called sailors and anybody could be given a sea job at any time. But I still come under the terms of my joining contract, so I stay at home – with my babies.'

'You never felt you would like to go to sea?'

'No! Those terrible goodbyes and the tearful waving from Devil's Point as ships disappear over the horizon. It makes me feel sick in my stomach to think about it.'

'The truth is, she can hardly get through the day without seeing the kids,' laughs Bob.

'Well, I'm not that bad' retorts Natasha, 'but I don't know how mothers leave their kids for any length of time. If they'd said I had to go to sea, I would never have joined up.'

'Mummy, look what I've painted,' says Daisy, holding up a picture of coloured daubs.

'*Beautiful*, darling,' says Tasha with feeling. 'Of course, I will see a bit less of the kids with this Field Gun Competition but that's only eight weeks, and it will just be a few late evenings. I won't be going away – except at the end when we go to Portsmouth for the actual competition itself – if I get selected for the team! God, I really want to get into that team!'

Over the following week the Devonport Field Gun Squad trains twice a day, every day – but this is all gymnasium work. Ian Binks puts his squad through repeated fitness circuits to build up strength and speed, but so far there is not a field gun in sight.

Another week passes before this happens. The gun arrives from Portsmouth and is delivered one morning to the Wyvern gym. The 12-Pounder Field Gun barrel weighs 900 lbs, its carriage another 365 lbs and its wheels 120 lbs each. The limber, which the gun hooks up to, weighs 365 lbs and its wheels again weigh 120 lbs each. The total weight of the gun and limber combined is 2,110 lbs or nearly a ton.

Everybody assembles on the road outside the gym. 'Gather round everyone!' shouts Number One. 'I am going to run through, in simple terms, what the race consists of. That is, what you have to do, so pay attention. Then we will walk it through. Happy?'

'Yes, Number One!'

'Right, the gun will be placed forty metres from the starting line. The limber will be taken off its wheels and all will be laid on the ground twenty metres from the start line. At the off, which will be a thunder-flash on the day, you will run as fast as you can – some to the gun and some to the limber. The limber team will then build the limber by picking up the wheels and placing them on the axles – someone either side of the limber will then place lynchpins into the axle heads to hold on the wheels. This is the limber lift. So far so good?'

'Yes, Number One!'

'Right! Then the limber party will run like hell, pulling the limber with them up to the gun, where you will exchange wheels between the limber and gun. You will then connect the gun to the back of the limber – this is the 'hook up'. Then you will advance at top speed to the point we call the first action at the seventy-metre mark. Here, the gun is unhooked, the limber is spun to face the start. Its wheels are removed and dropped to the ground. The gun is run to the end of the track at 100 metres where it is turned and stopped. The gun is then fired three times, each shell being run to the gun from the limber by the fastest man in the crew . . .'

Ian Binks continues to talk his squad through the highly complicated procedures that are involved with running the gun. It is a strangely surreal scene: in the middle of a dockyard boasting some of the most advanced state-of-the-art warships and submarines in the world, thirty sailors, each with a modern technical specialisation of some sort, are agonising over the fastest way to assemble a nineteenth-century howitzer and run with it over a course of 170 metres. But then, the Field Gun Competition is central to naval culture for many reasons – and is capable of inspiring enormous and sometimes even death-defying passion.

It all goes back to the Boer War – in particular the epic 119-day siege of Ladysmith in 1899, where those defending, needing urgent reinforcement, were relieved at the last minute by the arrival of Captain the Hon. Hedworth Lampton of the Naval Brigade with his 280 Blue-Jackets, four 12-pounders and two 4.7-inch guns. Special carriages and mountings for these guns had been improvised by Captain Percy Scott of the cruiser HMS *Terrible*, and despatched in HMS *Powerful* to Durban. After the siege of Ladysmith was finally lifted on 28 February 1900, Queen Victoria sent a telegram: 'Pray express to the Naval Brigade my deep appreciation of the valuable services they have rendered with their guns.' Later that same year, the idea of the Field Gun Competition was conceived.

For many years, the Inter Command Field Gun Competition became a regular feature at the Royal Tournament in Earls Court, until it was abolished in 1999 because of concerns over the manpower it required over many months of training and preparation. The Royal Navy Field Gun Competition continued, however, and now of course is the premier competition and is promoted throughout the Navy as a spectacle of toughness, courage, discipline and teamwork. As I said, it inspires extraordinary passions.

'. . . the limber wheels are shipped and it is run to the gun where it is hooked up again,' continues Ian Binks. 'Both are run towards the start, then stopped again for another wheel exchange. At this point the gun will feel very heavy, so beware – if you drop it now, you're in trouble. The gun and limber are run further towards the start line, separated and stopped for the second firing – again, three shells in double-fast time. Finally the limber is run back and hooked to the gun, then every one of you will run for home.'

Number One raises his voice for emphasis.

'You will sprint like the blazes for the start line, which is now your finishing line, pulling gun and limber with you. This is not the best time to fall in front of the gear, people, because it is very heavy and cannot be stopped!'

Natasha looks over to me with a wide-eyed expression that suggests a cross between true fear and genuine excitement.

'The world record, by the way, is 1 minute 18.88 seconds, achieved in 2001 by HMS *Collingwood* – the Maritime Warfare School,' adds Ian Binks. 'OK, people, we will give it a try. We will walk through it first, split it into its integral parts, and then we will try a couple of complete runs, so everyone in the squad can have a go. Everybody clear?'

'Yes, Number One!'

Ian Binks goes through the race stage by stage, explaining every transition and allocating specific tasks as he goes – the biggest and strongest are put on the heaviest items such as the gun barrel and the wheels. Some will be limber lifters and others will be runners – some pushing, some pulling. Tash's responsibility will be the lynchpin that keeps the right-hand wheel on the limber. It has to be taken out quickly and quickly replaced during wheel exchanges. She will also have to ensure on her side that the shackle of the drag rope that people use to pull the limber and gun with is firmly in place.

At the end of the training session, the squad prepares to attempt a couple of complete runs. Tash is in the first.

Ian Binks stands at the start line.

'I don't want you to run at full speed – just three-quarter pace. Stand by!'

The team line up and prepare for the off.

'Devonport field gun team!' shouts Ian Binks. 'Five, four three, two, one, GO!'

Tash and seventeen men sprint towards the limber and gun. As soon as the limber is assembled, it is hooked with the gun and accelerated up the track.

'Just eighty per cent everybody!' shouts Ian Binks. 'Do not run to your maximum yet! Concentrate on technique!'

Even at eighty per cent, the drill is an extraordinary sight. The limber builds, the manhandling of the heavy gun, the fast firing, the turns and the hook-ups are thrilling – but the final run for home is truly exhilarating, a final surge of speed and strength as eighteen sailors strain to get the gun home. The roar of the clattering wheels on the tarmac is deafening, and all the time Ian Binks shouts a constant stream of orders and directions.

'Oh my God!' exclaims Tasha, desperately trying to suck in oxygen. 'That was . . . that was . . . really . . . scary!'

'Not bad!' says Ian Binks. 'One minute 34 for your first run. Lots of work to do though!'

One runner is taken inside to have attention to a bruised leg and another for a crushed toe.

Over the following five weeks the squad trains twice a day, every day. Fitness increases, technique gets slicker, confidence grows and the running time gets quicker and quicker. The squad's personal best has come down to 1 minute 25, but now, with just a week to the competition, it is time for the final team of just eighteen to be selected from the squad of thirty. At the end of a lunchtime training session, Binks and the squad captain Lieutenant Alan 'Cruisy' Nekrews retire to consider their options.

'I really, really want to be in the team,' says Tasha looking nervous. 'I was frightened the first time we ran, but now, after all the training, I love it! And the guys are amazing. This is one of the best things I have ever done!'

An hour later, Ian Binks emerges from his deliberations and calls the squad together.

'I am now going to read out the final team that will run at HMS *Collingwood* in Portsmouth on Saturday week. Some of you are going to be disappointed – I know that.'

Tasha buries her head in her hands.

'But you are still in the squad, and injuries could occur at any time, so keep the faith. Right this is the team: Gilly Gillham, Stevy Stephenson, Cruisy Nekrews, Paddy Kerr, Dinger Bell, Robbie Burns, Paul Pridmore, Mac McClusky, Jan Phillips, Tom Sheehan, Tony Shone, Tasha Pulley . . .'

Tasha twitches as her name is announced, but manages to contain herself. She wants to explode but keeps her surprised and astonished delight to herself.

' . . . Jakey Foran, Winnie Wincott, Johnny Vaughan, Jazz Jary, Neil Crawford and Darbs Derbyshire. That will be the running team. Congratulations to all those selected, but remember, the moment you fail to deliver there is someone in the squad breathing down your neck who wants your place. Protect it with your life – and those of you not picked, fight back, wrestle that place back if you really want it!'

He knows how to fire people up.

Tasha waits till she is out of sight and earshot of the others before she punches the air and screams with joy.

'YEEEES!!! I'M IN!!!! WHEEEEEEE!!!!!! I *so* wanted that place. I can't tell you. Now we have just got to win the competition. We have just *got* to!'

Location: HMS *Collingwood* Maritime Warfare School
Date: 13 June 2005
Time: 09.00

The team, reserves and support squad have moved from Plymouth to HMS *Collingwood* in Portsmouth. The competition is next Saturday, so they have a week to practise where the competition will be run: a huge drill ground divided into six tracks side by side. Seventeen teams will be competing, including those from the Royal Navy based in Gibraltar, Cyprus and Scotland. Also, despite this being a traditionally naval competition, teams have been entered this year by the 7th Battalion Royal Engineers, as well as the Royal Air Force.

Every day of the week the teams practise on the competition ground, trying their runs on each of the six tracks. Every team meticulously times each stage of its run, to see where they can improve by snipping a second here or half a second there. The Devonport team have their personal best down to 1 minute 23 – less than five seconds outside the record. Ian Binks is supremely confident.

'We're in very good shape,' he says to me on track three, as the team prepare for another run. 'The Portsmouth team looks good; so does Caledonia, the team from Scotland; and the Army are moving quite well – but none of their times compare with ours and, just looking at them, I can see they just don't have our technique.'

It is true. The Devonport team is streets ahead in technique, speed and strength. Confidence is sky high. Every run produces yet another personal best.

'Devonport field gun team! Five, four, three, two, one, GO!'

The team and their gun thunder down the track. The other teams look over in awe at what they are seeing. Many actually applaud the Devonport team for their sheer skill and athleticism.

'One minute 23.4!' shouts Ian Binks. 'But there is still room for improvement in the first limber build, the big lift and the final hook-up!'

The team line up to march off the ground pulling their gun with them, and he joins them on their right-hand side.

'Devonport field gun team . . . by the right quick march! Left . . . left . . . left right left.'

The team, now clear favourites, move forward in perfect step.

'Heads up, Devonport!' shouts their Beast Master. 'Chests out! Be proud!'

Location: HMS *Collingwood* Drill Ground
Date: 17 June 2005
Time: 14.20

It is Friday afternoon, the day before the main competition, and time for the preliminary heats – a chance for all the teams to mark their cards and secure a place in tomorrow's main competition. Losers today will have to make do with the Plate Competition tomorrow. Also, if it rains tomorrow the competition will be cancelled – it is far too dangerous to run in the wet – so today's times will count as the final result. It is also an opportunity for the teams to sharpen their techniques and hone their performances in the heat of competition for the first time.

Each heat will see six teams going head to head. Devonport prepares to march out with all the other teams to the competition ground. First they form a circle, hug each other tight and sing their adopted team song entitled 'Men of Devon', although it is actually a slightly adapted version of the hymn 'Guide me, O thou great Redeemer', the change coming in the last three lines:

> Guide me, O Thou great Redeemer,
> Pilgrim through this barren land.
> I am weak, but Thou art mighty,
> Hold me with Thy powerful hand.
> Men of Devon, men of Devon,
> Feed me till I'm six foot four!
> Feed me till I'm six foot four!

One of the gun lifters, Big Jakey Foran, has good reason to make the heat times as quick as possible. His wife, back in Plymouth, went into labour late this afternoon. Knowing he could ruin the chances of his team if he leaves before the heats, he has elected to run this evening. His wife has been given Syntometrin in the hope of slowing the contractions to delay the birth and he will leave for Plymouth as soon as Devonport's race is run. He will, subject to no complications, be returning tomorrow for the main competition day.

On the order of a presiding chief petty officer, the gun carriage teams start the two-hundred-metre march to the start line of their allotted tracks. Six field guns roll forward one behind the other. Devonport will be running in track two.

'Devonport!' shouts Ian Binks at the top of his voice. 'By the right quick march!'

Seventeen towering men stride out and with them one small woman who is as brimming with pride as any of them.

'Swing those arms high,' says Ian Binks. 'Heads up, Devonport! Chests out! Be proud!'

Before the race starts the team has to disassemble the limber and put its constituent parts on the track. The gun is placed a further forty metres up the track, ready for the first hook-up with the limber. The team then warms up in a tight circle facing each other. 'Cruisy' Nekrews gives a final rallying pep talk before leading his team to the start line. The battery commander standing in the middle of the ground calls to each team to make sure they are ready. When he is satisfied, he reports the fact to the senior officer on parade, who then gives permission for the race to commence. A Marine bugler calls the alert, whereupon the battery commander lights the thunderflash and throws it to the ground. Five seconds later it explodes and the teams sprint off their lines.

HEADS UP, CHESTS OUT, BE
PROUD

NATASHA PULLEY PUTS
EVERYTHING INTO THE
FIRST HEAT

Devonport is ahead by the first limber build, further ahead by the hook-up and even further ahead by the first firing. The team is in complete harmony. Tasha darts in and out with the wheel lynchpin at exactly the right times, with no hesitation and no delay, and everybody else performs their allotted task in a near-perfect execution of the drill. By the 'run for home' Devonport has victory assured.

The heats go like a dream for the Devonport team. By the end of competition they are the clear leaders with a personal best time of 1 minute 20.54. If it rains tomorrow, Devonport are already the winners.

Jakey bids his team-mates goodbye and hightails it to Plymouth and his exceptionally patient, understanding and very pregnant wife.

Location: HMS *Collingwood* Drill Ground
Date: 18 June 2005
Time: 11.00

Saturday arrives. It is a day of destiny for the Devonport team. Every man (and one woman) knows it.

'I have never been this nervous about anything in my life,' says Tasha, sheltering in the shade from a sweltering sun. 'It's dry – so we're running for gold today. We've got three more heats and then it's the final.'

'Any news of Jakey?' I venture.

'Yes! He had a little girl at 11.30 last night. He's back and he hasn't slept a wink, but he's rarin' to go. Apparently, someone said he wants to call the poor little thing "Limber"!'

The crowd starts to arrive at 11.00. Five thousand people are expected today. There is a fairground, souvenir tents, food canteens and a bouncy castle for the children. The Royal Navy Raiders parachute display team drop out of the sky to land on the competition ground, and a motorcycle display team do their stuff – and for good measure, there is also a dog display and a falconry display – but it is all a build-up to one thing – the Field Gun Run. Every team is pumped up and ready.

'Listen up!' says the ever-determined Ian Binks to his Devonport team. 'You are running superbly. You are clear leaders from the heats yesterday, and you have recorded the fastest time overall as well as the best aggregate time. But guess what? You haven't won a bloody dicky bird. Not yet. You still have to get to the final, and then you have to win that. Only then can you relax. Don't be complacent because, even now, you could end up with bugger all. Understood?'

'Yes, Number One!'

At 13.35, the Devonport Field Gun Team marches out to take part in the first of three heats that could lead to a place in the grand final. They place their field gun and limber on the track, warm up in a circle and then take their position alongside the four other teams in the heat. The thunderflash explodes and the team sprints into meticulous action.

Split-second timing, raw power and a finely honed technique secure another triumph. Devonport are in the final.

'Well done!' says a delighted Ian Binks. 'You are in the final – 1 minute 20.7. That is less than two seconds away from the record, and I reckon the first limber lift was pretty slow, too. The Plate Competition starts now, so you have a couple of hours till you are on again at 16.30. Go and relax, people. Get your heads together. I want you back for a team talk at 16.00.'

Natasha Pulley goes for a stroll over to one of the ice-cream vans and buys an orange ice lolly. She then sits in the sunshine and ponders the last eight weeks.

'I've loved every minute of it,' she says, 'and I love these guys. They are real men's men, but they have so welcomed me into their ranks. They josh with me of course – that's the Navy way. My nickname is 'Chick' and they say they like me to wear sexy perfume to take the edge off their more naturally sweaty aroma during training sessions, but they know I got my place on merit and they respect that. And I tell you what – if anybody in the Navy was ever in a tight spot, you know in a war situation with the chips stacked against them, they would do a lot worse than have a field gunner around!'

NATASHA PULLEY AT THE
FIELD GUN COMPETITION

At four o'clock the team assembles in their allotted changing room. Ian Binks comes in with a big cardboard box and places it on a table.

'Gather round, everyone. I am now going to call you up one by one and present you with your special competition shirt for the final. Wear it with pride. You are going into the final better prepared than any other team I have ever been involved with – and that has been quite a few. I will tell you now you are awesome. Every man of you – plus woman – represents the epitome of what it is to be a field gunner. You have shown courage, stamina and discipline, but above all teamwork. Just think on this – the winners out there today will be able to call themselves the "best of the best". It's up to you now.'

He proceeds to call up each team member, to present them with a competition shirt – red with black trim and the name of their sponsors, The Plymouth Chamber of Commerce, emblazoned across the chest. Every gunner receives a hearty cheer from the rest of the team.

Half an hour later, it is time for the final march to the start line. First the team gathers in a huddle to sing their anthem. Then, on the order, they march forward, together with the other finalists. In track one will be HM Naval Base Portsmouth, track two HM Naval Base Devonport, track three HMS *Heron*, the naval Air Station at Yeovilton, track four HMS *Collingwood*, the Maritime Warfare School, track five HMS *Caledonia*, the naval base at Rossyth, and track six the 7th Battalion Royal Engineers. As usual Ian Binks marches at Devonport's side, shouting out his familiar battlecry over the deafening rattle of the field guns and limbers moving forward: 'Heads up, Devonport. Chests out. Be proud!'

The crowd has now swollen to well over five thousand and they applaud and cheer loudly as the teams stride out for the final confrontation – the race that will decide who really is the 'best of the best'.

The preliminary procedures are followed as usual. The limbers and guns are placed on the tracks. Each team warms up, but now with a greater intensity of purpose. Every team comes together for a final huddle, but this time they take that bit longer over it and squeeze each other that bit harder. Eventually, all the teams come to the line and wait. I watch the Devonport team faces with fascination – they are all unblinking and single-mindedly staring down the course.

Eventually, after the Marine bugler sounds the alert, the battery commander pulls the fuse from the thunderflash and throws it to the ground. Every member of every team strains to get away but has to wait for the explosion. Ian Binks counts under his breath – five . . . four . . . three . . . two . . . one . . . BANG! The explosion reverberates round the ground and the teams leap into instant action, sprinting towards the limber and gun for the first wheel change. Within ten metres everyone is neck and neck. Within twenty metres Devonport appears to be inching ahead – almost imperceptibly at first, but every stride seems to stretch them away from the field. Already the limber team has reached the limber, and the gun crew are hurtling towards the gun. The wheels of the limber are picked up and thrust on to the axles. The lynchpins go in

and now the drag ropes go on . . . then suddenly, shockingly, unbeliev-
ably, incredibly, as the limber team surge ahead towards the gun they
stop! A drag rope has come adrift. The smallest mistiming in the lifting
of the limber and the insertion of the wheels on to the axles caused
a slight hesitation in the attachment of the drag rope. It was no one's
particular fault, but a combination of factors that have cruelly cost the

GOING FOR GOLD!

Devonport team at least five seconds at the first wheel change. The drag
rope is quickly re-attached and the team moves forward with a jaw-
clenching determination to gain the lost ground. The faces of the
Devonport team become distorted by the renewed effort, but also by the
agony of realisation that a possibly fatal mistake has been made. Every
member of the team tries desperately to catch up with the other teams
who are now metres in front. It is as if destiny itself has been nudged off
balance by some malicious, spiteful, impish force that has decided to
distort the natural order of things for the sheer mischief of it. I watch in
disbelief as Devonport struggle to reclaim the race that should so right-
fully be theirs.

Ian Binks continues to run by the side of his team, continues to
shout out encouragement. Slowly, the team makes some ground on the
ones in front, but a margin of five seconds in the field gun final is virtu-

ally impossible to make up. The only chance for them is if all the other teams make a mistake, but that is unlikely as every team is well practised and rehearsed.

The 'Men of Devon' run valiantly to the end but, despite an impressive catch-up, they still come in last. The odds-on favourites are not the victors. They are the losers, and the fact of it is etched on every face.

'To the line!' screams Ian Binks. 'Devonport, come to the line!'

All the teams return to their starting line, where they have to kneel until it is decided that there are no penalty points to be awarded. The referees confer. All the runs are considered to be clean. No penalties. The result stands. For the first time in the history of the Field Gun Competition, the main trophy, known as the Brickwoods Trophy, is going out of the Navy. The 7th Battalion of the Royal Engineers crossed the line first in 1 minute 22.3 seconds. Devonport clocked a time of 1 minute 34 .29.

'Stay on the line, Devonport!' says Ian Binks to his team. They are all breathing heavily and dripping with sweat. Tasha is inconsolable, but not the only one in tears – clearly everyone is feeling the agony of defeat.

'What happened, happened,' says the Beast Master gently. 'You are gutted. I am gutted. But now is the time to show your metal. On the day, it was not to be. Accept it, deal with it and move on. There is always next year. Heads up . . . Chests out . . . Be proud!'

Devonport won every other trophy going that day: the Powersport Cup for the best aggregate time over seven competition runs – 9 minutes 45.18 seconds; the HMS *Powerful* Cup for the least penalties – none incurred; the Plymouth Area Cup for the fastest West Country Crew, and the *Powerful* Trophy for the fastest time in the competition, with a run of 1 minute 20.54 seconds. It was a clean sweep bar one – but it was the one that really counted.

By the evening, in the beer tent, Tasha has come to terms with the unexpected defeat and is beginning to put it in perspective.

'It is gutting but, as Number One said, we have to move on. The thing is, we were technically the best team and if you take all our best times of the separate stages and add them up, the time comes to one minute 16.54. That's two seconds under the world record. But we did not deliver in the race that mattered – end of story!'

She pauses and then screws up her face.

'The worst of it, though, is that the Pongos won! The Army won the Naval Field Gun!'

THE FATEFUL
FIELD GUN FINAL

Location: Devonport Naval Base
Date: 30 June 2005
Time: 20.00

Two weeks later I attend a celebration dinner for the Devonport field gun team, held in the senior rates' mess, back in Devonport dockyard. Every member of the team, the reserves and the back-up team is present. Speeches are made, souvenir pictures are handed out, and everybody sings 'Men of Devon' with as much passion as ever. This group of people has been forged into a real team and none of them will forget each other. They knew they were the best, and so defeat was all the more bitter when it occurred but they have dealt with that in their own way and put it behind them.

'Gentlemen and Lady,' says Ian Binks. 'Next year we will come back. Next year we will try again. Next year we will win the cup back for the Royal Navy. Heads up, Devonport! Chests out! Be Proud!'

CHAPTER FOURTEEN

The Immortal Memory

Location: The English Channel
Date: 20 May 2005
Time: 10.45

Daily Orders. Our Mission: 'Simply to come home!'
Notes: Enjoy the day – and well done!

HMS *Chatham* is cutting through the grey but familiar waters of the English Channel. After six months away she is returning to her home base at Devonport. Like thousands of ships before her, she is steaming towards the flashing light atop the Eddystone Rock Lighthouse, a granite tower standing some 135 feet high. This is visible to mariners for twenty-four miles and is the first sign of the approach to the Plymouth Sound.

'Six bleedin' months!' says Rab Butler standing on the foc's'le and looking at the distant outline of the English coast. 'So much has 'appened. Gulf patrol, Sri Lanka, Dubai, Alexandria, Gallipoli, and here we are again, back where we started. Some of the blokes down at the boxing gym probably haven't even noticed I've been away! Weird ain't it?'

HMS *Chatham* has certainly had a full and exciting deployment. She left to do a routine patrol of the Gulf, but ended up being diverted to help with the humanitarian relief necessitated by the Boxing Day tsunami. This was not on the itinerary; this was not expected; but the ship had to react and react she did.

'I reckon our time in Sri Lanka was the best,' says Rab. 'Horrible that the tsunami 'appened, but thank God we were there to lend a hand. Most of the lads and lasses think the same. We feel proud to have helped.'

Down below, in her cabin, Dr Alison Dewynter is preparing for the homecoming and seeing her Royal Marine husband, who will be waiting on the quayside.

'I'm nervous!' she confides. 'I'm dying to see Rich of course, but I'm frightened of suddenly not having everybody on the ship around me. We get very used to each other on board, and in a way come to depend on each other. It will be strange not to have some of them around.'

On the flight deck, Toby Clay and John Turner are about to fly their Lynx to its base at Yeovilton. 'We always have to do this,' says Toby, 'jump ship before anybody else, but we have to get the aircraft back to where she belongs.'

'It's a pity in a way,' says JT, 'because we never get to enjoy the actual homecoming and see all the waiting families on the jetty, all the waving flags and banners.'

Ten minutes later, the Lynx takes off for the last time in this deployment. Toby climbs, turns towards the ship, and buzzes it once down the starboard side as a way of saying goodbye. He then heads off towards the mainland.

Captain Steve Chick is on the bridge peering through the rain-spattered windows at the breakwater which marks the entrance into Plymouth Sound.

'I am very proud of my ship and very proud of my ship's company. They delivered everything I asked of them and more. HMS *Chatham* can hold her head up high, and soon everyone can enjoy some leave – they deserve it.'

Also on the bridge is John Gardner, the XO and second in command, who has worked so hard to maintain morale throughout the long deployment.

'It has been a really happy ship, but then, a successful ship normally is happy. Morale has always been high and that is a reflection of the nature of our ship's company from top to bottom. One is always proud of one's ship, of course, but I am *really* proud of *Chatham*.'

Most people will be getting immediate leave for about five weeks. The ship will not shut down during that time because important maintenance has to be carried out, but that will be done by the advance par-

HMS *CHATHAM* RETURNS

ties who were sent home early from Souda Bay in Crete and later from Barcelona. Ginge Grieveson was one of the party who left from Spain – at last able to finish his clock-watching and get home to Amanda and the boys.

Ratz Rackcliff, of course, left the ship in Alexandria to come home on paternity leave, ready for the birth of his first child. He promised to be waiting on the quayside with the baby when the ship returned.

The ship's company lines the upper deck, ready for the final approach into Devonport. The ship, now joined by two tugs to see us in, glides past Drake's Island and Plymouth Hoe. Some people have gathered at Devil's Point and are waving vigorously at anyone willing

THE GRAND RETURN

FAMILIES WAIT FOR
HMS *CHATHAM*

to wave back. Soon we are passing the Torpoint Ferry jetty, North Yard
and HMS *Drake*. Then, at last, we reach Weston Mill Lake where we turn
hard to starboard and enter Frigate Alley. Here, for the first time, we
see the mass of people waiting to greet the ship at Wharf 14. Flags and
banners are waving in the freshening wind and now driving rain, but
nothing is going to dampen the ardour of the moment. A Royal Marine
band is playing, but can hardly be heard above the cheers now echoing
across the water.

RAB – HOME AGAIN!

ROYAL MARINE BAND
WELCOMES HOME
HMS *CHATHAM*

'Blinding!' says Rab, still on the fo'c'sle. 'My Mel is amongst that lot somewhere!'

Nudged by the tugs, HMS *Chatham* edges slowly in to the quayside. One by one, sailors spot their families and start waving frantically. Soon the gangway is craned into place and secured, whereupon a blue tide of sailors flows – no, cascades – off the ship and into the arms of wives, husbands, girlfriends, boyfriends, mothers, fathers, brothers, sisters and friends.

Rab has found a tearful Mel who he is holding tightly in one arm, whilst his other arm is around his brother who he has not seen for two years.

Ratz Rackliff is there, greeting all his shipmates with his wife Theresa and a small pink version of himself called Jake.

Alison Dewynter is holding on for dear life to her husband Rich, who cannot stop kissing her.

As her ship's company are reuniting with their families in front of her, HMS *Chatham* sits quietly at the quayside. She looks weathered and her paintwork is rust-stained after a tough six-month deployment that has taken her halfway across the world, but she has delivered her people safely home. Job done.

ALI DEWYNTER GREETS HER
HUSBAND RICH

This is not quite the end of the story, however, because HMS *Chatham* has one more important duty to perform – not now but in a few weeks' time. She has been awarded the singular honour of being the Queen's escort ship at the International Fleet Review to mark the 200th anniversary of the Battle of Trafalgar – the first fleet review since the Silver Jubilee of 1977.

Location: Portsmouth
Date: 28 June 2005
Time: 09.00

Daily Orders. Our Mission: 'To escort HMS *Endurance* carrying HM the Queen for the IFR'
Notes: HMS *Chatham* will be firing a 21-Gun Salute as HM the Queen arrives at HMS *Endurance*.

HMS *Chatham* is tied up alongside at Portsmouth Naval Base. In front of her is the Antarctic Patrol Ship HMS *Endurance* which will be carrying Queen Elizabeth, the Lord High Admiral of the United Kingdom, to review the Fleet. As the Royal Escort Ship we will follow *Endurance* as she sails past more than 167 ships and 25,000 sailors from fifty-seven navies.

'We gotta stand here like bleedin' lemons for three hours,' complains Rab Butler, as he takes his place in the fo'c'sle party again, but this time in sweltering sunshine.

'You complaining again, Rab?' I say tauntingly.

'Yes I bloody am!' he snaps in mock anger. 'It's gonna get bloody hot today, and we have to stand to attention for three hours as we go round the friggin' fleet.'

Rab, I have come to understand, is really only happy when he has something to complain about, so right now I conclude he must be nearly ecstatic. It is certainly going to be hot today, close and humid too.

The Queen duly arrives at HMS *Endurance,* and HMS *Chatham* fires a 21-Gun Salute, using two ceremonial guns positioned on the upper-deck waists. After this, both *Endurance* and *Chatham* leave the wall and start the long passage past the fleet, which is deployed in four lines, each five miles long.

The tradition of the fleet review is as old as Britain's mastery of the seas. In their earliest incarnation, reviews were essentially practical

FACING PAGE:
CHATHAM FOLLOWS
THE QUEEN AT THE
INTERNATIONAL
FLEET REVIEW

SHIPS FROM ALL OVER THE
WORLD GATHER AT THE
2005 INTERNATIONAL FLEET
REVIEW

affairs, to ensure the seaworthiness of ships whose job was to transport huge numbers of men in armour, their horses, squires and bowmen, across the Channel, invariably to confront the French.

Since then, however, the fleet review has been more a way of displaying Britain's awesome naval power, both to impress the British populace as well as to intimidate potential enemies. In short, it was a very British way of flexing the country's considerable maritime muscle.

Today, of course, the review is more symbolic than jingoistic. Even though it marks the great victory at the Battle of Trafalgar by the Royal Navy over the French and Spanish navies during the Napoleonic wars, less than half of the ships to be reviewed by the Queen are from the Royal Navy. The rest are provided from other world navies, from places as far afield as Japan, South Korea, Russia, Canada, Australia, India, Pakistan, Poland, Oman, Morocco, Nigeria, Algeria, Turkey, Greece, Germany, Italy, Ireland and, of course, Nelson's old enemies Spain and France. Indeed it is ironic that the French have sent six ships to stand in the

review, including the pride of their navy – the nuclear-powered aircraft carrier *Charles de Gaulle* – twice as big as anything the Royal Navy has.

'Why the 'ell 'ave the French sent their biggest ship to a celebration of the bloke what did for 'em?' asks Rab Butler.

Vice Admiral Jacques Mazars, the senior French officer attending today, answered that earlier, by telling journalists, 'We were invited. When you are invited to your cousin's wedding, you wear your best dress. That's what we have done.'

'Whatever!' exclaims Rab. 'I reckon it's a case of "ours is bigger than yours" – cheeky buggers!'

HMS *Endurance* carries Queen Elizabeth past a seemingly endless line of international warships, each one of which salutes and cheers as she draws level.

'Well, you gotta admit it's pretty bloody impressive!' says Rab as we pass the huge American amphibious carrier USS *Saipan*. 'That's a big "mother" too, ain't it?'

'Yeah, but they've got bigger ones,' says someone else in the fo'c'sle party.

'Bloody right, mate! Some of their flat tops are the size of small countries!'

We are now passing HMS *Ocean*, the Royal Navy's largest ship, and I am looking to see if I can spot Mike Brotherton or Tony Johnstone-Burt. I can't, but I can see 700 sailors and Royal Marines lined up on the upper deck, giving the Queen a rousing cheer.

Before us now is a magnificent panorama of warships, but it cannot have escaped the Queen's attention how much her own fleet has shrunk since she last reviewed it in 1977, when more than 100 warships were in service. The Royal Navy now stands at almost a quarter of that strength – a shadow of the force which once dominated the oceans of the world.

I look over at HMS *Bulwark*, Jerry Stanford's amphibious assault ship, the newest addition to the Royal Navy. Just to her side is a magnificent tall ship with sailors standing proud along the yardarms. The old and the new side by side. It makes me think about something somebody said to me, before I started my year with the Royal Navy. 'Why do we need a navy?' they said. 'There are no battles at sea any more – so what does the Navy do exactly?'

Now – today – at the end of my year with the Navy and its people, I consider the question again, and I consider it in the context of today's celebration of the greatest sailor this country has ever produced.

It is true – there are no more battles to be fought at sea. There is no more need for battleships with massive guns to blast other battleships out of the water – but then, there has not been that need for a while now. A modern Navy has to remain just that – modern. To do that it needs to adapt continually – both its hardware and, more importantly, its personnel.

Today, the Royal Navy is experimenting with advanced techniques in littoral warfare – that is, warfare involving coastlines – anywhere in the world. That is why the Navy is investing in 'amphibious platforms' like HMS *Ocean*, HMS *Bulwark* and her sister ship HMS *Albion*. Ships like these can deliver troops, aircraft, arms, military equipment to any coastline at any time. By the same token, of course, they can also deliver bags of rice, shelter and medical supplies where they are needed.

The world is now threatened by terrorism – what military people call the 'asymmetric' threat, a reference to the scale of destruction that can be achieved by relatively small assets, whether they be bombs planted in crowded trains, or suicide bombers causing havoc in crowded streets, or small boats packed with explosives coming alongside a cruiseliner. The Navy has identified piracy in eighteen parts of the world, which threatens international trade and security. Arms running, drug smuggling, people smuggling are all taking place on the world's international highway – the sea – and few could argue that the sea does not need to be policed. This is what HMS *Chatham* was doing in the Gulf, as part of a multi-national effort to counter the international terrorist groups that use the sea for their own advantage.

Commanding officers in the Royal Navy, it seems to me, have to be innovators. Nelson, of course, was the ultimate innovator. When he considered a battle or a campaign, he always tried to minimise the element of chance, so that he held all the advantages whilst the enemy were deprived of their options. At the Battle of the Nile, some victims of which HMS *Chatham* buried in Alexandria, the French firmly believed that they would not be attacked from the coastal shallows of Abu Qir Bay, but it was Nelson himself who went off in a boat to do the soundings that made it possible for his ships to go in close to land and attack from behind.

ON *CHATHAM* AT THE FLEET REVIEW

Nelson also used to say that the best negotiator in Europe was a fleet of battleships and, whilst that is too bellicose a stance to adopt today, it remains true, I think, that the best way to fly the national flag is from the sharp end of a British warship – whether that be in the Arabian Gulf, off the coast of Sri Lanka or in the Dardanelles under the shadow of the Gallipoli war memorials.

The Royal Navy is certainly not without its problems. Defence cuts do threaten its replacement programme, recruitment problems do compromise its manpower projections, but it is still a world-class navy – and it has five hundred years of tradition to underpin it.

The corporate RN strap line for the Trafalgar celebrations is 'Past Glories – Future Horizons', although Admiral Chris Parry, someone I met at the very beginning of my initial research for this project, sums up the Navy in another way: 'In footballing terms the Royal Navy is the

AN EXPLOSIVE END TO THE
INTERNATIONAL FLEET
REVIEW

Brazil of naval war fighting – we always get to the final.' With this in
mind my first team selection is as follows:

Rab Butler, Ginge Grieveson, Ratz Rackliff, Alison Dewynter, Toby
Clay, John Turner, Steve Chick, John Gardner, Tommy Goodwin, Mike

Brotherton, Tony Johnstone-Burt, Jerry Stanford, Paul Ransley, Sam Yarnold, Scouse Ashton, Russ Eatwell, Tasha Pulley, Ian Binks and the Devonport Field Gun Team, George Hebron, Chris Lewis and, of course the Forty-Sixers.

SHIPMATES ALL